Frank Smith

Ontario Institute for Studies in Education

UNDERSTANDING READING

a psycholinguistic analysis of reading and learning to read

second edition

HOLT, RINEHART AND WINSTON
New York   Chicago   San Francisco   Dallas
Montreal   Toronto   London   Sydney

Library of Congress Cataloging in Publication Data

Smith, Frank, 1928–
  Understanding reading.

  Includes bibliographical references and indexes.
  1. Reading. I. Title.
LB1050.S574 1978   428′.4   77-19260
ISBN 0-03-020866-1 (pbk.)
ISBN 0-03-041765-1

PREFACE

This book attempts to shed light on some of the fundamental aspects of the complex human skill of reading — linguistic, psychological, and physiological — and on what is involved in learning to read.

This is not a book about reading instruction. There is no comparison of instructional methods nor is there any effort to promote one method at the expense of another. Current instructional methods are probably not much different from the methods that will be developed as we learn more about learning to read. So many instructional methods have been tried, and so many succeed (in some instances at least), that further permutations in the game of instructional roulette are unlikely to produce any great gain, either by chance or design. What will make a difference is an understanding of the reading process.

Part of the process of enlightenment is to demonstrate that fluent reading is more complex than is frequently believed, and learning to read more involved. Fortunately, children can overcome instructional deficiencies and seek for themselves the information that will help them acquire reading skills — if given the chance — far better than they are given credit for.

The process of reading is still not very well understood. Researchers do not yet know enough about the developed skills of the fluent reader, the net product of the instructional process, let alone the process of acquiring these skills. But researchers are beginning to realize that reading will not be completely understood until there is an understanding of all the perceptual, cognitive, linguistic, and motivational aspects not just of reading but of thinking and learning in general. Advances are being made in the study of all these, but all too often the results of these advances are not available to those assisting a child who is learning to read — especially the reading teacher. The first step towards understanding is to accept that many questions remain unanswered — that there is no justification for dogmatism about reading or learning to read. The second step is to dissect the reading process as carefully as possible, to examine all the parts and requirements of this complex process, and to develop at least an idea of what is involved.

That is the precise purpose of this book — to provide an idea of what must be involved in reading and learning to read. The aim is not to propagandize but to offer insights. One insight that this book will attempt to give is that the child is not as helpless in face of the task of learning to read as we sometimes think. A feeling for what children can do, and what they need, can be a most important insight that can develop from a clearer understanding of what reading involves.

My reluctance to be dogmatic about instructional methodology is based on more than academic puritanism. It is an open question whether classroom "experts" who make uninformed pronouncements about linguistics and psychology cause more confusion than linguists and psychological theorists who make categorical assertions about how reading should be taught, especially if these assertions are given a false authority by a reputation that is irrelevant to the classroom.

The reading process and reading instruction are two quite independent domains of inquiry. Workers in each area should influence each other, perhaps much more than they do, but only by sharing information and stimulating hypotheses; they cannot pass judgment on each other's methods. A theory is useful as a summary and framework for what is known, and as a source of new ideas; a theory is tested by data acquired under rigorously controlled laboratory conditions. Instructional techniques, on the other hand, are of value only if they are proved to be effective in the classroom by the achievement of instructional and other educational objectives. Nothing in this book should be interpreted as a direct condemnation or justification of a particular technique, although I hope teachers will find a better understanding of why some methods may be successful, and how they might be improved.

An understanding of reading requires some acquaintance with research in a variety of disciplinary fields; that is why more than half of this book is devoted to such topics as language, communication, learning theory, the acquisition of speech, and the physiology of the eye and brain. These topics are discussed in an attempt to make them understood, which means that there is an assumption that the reader of this book may have neither the experience nor the time to undertake deep or specialized study in these areas. After stressing that reading is more complicated than we generally allow, and that our ignorance of it is more profound than we usually admit, I owe it to my own readers not to make the issue more confusing by blinding them with reflected scholarship or losing them in fields of footnotes. At the risk of offending the specialist, diverse subject areas have been covered only to the extent that they are relevant to the topic of reading. For those who wish to pursue any topic further, some introductory sources are listed in the Notes at the end of the book.

This book is designed to serve as a college text for a basic course on the reading process, as a guide to relevant research literature on reading, and as an introduction to reading as an example of higher cognitive skills.

Some comments on the second edition

The preceding paragraphs are seven years old, lifted bodily — with a few minor editorial changes — from the preface to the first edition of *Understanding Reading*. These paragraphs are among the few parts of the original text that I have been able to carry through to the second edition without great compulsion to rewrite. Obviously my aims and basic attitudes have remained unchanged since 1971 but I have found new ways to analyze or explain my topics in what has become familiarly known as *SOUR* (for *Son of Understanding Reading*). Certainly my researches during the intervening years have served only to consolidate four themes that ran through the first edition:

(1) Understanding how children learn to read requires understanding reading and how children learn;

(2) Understanding reading requires understanding language generally and the functioning of the brain;

(3) From a reading point of view: information brought to reading by the brain is more important than information provided by the print;

(4) From an instructional point of view: children learn to read by reading.

There has been a great deal of recent interest and work in reading. Probably more research has been done in the name of reading during the past decade than in all of the preceding sixty years, following the publication of Huey's landmark book, still readable and relevant today, *The Psychology and Pedagogy of Reading* (Huey, 1908). This flowering of interest in reading among psychologists and linguists — the two groups of researchers who together contribute their insights and labors to the interdisciplinary field of study called psycholinguistics — is not I think simply a response to growing public concern about literacy (and the consequent availability of research funds). There has also been a theoretical liberalization as the behavioral sciences have continued to free themselves from constraints of behaviorism and ventured more into the realm of mental life, which is surely the arena of reading. As George Miller said in one of the first articles to introduce the transformational linguistics of Chomsky to psychologists, "Mind is something more than a four-letter Anglo-Saxon word" (Miller, 1962). There is still a great deal of research that I would consider peripheral to main issues in reading, studies that restrict themselves to eye movements and to letter or isolated word recognition. But there have also been many attempts, in linguistics and psychology as well as in education, to understand better the notions of meaning and comprehension, and it is these that I feel are contributing most to theoretical and practical issues in reading.

But then I am biased. Emphasis on comprehension also characterizes the direction my own work has taken since the first edition of this book. Comprehension was stressed in the first edition, but I had relatively little to say about it. The notion of *prediction*, which I now feel to be the basis of language comprehension, permeates the present edition but was not even listed in the original index. It has mainly been through a focus on processes of comprehension that I have tried to achieve twin aims with the second edition, (1) to make the text more readable, and (2) to bring it up to date. Comprehension, I hope, now provides a link for all the various aspects of reading to which I refer, and it also accounts for the bulk of the many new references that I have added. (Some specific detail about changes in this edition, of interest to instructors and others who might wish to compare the two editions, are given in a Note on page 197.)

Once again I have tried to provide an integrated discussion of reading, as opposed to a compendium of research. I have not attempted to cover all the research and theorizing, but have tried to indicate at least one source of evidence for every assertion that I make about language or the brain. The manner in which I interpret the evidence and try to construct a coherent picture reflects basically my own point of view. Alternative views are cited in the Notes to the final chapter. I still believe that detailed instructional implications of my theoretical analysis can and should be left to speak for themselves — teachers must make their own decisions in classrooms. Where I do make such comments — notably at the end of the final chapter — it should be clear that I am expressing personal opinions, although I am encouraged to do so because in general I have found them supported by the experience of many teachers with whom I have worked. The fact that there is little research to support (or to reject) general statements about instruction in a sense accords with my theoretical point of view, that the problem of helping children learn to read is more a matter of teacher understanding than of method. At best, instructional programs have only limited aims, and research serves only to show that they usually achieve these limited ends with some children at least. Whether in fact such programs help children to become fluent and interested readers is generally beyond the scope of both the instructional program and the related research. In contrast to the flurry of research relevant to theoretical issues in reading and comprehension, research into reading instruction has in my opinion demonstrated relatively little in recent years (Smith, in press). The question of the best method for teaching reading has, I think, not been answered because it is not the appropriate question; children do not learn because of reading programs, but because teachers succeed in preventing programs from standing in children's way. It is the wisdom and intuition of teachers that must be trusted, provided that teachers have the theoretical foundation to reflect upon the decisions that only they can make.

Concerning dedications

The first edition of this book was dedicated to George A. Miller, who challenged psychologists who wished in some way to promote human welfare "to give psychology away" by making its findings accessible to those to whom these findings would be most relevant. I also listed Miller as one of the intellectual inspirations for my work in language, and to that list I must now add the names of David Olson, Kenneth Goodman, and James Britton, focal figures among many friends, colleagues, and students who have helped and encouraged me. I owe particular thanks to Hugh Glenn and Dorothy Watson, together with a number of *their* students, for detailed comments on the first edition of this book, and to many thoughtful readers who have taken the trouble to write or talk to me about it. Dick Owen has been a patient editor and friend, and Ann Gonzalez an exceptionally helpful and efficient secretary. Four more names to mention — Mary-Theresa, who never fails to understand and support, and Laurel, Melissa, and Nicholas, who have changed the most since the first edition of this book. Scarcely children now, they have become remarkably sympathetic companions.

Too many people would deserve a share of the dedication of this book, so instead, I shall dedicate it to an activity. That this activity happens to be the topic of the book is coincidental — at this moment my concern is with the activity for what it achieves for me. I shall dedicate this book to *reading*, not as a subject for teaching but as a means of learning and source of pleasure, sharing ideas and ideals with people one might otherwise never meet.

Toronto, Canada   Frank Smith
December 1977

CONTENTS

CHAPTER 1

UNDERSTANDING
READING
perspective
and
outline

Reading involves a number of more general skills that cannot be ignored in any serious analysis of the subject. The frequent assertion, for example, that reading requires a special kind of visual discrimination completely overlooks fundamental facts about the role of the eyes in reading. No exceptional kind or degree of visual acuity is required to discriminate among printed letters or words; probably any child who can distinguish between two faces at ten feet has sufficient visual capacity to learn to read. A reader must discover minimal critical differences between letters and words, which is not so much a matter of knowing how to look as knowing what to look for. Because of quite general characteristics of the human visual system and of language, fluent reading, in fact, depends upon an ability to rely on the eyes as little as possible. As we shall see, such ability is not taught; it is acquired by children as they employ perceptual and cognitive skills common to many everyday aspects of visual perception.

Another persistent assertion is that reading is simply a matter of "decoding to sound" — of translating the written symbols on the page into real or imagined sounds of speech, so that learning to read becomes little more than memorizing selected rules for decoding and practising their use. But analysis of the relationships between print and speech not only confirms that the "rules" relating spelling to the sounds of speech are inordinately complicated and unreliable in English, but also that they are largely irrelevant to reading in any language. Reading is less a matter of extracting sound from print than of bringing meaning to print. The sounds that are supposed to reveal the meaning of sequences of letters cannot in fact be produced unless a probable meaning can be determined in advance. It is a universal fact of reading rather than a defect of English spelling that the effort to read through decoding is not only futile but unnecessary.

An understanding of reading therefore cannot be achieved without some general insights into the nature of language and of various operating characteristics of the human brain. Consequently, the first half of this book is devoted to a very broad consideration of such topics as vision, memory, knowledge, language, and learning. These opening chapters are by no means intended to be comprehensive or even balanced disquisitions upon the subjects covered; this is not a book about physiology, linguistics, or cognitive psychology. Instead, the chapters offer the minimum of background fact and theory that is necessary and relevant for an analysis of reading. A few suggestions are made in the Notes to chapters to set interested readers on the trail of more detailed sources.

Such a broadly-based approach to reading has some incidental advantages. The more that is said about general topics at the beginning, the less remains to be added about reading when the specific issue is broached. There is, in fact, nothing unique about reading. There is nothing in reading as far as vision is concerned that is not involved in such mundane perceptual activities as distinguishing tables from chairs or dogs from cats. There is nothing in reading as far as language is concerned that is not within the competence of anyone with a working ability to comprehend speech. Although the difficulty some children experience in learning to read is often attributed to some kind of minimal and undetectable brain damage, there is no convincing evidence even that a particular part of the brain is uniquely involved in reading. It is, of course, possible — though by no means as common as some reading authorities would suggest — for an occasional child to have a brain injury that would affect language ability, but such an injury would not interfere with reading yet leave the comprehension of speech untouched. Children can obviously have visual defects that will interfere with reading, but these are defects that would show up in other visual activities as well. None of this is to say that it is impossible for a child to fail to learn to read despite perfectly adequate vision and spoken language skill; there are enough counter examples in our schools. But there are many other possible reasons for reading difficulty apart from hypothetical brain disorders. Personal, social, or cultural conflicts can interfere critically with a child's motivation or ability to learn to read, and it is also possible for something to go wrong during instruction. Children can develop reading habits that make comprehension impossible.

A detailed analysis of reading will therefore be left to the second half of this book, by which time much of the basic ground will have been covered. Questions related to reading instruction will be left to the final chapter, partly because the pedagogical emphasis of this book is on enabling reading teachers to make informed decisions rather than on telling them what to do; partly because inferences about how reading should be taught become clearer as reading itself becomes more fully understood. The main instructional implication of the analysis of this book is that children learn to read by reading. Drills, exercises, and rote learning play little part in learning to read and in fact may interfere with comprehension. The function of teachers is not so much to *teach* reading as to help children read. How this can be done — and the resolution of the paradox that children must read to learn while learning to read — must of course eventually be faced. But for the moment it is more appropriate to postpone the ultimate issues and to look at the route by which the concluding portions of the book will be reached.

PREVIEW OF THE BOOK

Chapter 1, *Understanding Reading,* will continue after this preview with a very general outline of how reading takes place, demonstrating that what transpires behind the reader's eyes, in the reader's brain, makes a far greater contribution to reading than the print in front of the reader's face.

Chapter 2, *Communication and Information,* explains a few technical concepts and terms that will be used in the analysis of reading, emphasizing the active role that the reader must play and the kinds of influence that can interfere with "receiving messages" from print.

Chapter 3, *Between Eye and Brain,* goes behind the eyes to discuss some of the brain's limitations in dealing with information picked up by the eyes, and showing the importance of what is already known by the brain.

Chapter 4, *Memory,* is concerned with another prime source of both the brain's strengths and its limitations.

Chapter 5, *Knowledge and Comprehension,* attempts to elucidate what is already in the brain and discusses the manner in which prior knowledge is used to make sense of the world, whether through language or more directly.

Chapter 6, *Language — Spoken and Written,* examines some of the special demands that all forms of language make on listeners or readers, and also the rather complex relationships and subtle differences that exist between speech and print.

Chapter 7, *Learning about the World and about Language,* outlines some basic principles, since children are not equipped with (nor can they lack) special abilities for learning to read. Rather must they use quite fundamental learning skills to solve the problems of reading.

The next four chapters, 8 to 11, undertake a theoretical analysis of reading, and of aspects of learning to read, based on the preceding discussions.

Chapter 12, *Reading and Learning To Read,* consists of a review of the major points about reading, some additional perspectives on learning to read, and a consideration of the role of teachers.

TWO SIDES OF READING

Obviously, reading is not an activity that can be satisfactorily conducted in the dark. In order to read you need illumination, some print in front of you, your eyes open, and possibly your spectacles on. Reading, in other words, depends on some information getting through the eyes to the brain. Let us call this information that the brain receives from print *visual information.* It is easy to characterize the general nature of visual information; it goes away when the lights go out.

Access to visual information is a necessary part of reading but it is not sufficient. You could have a wealth of visual information in a piece of text before your open eyes and still not be able to read. For example, the text you are looking at might be written in a language you do not understand. Knowledge of the relevant language is part of information that is essential for reading, but it is not information that you can expect to find on the printed page. Rather it is information that you must have already, behind the eyeballs. It can be distinguished from the visual information that comes through the eyes by being called *nonvisual information.*

There are other kinds of nonvisual information apart from knowledge of language. Knowledge of subject matter is similarly important. Give many people an article on subatomic physics, the differential calculus, or the maintainance of jet engines, and they will not be able to read — not because of some inadequacy of the text, which specialists can read perfectly well, nor because there is anything wrong with their eyes, but because they lack appropriate nonvisual information. Knowledge of how to read is another kind of nonvisual information, and of evident importance in making reading possible, although it has nothing to do with the lighting, the print, or the state of one's eyes. Nonvisual information is easily distinguished from visual information — it is carried around by the reader all the time; it does not go away when the lights go out.

The distinction between visual and nonvisual information may seem obvious; nevertheless, it is so critical in reading and learning to read that I have put it into diagram form below.

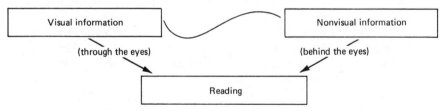

FIGURE 1.1   Two sources of information in reading

The reason that the distinction between visual and nonvisual information is so important is simply stated — there is a reciprocal relationship between the two. Within certain limits, one can be traded off for the other. The more nonvisual information a reader has, the less visual information the reader needs. The less nonvisual information that is available from behind the eyes, the more visual information is required. This reciprocal relationship is represented by the curved line between the two kinds of information in Figure 1.1.

Informal demonstrations of the trade-off between two kinds of information in reading are not difficult to give. They are provided by the common phenomenon that popular novels and newspaper articles tend to be easy to read — they can be read relatively quickly, in a poor light, despite small type and poor quality printing. They are easy to read because of what we know already; we have less need for visual information. On the other hand, technical materials or difficult novels — or even the same popular novels and newspaper articles when read by someone not so familiar with the language or the conventions of writing — require more time and more effort, larger type, clearer print, and superior physical conditions. The names of familiar towns on traffic signs can be read from further away than the same-size place names of unfamiliar localities. It is easier to read letters on a wall when they are arranged into meaningful words and phrases than the same size letters in the random order of an optician's test chart. In each case the difference has nothing to do with the quality of the visual information available in the print, but with the amount of nonvisual information that the reader can bring to bear. The less nonvisual information the reader can employ, the harder it is to read.

Now we can see one reason why reading can be so very much harder for children, quite independently of their actual reading ability. They may have little relevant nonvisual information. Some beginning reading materials seem to be expressly designed to avoid the use of nonvisual information. At other times adults may unwittingly or even deliberately discourage the use of nonvisual information. For whatever cause, insufficiency of nonvisual information will make reading more difficult.

Insufficiency of nonvisual information can even make reading impossible, for the simple but inescapable reason that there is a limit to how much visual information the brain can handle at any one time. There is a bottleneck in the visual system between eye and brain, as indicated in Figure 1.2 below.

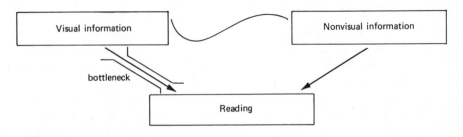

FIGURE 1.2   The bottleneck in reading

As a consequence of this bottleneck a reader can easily become, temporarily, functionally blind. It is possible to look but not be able to see, no matter how good the physical conditions. A line of print which is transparently obvious to a teacher (who knows what it says in the first place) may be almost completely illegible to a child whose dependence on visual information can limit perception to just two or three letters in the middle of the line.

Being unable to discern the words for the print is not a handicap that is restricted to children. Fluent readers may find themselves in exactly the same situation for essentially the same reasons — by being given difficult material to read, by being required to pay a lot of attention to every word, or by being put into a condition of anxiety, all of which increase the demand for visual information and have the paradoxical consequence of making it harder to see the text.

In Chapter 3 I shall show how the relative proportions of visual and nonvisual information required in reading can be assessed, and also indicate how narrow the bottleneck is; so narrow, that at least three quarters of the visual information available in text must usually be ignored. As psychologist Paul Kolers (1969)[1] wrote, "Reading is only incidentally visual." Because nonvisual information lies at the core of reading, a large part of this book will be concerned with its nature, development, and use.

Some Basic Distinctions

Books on reading often open with an attempt to define the term, a formal statement such as, perhaps, "Reading is extracting information from print." But such an assertion does not really say anything that anyone is unlikely to know, nor does it indicate whether and how the author intends to use a word differently from everyone else. Formal definitions have utility only if words are being used in a very specialized, narrow, or otherwise unpredictable way, and even then they may cause more trouble than they are worth because readers prefer to interpret familiar words in familiar ways. The fact is that common, easily understandable words tend to have a multiplicity of meanings — an interesting aspect of all languages with which we shall later be concerned — and what usually gives a word its unambiguous meaning is neither prior agreement nor fiat but the particular context that it happens to be in.

Take the question of whether "reading" necessarily involves

---

[1]References are indicated by year of publication in parentheses and given in full in a list at the end of the book, beginning on page 244.

comprehension. Such a question does not ask anything about the reading act, only about the way in which the word is used. And the only possible answer is that sometimes "reading" certainly implies comprehension — as when we ask if someone is enjoying reading a book — and sometimes it does not — as when they reply that they have been reading the book for two hours and scarcely understood a word. Such flexibility does not illustrate a flaw of language but rather its boundless productivity. Context generally does serve (and always should serve) to make meaning clear, preserving us from the undesirable necessity of using familiar words in unfamiliar ways or of inventing unfamiliar words for familiar purposes. Definitions are not usually useful.

I do, however, want to note a distinction between reading with comprehension and reading — or whatever else one might want to call it — without. It is, of course, possible to recite a series of words without understanding anything about them at all — what has been called "barking at print" (Wardhaugh, 1969). When there is no possibility of the comprehension of a meaning and it is important to make the situation clear, I shall avoid using the word "reading" but talk about "word identification" instead. Occasionally — because I want to make a comparison or contrast — I shall refer to comprehension as "meaning identification". But, in general, I shall use the terms "reading" and "comprehension (of print)" interchangeably. To my mind, reading is something that makes sense to the reader.

An important distinction that I must comment upon is between learning and teaching. The difference might seem obvious enough, but in occasional educational circles and textbooks it seems to be assumed that the two are completely correlated. As a consequence, the achievement of children can be underrated. For example, it may be taken for granted either that parents teach children to talk (since most children quickly acquire that skill) or that there is nothing very remarkable about being able to talk (since few parents seem to bother to teach it). Both points of view are incorrect. Learning to talk is a remarkable intellectual feat, equalled only by the ease with which children make sense of many of the other patterns of sounds, sights, smells, and other kinds of events in their environment. It is indeed fortunate that children can learn without a teacher, since a large part of what we expect them to learn — including reading — cannot in fact be the subject of formal instruction.

On the other hand, teaching all too often takes place in the absence of learning. And when teaching and learning appear to be going on at the same time, teaching may get undeserved credit. Ask many people how they first learned to read, and they are likely to reply that someone taught them the names and sounds of letters. This kind of romanticism underlies many of the assertions that the way to improve reading is to "get back to the basics". But apart from the fact that few adults have a reliable memory for the specific detail of the first half dozen years of their lives (nor did they understand very well what their teachers were doing with them at that time) it happens to be the case that no one learns to read simply by knowing the names and sounds of letters. So if the teacher is to get the credit, it must be for doing something else with a significance that escaped the child and possibly the teacher as well. Teachers may on occasion do the right thing for the wrong reason, or when they think they are doing something else, and children can be very adept at profiting from any useful information that comes their way.

It is to underline the distinction between learning and teaching that questions of instructional practice are left to the final chapter of this book. On the frequent occasions when I talk about learning before that point, I would not want it to be inferred that formal instruction is necessary or even possible. In fact, my usual intention will be the opposite; the kind of learning that I shall emphasize cannot be taught. Teachers have an important role in helping children learn to read, but it is rarely by dictating what and when a child should learn.

While I stress the possible gulf between learning and teaching, another distinction that is quite often made I must, in fact, reject. I want to argue that there is no essential difference between learning to read and reading. There are no special kinds of skill that a child must learn and exercise that are not involved in fluent reading, nor is there any part of fluent reading that is not a part of learning to read. There is no magical day in the life of children when they cross the threshold from "learner" to "reader". Everyone must read in order to learn to read, and every time we read, we learn more about reading. At no time is a reader "finished". The main difference between beginning to read and fluent reading is that the beginning is very much harder. Even skilled readers will have great difficulty in reading some material, although they can always learn to do better with more experience.

The previous paragraph helps perhaps to explain why I may seem to be discussing fluent reading most of the time. It is not that I think learning to read is a less interesting or less important topic. My justification for concentrating on what fluent readers are able to do is that this is precisely what beginning readers must learn to do. By focusing on fluent reading, I can in fact try to make this book relevant to those concerned with reading or with teaching reading at all ages and levels.

SUMMARY

The final part of each chapter is a brief Summary recapitulating the main points. Terms printed in **bold type** in the Summary are key terms that will be found in a glossary at the back of the book, beginning on page 239.

Reading is not just a visual activity, nor a simple matter of decoding to sound. Two sources of information are essential for reading, **visual information** and **nonvisual information.** While there is a trade-off between the two, there is a limit to how much visual information the brain can handle in making sense of **print.** Therefore, the use of nonvisual information is crucial in reading and learning to read.

NOTES

I shall try to keep the introduction and development of the theme of each chapter as informal and nontechnical as possible. Experimental detail and descriptions of key research that has been done (or perhaps should be done) in specific areas will be held back to Notes on each chapter at the end of the book, beginning on Page 197. These Notes, which may also include reference to alternative points of view, could be skipped on a first pass by readers concerned with getting a preliminary feel of the book or trying to follow the main themes without too great a burden on their nonvisual information. But the Notes should be examined with care by students and others who want to test the merits of the arguments or achieve a deeper grasp of the issues. At the conclusion of the Notes for each chapter will be suggestions for further reading.

CHAPTER 2

INFORMATION
AND
COMMUNICATION

We shall need a language with which to talk about reading. Since reading may in very general terms be considered as part of a process of communication in which information travels between a transmitter and a receiver — whether the reader is a scholar deciphering a medieval text or a child identifying a single letter on a chalkboard — we shall begin by seeing what can be borrowed from theories of communication and information. We shall find that these theories offer some useful basic concepts for the construction of a theory of reading and a terminology that can increase the clarity of its expression. But we shall also find that reading is not reducible to a simple matter of readers "decoding" messages that are transmitted by writers. Instead the present chapter will emphasize the following important points:

1. Reading is not a passive activity — readers must make a substantial and active contribution if they are to make sense of print.
2. All aspects of reading, from the identification of individual letters or words to the comprehension of entire passages, can be regarded as the reduction of uncertainty.
3. Fluent reading requires the use of redundancy — or of information that is available from more than one source — so that prior knowledge can reduce the need for visual information.
4. Reading can be a risky business.

THE COMMUNICATION TRANSACTION

Communication requires the interaction of two participants, who for the sake of generality can be called the transmitter and receiver of information. The transmitter might be a speaker or a writer, and the receiver, a listener or a reader. The transmitter sends, or produces, and the receiver tries to comprehend. The opening statement about the need for *interaction* between transmitter and receiver should be regarded as more than an assertion of the obvious — that there has to be a listener around for a speaker to get the point across, or that writing has no purpose without a reader. The receiver, whether listener or reader, must make a contribution at least as great as that of the transmitter if communication is to occur. In fact, the receiver must provide more information than the amount which is actually available in the sound waves that pass through the air or in the printer's or writer's marks on paper.

In some senses, the task of the receiver is more difficult than that of the transmitter. Not only must receivers have skills of language comprehension compatible with the skills of language production employed by a transmitter, but they may also need to interpret information that includes elements of structure or content quite foreign to their own experience. That is, speakers or writers never have to go beyond their own vocabulary and syntax, and are generally presumed to know what they are talking about. Transmitters can afford to be discursive because they know the point they are eventually going to make. But receivers have none of these advantages; everything that the transmitter takes for granted receivers have to figure out for themselves. The receiver has the additional disadvantage that while transmitters can speak or write at their own pace, the listener can rarely demand a replay or even the slowing down of delivery, and the reader is usually constrained to read in the order in which writers choose to present their thoughts and, as we shall see, function under time constraints that do not necessarily disturb writers. On the other hand, receivers can often ignore much of the information the transmitters are expected to provide.

We shall make a closer study of the active role that the receiver must play in listening and reading when we consider language and its comprehension, examining discrepancies between the sound (or written representation) of language and its meaning that can be bridged only by the contribution of additional information from the receiver.

The Communication Channel and Noise

The transmitter and receiver may be regarded as the two ends of a communication channel along which information may flow in a variety of forms. In a telephone system, for example, the channel of communication between speaker and listener includes the vocal apparatus of the speaker, the microphone and speaker in each of the telephones, the cable linking the two telephones, and the auditory apparatus of the listener. In passing through this communication channel, information takes the forms of complex sequences of neural impulses organizing the message of the speaker, of patterns of vibration in the molecules of the air (sound waves), of electrical impulses in the telephone cable, and of sound waves again on the way to the listener's eardrum, after which it goes through a complicated series of changes on the way to being transformed to another set of nervous impulses directed into the listener's brain. At every stage in this channel, information can be regarded as being embedded in a pattern of signals, structured in both space and time. The problem for the receiver is to interpret the final pattern, the sequence of nervous impulses, and extract a message.

At each part of the communication process there is the possibility that information will be changed in some way. There can be losses because particular sections of the channel are not able to transmit all the signals coming into them. A channel may perhaps be incapable of responding to some aspects of the signal, just as a loudspeaker may not be sensitive enough to produce with fidelity some of the lowest or highest tones of music. Or parts of a signal may be lost because a channel cannot pick up and pass on information as fast as it arrives. The limit to the amount of information that can pass through any communication channel is referred to as *channel capacity*. Channel capacity may clearly be independent of the skill of the receiver, although the limitation may also be part of the communication channel inside the listener — for example, an inability to handle more than a certain amount of information at one time. Such a limitation, which we are all heir to, is sometimes referred to as a limitation on the *information-processing capacity* of the human brain.

In addition, extraneous signals called *noise* may degrade or confuse the message. The concept of noise is not restricted to acoustic events, but can be applied to anything that makes communication less clear or effective, such as a difficult-to-read type face for printed material, or poor illumination, or distraction of the reader's attention. The *static* that sometimes interferes with television reception is visual noise.

More formally, noise may be regarded as a signal that conveys no information, in contrast to the actual information-bearing signal. The receiver must separate the informative signal from the noise, and whenever there is failure to do so part of the message will be lost. Any part of a message that the receiver lacks the skill or knowledge to comprehend obviously becomes noise. The present chapter offers information to readers who understand its language and general theme, but it is literally only noise for anyone else. And noise cannot be easily ignored; it is not an absence of information but rather a negative, information-reducing component of communication. Because communication channels have limited capacities, noise contributes quite uselessly to overloading the system and can interfere with the reception of informative signals.

Because anything becomes noise if one lacks the skill or knowledge to understand it, reading is intrinsically more difficult for the novice than for the experienced reader. For the beginner, everything is much noisier.

There are other ways in which the concepts of limited channel capacity and of noise will be relevant to our consideration of both the fluent and the novice reader. For example, we shall see that there is a limit to the speed at which the eyes can gather information from a passage of text and to the amount of information from the eyes that the brain can handle. Both of these are limitations of channel capacity iɪ. the communication system of the reader. We shall also see that one problem for the beginning reader is to discover which aspects of the visual information of letters and words actually serve to distinguish them from one another — in other words, which are their "distinctive features". Features that are not distinguishing, which do not make a contribution toward differentiating alternatives, such as the elegant ornamental embellishments of some capital letters, are other examples of noise.

Figure 2.1 summarizes in graphic form the main concepts that have been discussed. You may notice that the entire diagram is an alternative way of representing the situation on the left hand side of Figures 1.1 and 1.2 — the relation of visual information to reading. But the right sides of Figures 1.1 and 1.2 also indicate how Figure 2.1 is inadequate as a representation of reading. Figure 2.1 does not represent the other information that the receiver requires to understand a message — the information that does not come through the communication channel.

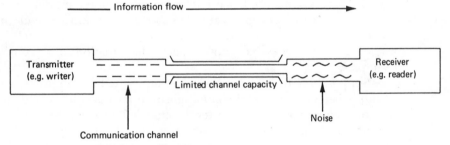

FIGURE 2.1   Concepts in communication

Information and Uncertainty

One contribution that the study of communication systems has made to the study of human behavior has been a clarification of the concept of information, together with a technique by which information can actually be measured. We have seen that information assumes a variety of guises as it passes through different portions of a communication channel, but there has been no clue about what remains constant through all these different manifestations. What is this "information" that flows in the form of patterns of sound waves through the air, light waves through space, and pulses of energy through electric or neural cables? The statement that *information is the reduction of uncertainty* may not appear to make much progress towards clarification until we have a definition of uncertainty. But such a definition is not difficult to find.

Uncertainty can be defined and measured in terms of the number of alternatives confronting the decision-maker. If you are confronted by a lot of alternatives you have a great deal of uncertainty; there are many different decisions you could make. If you have fewer alternatives, it may be just as hard for you to make up your mind but theoretically your uncertainty is less; there are fewer alternative decisions you might make. The argument has nothing to do with the *importance* of the decision to you, only with the number of alternatives. Theoretically, your uncertainty is the same whether you must decide for or against major surgery or for having your morning eggs scrambled or fried. The number of alternatives is the same in each case, and so therefore is your uncertainty.

And now information can be defined more fully: Information is the reduction of uncertainty by the elimination of alternatives. Information, very reasonably, is anything that moves you closer to a decision. It is beside the point whether the decision concerns the identification of particular objects or events or the selection among various choices of action. Uncertainty and information are defined in terms of the *number* of alternative decisions that could be made no matter *what* the alternatives are. However, it is easier to reach an understanding of these concepts if particular situations are taken as examples.

Suppose that the message to be communicated is a single letter of the alphabet. Or to put it in plain English, suppose a child is given the task of identifying a letter written on the chalkboard. There are 26 alternatives available to the transmitter and the receiver — the 26 letters of the alphabet. The receiver's uncertainty involves a decision or choice among 26 possibilities. If the situation involves bidding in a bridge game, then the uncertainty may perhaps concern a player's strongest suit, and the number of alternatives will be four. For the simple toss of a coin, the number of alternatives is two; for the roll of a die, it is six. Sometimes the exact number of alternatives cannot be known, for example, if a name or a word is being transmitted. But it may still be possible to determine when this indefinite amount of uncertainty has been reduced — for example, when the receiver learns that the name or word begins with a particular letter or is of a particular length, either of which will reduce the number of alternative possibilities.

We can now return to the definition of "information" as the reduction of uncertainty. Just as the measure of uncertainty is concerned with the number of alternatives among which the receiver has to choose, so information is concerned with the number of alternatives that are eliminated as a result of the message. If the receiver is able to eliminate all alternatives except one, and thus can make a decision, then the amount of information transmitted is equal to the amount of uncertainty that existed. A card player who receives the information that the partner's strongest suit is red has had uncertainty reduced by a half; if the information is that the strongest suit is hearts, uncertainty is reduced completely. Similarly, a child who knows the letters well enough to decide that the letter on the board is a vowel has acquired information reducing uncertainty from 26 alternatives to five. If the letter is correctly identified, then the information in the letter is equal to the original uncertainty.

Reading can be considered similarly to any other process of acquiring information, namely as the reduction of uncertainty. And we have discovered a way in which the conventionally disparate areas of reading such as letter identification, word identification, and "reading for comprehension" can be considered in the same light. In each of these aspects, information is acquired visually to reduce a number of alternative possibilities. The exact number of alternatives can be specified for letters, an approximate figure can perhaps be put to the number of words, but the number of alternatives for comprehension, if it can be estimated at all, must obviously be closely related both to the passage being read and the particular individual who is doing the reading. However, it is not necessary to specify the exact amount of uncertainty in order to discuss the informativeness of a message — that is one of the advantages of expressing both uncertainty and information in relative terms. We may not know how much uncertainty an individual has about the identity of the sovereign of England in the year 1900, but we do know that uncertainty must be reduced if a message is read and comprehended that the sovereign was a woman. In fact there are quite reliable ways of estimating the amount of information in a particular statement by using what is known about the channel capacity of human perceptual systems as a yardstick.

Redundancy

Redundancy is one of the most important concepts that I shall discuss, although it is a concept that occurs infrequently in the literature on the psychology of reading. Redundancy exists whenever information is available from more than one source. Or we can say — to use the earlier definition of information — that there is redundancy whenever the same alternatives can be eliminated in more than one way. And one of the basic skills of reading is the elimination of alternatives through the use of redundancy.

An obvious way to provide redundancy is to repeat everything;

with this method the alternative sources of information are the two successive sentences. A different method of presenting the same message twice would be to present one version to the eye and the other to the ear — an audiovisual or "multimedia" approach. Repetition is an eminently popular technique in advertising, especially in television commercials, exemplifying one of the practical advantages of redundancy that it reduces the likelihood that receivers will make a mistake, or overlook anything, in their comprehension of the message. There are other aspects of redundancy, however, that are not always as obvious but that play a very important role in reading.

Very often the fact that some of the same alternatives are being reduced by two sources of information is not apparent. As an example of two overlapping sources of information that also each contain some unique information, consider the following pair of sentences:

1. The letter of the alphabet that I am thinking of is a vowel.
2. The letter I am thinking of is from the first half of the alphabet.

At first glance the two statements might appear to provide complementary pieces of information telling us that the letter is a vowel in the first half of the alphabet. However, if we look at the alternatives that each of the two statements eliminates, we can see that they actually contain a good deal of overlapping information. Statement 1 tells us that the letter is not $b, c, d, f, g, h, j, k, l, m, n, p, q, r, s, t, v, w, x, y, z$, and statement 2 tells us that it is not $n, o, p, q, r, s, t, u, v, w, x, y, z$. Both statements tell us that the letter is not $n, p, q, r, s, t, v, w, x, y, z$, and it is to this extent (the extent to which the excluded sets of alternatives intersect) that the statements are redundant. In fact, the only new information provided by statement 2 is that the letter is not o or u; all the other information is already provided in statement 1.

There are frequent examples of redundancy in reading. As an illustration, consider the unfinished sentence (which could possibly appear at the bottom of a right-hand page of a book):

The captain ordered the mate to drop the an-

We shall consider four ways of reducing our uncertainty about the remainder of that sentence, four alternative and therefore redundant sources of information. First, we could turn the page and see how the last word finished — we can call this visual information. But we can also make some reasonable predictions about how the sentence will continue without turning the page. For example, we can say that the next letter is unlikely to be $b, f, h, j, m, p, q, r, w,$ or z because these letters just do not occur after *an* in common words of the English language; we can therefore attribute the elimination of these alternatives to *orthographic* (or spelling) information. There are also some things that can be said about the entire word before turning the page. We know that it is most likely to be an adjective or a noun, because other types of words such as articles, conjunctions, verbs, and prepositions, for example, are most unlikely to follow the word *the;* the elimination of all these additional alternatives can be attributed to *syntactic* (or grammatical) information. Finally, we can continue to eliminate alternatives even if we consider as candidates for the last word only nouns or adjectives that begin with *an* plus one of the letters not eliminated by the orthographic information already discussed. We can eliminate words like *answer* and *anagram* and *antibody* because although they are not excluded by our other criteria, our knowledge of the world tells us these are not the kinds of things that captains normally order mates to drop. The elimination of these alternatives can be attributed to *semantic* information. Obviously, the four alternative sources of information about the incomplete word in the above example, *visual, orthographic, syntactic,* and *semantic,* to some extent provide overlapping information. We do not need as much visual information about the next word as we would if it occurred in isolation because the other sources of information eliminate many alternatives. The four sources of information, therefore, are all to some extent redundant. And the skilled reader who can make use of the three other sources needs much less visual information than the less fluent reader. The more redundancy there is, the less visual information the skilled reader requires. In passages of continuous text, provided that the language is familiar and the content not too difficult, every other letter can be eliminated from most words, or about one word in five omitted altogether, without making the passage too difficult for a reader to comprehend.

One last point. I have been talking of redundancy in reading as if it exists in the written words themselves, which of course in a sense it does. But in a more important sense, redundancy is information that is available from more than one source only when one of the alternative sources is in the reader's own head. Put another way, there is no utility in redundancy in the text if it does not reflect something the reader knows already, whether it involves the visual, orthographic, syntactic, or semantic structure of written language. Redundancy, in other words, can be equated with prior knowledge. In making use of redundancy, the reader makes use of nonvisual information, using something that is already known to eliminate some alternatives and thus reduce the amount of visual information that is required. Redundancy represents information you do not need because you have it already.

HITS, MISSES, AND CRITERIA

The picture that is being developed is of a fluent reader who does not require a fixed amount of information in order to identify a letter or a word. Such readers make their decisions on more or less visual information depending on their access to information from other sources.

Exactly how much information a reader will seek before making a "decision" about a particular letter, word, or meaning will depend on the difficulty of the passage (which must always be defined with respect to a particular reader), on the reader's skill, and on the "cost" of making a decision.

A useful term for the amount of information that individuals require before coming to a decision is their *criterion*. If the amount of information about a particular letter, word, or meaning reaches a reader's criterion for making a decision, then a choice will be made at that point, whether or not the reader has enough information to make a decision correctly.

An important consideration, of course, is how a person decides at what level to establish a criterion — ranging from a supercautious attitude requiring almost an absolute-certainty amount of information before deciding, to willingness to take a chance and make a decision on minimal information, even at the risk of making a mistake. But in order to understand why a particular criterion level is established, it is necessary to understand what the effect of setting a high or low criterion might be.

The concept of criterion developed in the present section comes from an area of study called *signal detection theory,* which has upset quite a number of venerable ideas about human perception. It is traditional to think, for example, that one either sees an object or one does not, and that there is no area of freedom in between within which the perceiver has no role in deciding what can be seen. Signal detection theory, however, shows that in many circumstances the question of whether an object is perceived depends less on the intensity of the object — on its "clarity", if you like — than on the attitude of the observer. Perception, in other words, involves decision-making, just like many other activities of the brain, such as reading. It is also traditional to think that there is an inverse relationship between correct responses and errors, that the more correct responses on any particular task — for example, the greater the proportion of letters correctly identified — the lower the number of errors must be. Signal detection theory, however, shows that the relationship is quite the reverse, and that in identification tasks (such as reading) the proportion of correct responses for a given amount of information can within limits be selected by the perceiver, but that the cost of increasing the proportion of correct responses is an increase in the number of errors. In other words, the more often you want to be right, the more often you must tolerate being wrong. The paradox can be explained by discussing in a little more detail what the theory is all about.

Signal detection theory was originally concerned literally with the detection of signals — with the ability of radar operators to distinguish between the "signals" and "noise" on their radar screens with the objective of identifying aircraft presumed to be hostile. As far as the actual situation is concerned, there are only two possibilities: a particular blip on the screen is either a signal or noise; an aircraft is present, or it is not. As far as the operator is concerned, there are also only two possibilities: a decision that the blip on the screen is an aircraft, or a decision that it is not. In an ideal world, the combination of the actual situation and the operator's decision would still permit only two possibilities: either the blip is a signal, in which case the operator decides that there is an aircraft, or the blip is merely noise, in which case the decision is that there is no aircraft involved. We may call each of these two alternatives *hits* in the sense that they are both correct identifications. However, there are two other possibilities, of quite different kinds, that can be considered errors. The first type of error occurs when no aircraft is present but the operator decides that there is — this situation may be called a *false alarm*. And the other type of error occurs when there is an aircraft present but the operator decides that there is not, that the signal is actually noise — a situation that can be termed a *miss*.

The problem for the operator is that the numbers of hits, false alarms, and misses are not independent; the number of one cannot be changed without a change in the number of another. For example, if the operator is anxious to avoid false alarms, and wants to get maximum information before deciding to report an aircraft, then there will be more misses. If, on the other hand, the operator wants to maximize the number of hits, reducing the possibility of a miss by deciding in favor of an aircraft on less information, then there will also be more false alarms. The situation is rather similar for a sentry on duty on a dark night who hears approaching footsteps but who cannot reveal his own position by asking questions. His alternatives are to shoot or hold his fire. If he shoots and the intruder is indeed hostile, then the sentry will get a medal. If he holds his fire and the stranger is friendly, his decision is also commendable. But a miss (letting through an enemy) or a false alarm (shooting a friend) will have less desirable consequences. Yet the nature of the world is such that sentries always have to settle for some level of probability for the undesirable consequences; the sentry anxious to stop every enemy is going to shoot a friend from time to time while the sentry anxious not to shoot a friend will occasionally let an enemy slip through. Error is unavoidable.

Of course, with increased skills of discrimination both the radar operator and the sentry can improve their level of efficiency and increase the ratio of hits to false alarms, just as increased clarity of the situation will make the task easier. But in any given situation the choice is always the same between maximizing hits and minimizing false alarms. Always the perceiver has to make the choice, to decide where to set the criterion for distinguishing signal from noise, friend from foe, *a* from *b*. The higher the criterion, the fewer will be the false alarms but the fewer also will be the hits. There will be more hits if the criterion is set lower, if decisions are made on less information, but there will also be more false alarms.

Now we can approach the question of the basis upon which the criterion is established: what makes the perceiver decide to set a criterion high or low? The answer lies in the relative costs and rewards of hits, misses, and false alarms. A radar operator who is heavily penalized for false alarms will set the criterion high, risking an occasional missed identification. On the other hand, a sentry who is highly motivated to eliminate every possible enemy, and excused for the occasional slaughter of an innocent friend, will set the criterion low.

Readers cannot afford to set a criterion level that is too high before making decisions. A reader who demands too much visual information will often be unable to get it fast enough to read for sense. The brain's channel capacity is limited. Readiness to take chances is a critical matter for beginning readers who may be forced to pay too high a price for making "errors". The child who stays silent (who "misses") rather than risk a "false alarm" may please the teacher but develop a habit of setting a criterion too high for efficient reading. Poor readers often are afraid to take a chance; they may be so concerned about not getting words wrong that they miss meaning altogether.

SUMMARY

Reading is not a passive aspect of communication. Because of the brain's information-processing limitations, readers must make use of all available forms of **redundancy** in written language — **orthographic, syntactic,** and **semantic** to reduce their dependence upon **visual information** from print. **Information** may be regarded as the reduction of **uncertainty,** which is defined in terms of the number of alternatives among which a reader must decide. One important factor that determines how much information a reader requires to make decisions is the reader's willingness to risk making mistakes. Readers who set a high **criterion level** for making decisions will find comprehension more difficult.

Notes to Chapter 2 begin on page 198.

CHAPTER 3

BETWEEN EYE AND BRAIN

The eyes are given altogether too much credit for seeing. The eyes do not see at all, in a strictly literal sense. The eyes *look*, they are devices for collecting information for the brain, largely under the direction of the brain, and it is the brain that determines what we see and how we see it. The brain's perceptual decisions are based only partly on information from the eyes, greatly augmented by information that the brain already possesses. I have referred to this dual basis of perception in the distinction between visual and nonvisual information in reading.

The present chapter is not intended to be a comprehensive physiology of the visual system, but it will outline a few characteristics of eye-brain function that make critical differences to reading. To be specific, three particular features of the visual system will be considered:

1. the brain does not see everything that is in front of the eyes;
2. the brain does not see anything that is in front of the eyes immediately;
3. the brain does not receive information from the eyes continuously.

Together these three considerations lead to three important implications for reading, and thus also for learning to read:

1. reading must be fast;
2. reading must be selective;
3. reading depends on nonvisual information.

The remainder of this chapter will consider the preceding six points in order.

LIMITATIONS OF VISION

The Brain Does Not See Everything

The fact that the eyes are open is not an indication that visual information from the world around is being received and interpreted by the brain. The brain does not *see* the world as its image falls upon the eye. How could it, when that image must often be a kaleidoscopic blur as the eyes flick from place to place in their fitful investigations of the world? But the argument is more complex than the relatively simple fact that the world we see is stable although the eyes are frequently in movement. The scene perceived by the brain has very little in common with the information that the eyes receive from the surrounding world.

What goes into the open eyes is a diffuse and continual bombardment of electromagnetic radiation, minute waves of light energy that vary only in frequency, amplitude, and spatial and temporal patterning. The rays of light that impinge on the eye do not in themselves carry the color and form and texture and movement that we see; all of these familiar and meaningful aspects of perception are created by the brain itself. The image that presents itself to the eyes is actually lost the moment it gets there. The light-sensitive area of the eyeball, the *retina*, consists of millions of cells that transform light energy into neural impulses by a marvelously intricate process involving the bleaching and regeneration of pigment in the retinal cells. As a result of this chemical transformation, bursts of neural energy begin a complicated and relatively long and slow journey along the optic nerve — actually a bundle of many individual nerve fibers — from the back of the eyeballs to the visual areas of the brain, some six inches away at the back of the head. The messages[1] that pass from the eyes to the brain undergo a number of analyses and transformations on the way. The patterned array of light that falls on the eye and the structured percept that is produced by the brain are linked by a train of nervous impulses that itself has no simple correspondence with the occurrences at either extreme of the visual system.

Not one nerve fiber runs directly from the eye to the brain; instead there are at least six interchanges where impulses along one nerve may cause — or may prevent — propagation of a further pattern of impulses along the next section of the pathway. At each of these neural relay stations there are large numbers of interconnections, some of which determine that a single impulse arriving along one section may set off a complex pattern of impulses in the next, while others may relay the message only if a particular combination of signals arrives. Each interconnection point is, in fact, a place where a complex analysis and transformation of signals takes place.

Three layers of interconnections are located in the retina of the eyes, which is, in terms of both function and embryonic development, an extension of the brain. A tremendous compression of information

---

[1] It is difficult to avoid referring to these bursts of neural energy as "messages" or "information" that the eyes send the brain about the world. But both terms are inappropriate, with their implication that some kind of meaningful content has been put into the messages in the first place. It might be more apt to refer to the neural impulses that travel between eye and brain as "suggestions" or "hints" about a world forever concealed from direct inspection. No scientist or philosopher can say what the world is "really like," because everyone's perception of the world — even when mediated by microscopes or telescopes, by photographs or x-rays — still depends on the sense the brain can make of neural impulses that have come through the dark tunnel between eye and brain. We can no more see the image of the world that falls on the retina than we can see the nerve impulses that the retina sends to the brain. The only part of vision of which we can ever be aware is the final sensation of seeing, constructed by the brain by its own private and mysterious processes.

takes place within the retina itself. When the nerve fibers eventually leave the eye on their journey to the brain (the pencil-thick bundle of nerve fibers is collectively called the *optic nerve*) the information from about 120 million light-sensitive cells in the retina where the neural messages originate has been reduced over a hundredfold; the optic nerve consists of barely a million neural pathways.

An interesting facet of this part of the visual system is that the retina of the eye would appear to have been constructed "the wrong way round" — probably because of the requirements of the process of constructing the retina from an extension of the similarly multilayered brain surface during prenatal development, beginning as early as three weeks after conception. All of the eye's three layers of nerve cells and their interconnections, together with the vessels that provide the retina with its rich blood supply, lie *between* the light-sensitive surface of the eye and the lens. The light-sensitive cells face the world through their own cell bodies, through two other layers of nerve cells, millions upon millions of interconnecting neural networks, and the curtain of their own neural processes as they converge upon one spot (the "blind spot") to pierce the shell of the eye at the beginning of the optic nerve.

The actual nature of the message that passes along this complex cable of nerves is also very different from our perception or belief of what the visual stimulus is really like. Every nerve in our body is limited to convey only one type of signal — either it fires, or it does not. The speed of the impulse may vary from nerve to nerve, but for any one nerve it is fixed; the response is "all or none". The nerve impulse is relatively slow; the fastest rate, for some of the long thick nerves that travel several feet along the body, is perhaps 300 feet a second (about 200 miles an hour), but the smaller nerves, such as those in the visual system and brain, transmit at only a tenth of that speed (about 20 miles an hour, compared with the 186,000 miles a second at which light travels to the eye). Many examples of the way in which the brain imposes stability upon the ever-changing perspective of the eyes are provided by what psychologists call the visual constancies. For example, we always see a known object as a constant size; we do not think that a person or automobile moving away from us gets smaller as the distance increases, although the actual size of the image on the retina is halved as the distance doubles. We do not think the world changes color just because the sun goes in or see a lawn as two-tone grass because part of it is in the shade. The constancy of the visual impression belies the variations in the light information received by the eye. We "see" plates and coins as round, although from the angle at which such objects are usually viewed the image hitting the eye is almost invariably one form of oval or another. A cat that hides behind a chair is recognized as the same cat when it comes out again, although that information is certainly not present in the input to the eye. In fact, the distinctive forms of cats, chairs, and all other objects do not organize themselves neatly for the eye — we can distinguish them because we already know the forms we want to separate. Why else should we perceive Th as T and h and not as Tl and ח or any other arrangement of parts?

One might think that at least the perception of movement is determined by whether or not the information that falls on the retina is moving, but that is not the case. If our eyes are stationary and a moving image falls across them, we do indeed normally see movement. But if a similar movement across the eyes occurs because we move our eyes voluntarily — when we look around a room, for example — we do not see the world moving. Our perception of whether something is moving or not depends as much on the knowledge we have about what our eye muscles are doing as on the visual information being received by the eye. We can easily fool our own brain by sending it false information. If we "voluntarily" move an eye from left to right by the use of our eye muscles, we do not see the book or wall in our field of vision as in motion, but if we move the eye in the same way by poking it with a finger — moving the eye without moving the eye muscles — then we do see the book or wall in movement. The brain "thinks" that if the eye muscles have not been actively involved, then the changing image on the eye must mean external movement, and constructs our perception accordingly.

Tachistoscopes and Tunnel Vision

The preceding discussion was not intended merely to acquaint you with some of the intricacies of the visual system — about which we can do very little in the classroom in any case. The aim was to illustrate that what we think we see at any one time may be very different from what we are actually detecting visually from the world around us. It is important to know that seeing is not a simple matter of an inner eye in the brain examining snapshots or television pictures of complete scenes from the outside world. The brain may generate a feeling that we are able to see most of what is in front of our eyes most of the time, but that is what it is — a feeling, generated by the brain. Upon analysis we may find that in fact we see very little. The eyes are not windows, and the brain does not look through them. Not only what we see, but our conviction of seeing, is a fabrication of the brain.

For a particular example, take the case of reading. When we look at a page of print we probably feel that we see entire lines at a time. In practice, we probably see very much less. And in extreme circumstances we may be almost blind. Paradoxically, the harder we try to look, the less we may actually see. To understand the research that underlies these assertions, it is necessary to acquire some familiarity with a venerable piece of psychological instrumentation and with a rather precise way of talking about very small units of time. The small unit of time is the *millisecond,* usually abbreviated to *msec.* One millisecond is a thousandth part of a second; ten milliseconds is a hundredth of a second; 100 msec is a tenth; 250 msec, a quarter; 500 msec, a half a second; and so forth. Ten milliseconds is about the amount of time the shutter of a camera requires to be open in normal conditions to get a reasonable image on a film. It can also be sufficient time for information to be available to the eye for a single perceptual experience to result. Much more time is required for a message to get from the eye to the brain, or for the brain to make a perceptual decision.

The venerable piece of psychological equipment is the *tachisto-scope,* a device that presents information to the eyes for very brief periods of time. In other words, a tachistoscope is a device for studying how much we can see at any one time. It does not allow the reader a second look.

In its simplest form, a tachistoscope is a slide projector that throws a picture upon a screen for a controlled amount of time, usually only a fraction of a second. One of the first discoveries made through the use of the device during the 1890s was that the eye had to be exposed to visual information for very much less time than generally thought. If there is sufficient intensity, an exposure of 50 msec is more than adequate for all the information the brain can manage on any one occasion. This does not mean that 50 msec is adequate for identifying everything in a single glance; obviously it is not. You cannot inspect a page of a book for less than a second and expect to have seen every word. But 50 msec is a sufficient exposure for all the visual information that can be gained in a single fixation. It will make no difference if the source of the visual information is removed after 50 msec or left for 250 msec; nothing more will be seen. Eyes pick up usable information for only a fraction of the time that they are open.

The second significant finding from the tachistoscopic studies was that what could be perceived in a single brief presentation depended on what was presented and on the viewer's prior knowledge. If random letters of the alphabet were presented — a sequence like *KYBVOD* — then only four or five letters might be reported. But if words were presented, two or three might be reported comprising a total of perhaps 12 letters. And if the words happened to be organized into a short sentence, then four or five words, a total of perhaps 25 letters, might be perceived from the one exposure.

The preceding paragraph reports a most important finding and one that is central to an understanding of reading. To underline its importance I shall reiterate the main points in the form of a diagram.

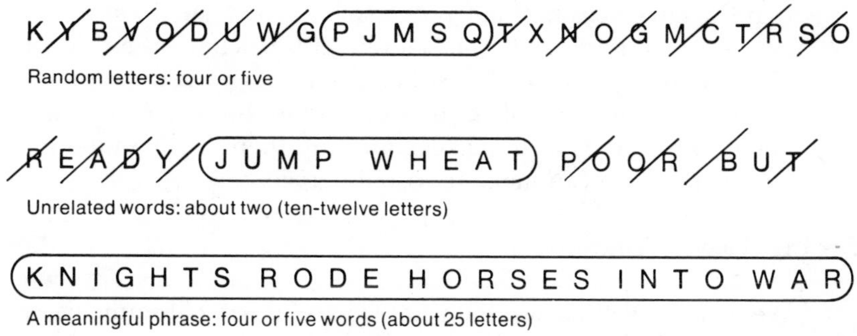

K X B X Q D U W G (P J M S Q) T X N O G M C T R S O

Random letters: four or five

R E A D Y (J U M P   W H E A T) P O Q R B U T

Unrelated words: about two (ten-twelve letters)

(K N I G H T S   R O D E   H O R S E S   I N T O   W A R)

A meaningful phrase: four or five words (about 25 letters)

FIGURE 3.1   How much can be seen in one glance?

In the Notes section at the end of this book, I shall show that the eye and brain are doing the same amount of work in each of the above three situations. The eyes are sending the same amount of visual information to the brain and the brain is making sense of the same proportion of it. But the more sense the letters make — which means the more the brain is able to use nonvisual information — the more can be seen. The difference lies in the number of alternatives confronting the brain in making its perceptual decisions. When the letters are random — or as good as random to the person trying to read them — they are basically unpredictable and demand a good deal of visual information for each identification decision. The reader consequently sees very little and is in a condition known as "tunnel vision" (Mackworth, 1965), very similar to trying to examine the world through a narrow paper tube. Everyone can have tunnel vision sometimes; it has nothing to do with the health or efficiency of the eyes. Tunnel vision is a result of trying to process too much visual information. Airline pilots can suffer from tunnel vision, especially when they have so much to attend to in trying to land a big jet. That is why it takes more than one pilot to fly such planes. All readers can be afflicted with tunnel vision when the material they are trying to read is unfamiliar, opaque, or otherwise difficult — or when through the particular demands of the task or sheer anxiety they try to handle too much visual information. Beginning readers are prime candidates for having tunnel vision much of the time, especially if the books they are supposed to read from make little sense to them. Tunnel vision, in other words, is caused by information overload.

On the other hand, if the text is easily comprehended, entire lines can be seen at a time. So for a teacher who points to some words in a book and says to a child, "There, you can see that clearly enough, can't you?" the answer is probably "No." The teacher who can see the entire line probably knows what the words are in the first place. The fact that the teacher is pointing can make the situation even worse and ensure that the child sees nothing very much beyond the tip of a finger.

You cannot read if you see only a few letters at a time. Tunnel vision makes reading impossible. And the situation cannot be retrieved by trying to look at the words more often. Because, as we are about to consider, seeing takes time, and there is a limit to the rate at which the brain can make its visual decisions.

Seeing Takes Time

We usually feel that we see what we are looking at immediately. But this is another illusion generated by the brain. It takes time to see anything because the brain requires time to make its perceptual decisions. And the time that is required is again directly related to the number of alternatives confronting the brain. The more alternatives the brain has to consider and discard, the longer it takes the brain to make up its mind, so to speak, and for seeing to occur.

The situation is quite analogous to how quickly you can identify your own car in a parking lot. No matter how well you know your own vehicle, and no matter how close you are standing to it, the time it will take you to realize "That's mine" will vary with the number of other cars in the park. Only two cars in the park, and you will spot yours in a fraction of a second. Ten cars, and it will take considerably longer. A hundred cars, and you can be quite delayed.

For an experimental demonstration that the number of alternatives determines the speed of perception, the tachistoscope can again be used. If a single letter of the alphabet is briefly but clearly displayed, say *A*, the delay before the viewer succeeds in saying "A" will depend on the number of letters that could have occurred instead of *A*. Give the viewer no clue, so that the letter might be any one of 26, and the delay — the "reaction time" — can be as long as 500 msec, half a second. Say in advance that the letter occurs in the first part of the alphabet, or that it is a vowel, and the reaction time will be much briefer. Tell the viewer that the letter is either *A* or *B*, and reaction time may drop to as little as 200 msec. With fewer alternatives the brain of the viewer has much less work to do, and the decision comes very much faster.

In reading, it is imperative that the brain should make use of anything relevant that it already knows — of nonvisual information — in order to reduce the number of alternatives. The rather slow rate at which the brain can make decisions can be extremely disruptive. If the brain has to spend too long deciding among the alternatives, the visual information that the eye makes available to the brain will be gone. That is the explanation of tunnel vision — the brain loses access to visual information before it has had time to make many decisions about it.

Visual information does not stay available to the brain for very long after being picked up by the eye. Obviously, visual information remains somewhere in the head for a short period of time, while the brain works on the information collected by the eye in the first few milliseconds of each look. Psychologists have even coined a name for the place where this information is supposed to reside between the time it has been sent back from the eye and the time the brain has made its decisions. This place is known as the *sensory store,* although it so far has remained a purely theoretical construct without any actual known location in the brain. But wherever and whatever the sensory store might be, it does not last very long. Estimates of its persistence vary from half a second to — under optimum conditions — two seconds. But it is just as well that sensory store does persist briefly because a full second is required for the brain to decide even about the limited amount that it is usually able to perceive in a single glance. The visual information that can be utilized in a single glance or tachistoscopic exposure — resulting in the identification of four or five random letters, a couple of unrelated words, or a meaningful sequence of four or five words — in fact requires a full second of "processing time". The title of Figure 3.1 could be amended to read not just "How much can be seen in one glance?" but also "How much can be seen in one second?" This basic physiological limitation on the rate at which the brain can decide among alternatives seems to put the limit on the speed at which most people can read meaningful text aloud, which is usually not much more than 250 words a minute (about four words a second). People who read very much faster than that rate are generally not reading aloud and not delaying to identify every word.

Information is not usually allowed to stay in sensory store for its full term of a second or so. Every time the eyes send another portion of visual information to the brain — which means every time we shift our gaze to a new focal point, or at least blink to take a second look at the same place — then the arrival of new visual information erases the previous contents of sensory store. This phenomenon is referred to as *masking.* It is by the controlled use of masking in tachistoscopic experiments that psychologists have determined that the brain does indeed require a substantial amount of time to make perceptual decisions. The experiments I have discussed to illustrate how much can be seen in a single glance only work if a second exposure to visual information does not follow the first before the brain has had time to make sense of it. If a second exposure is presented less than half a second after the first, the viewer is unlikely to report the full four or five random letters or words that would otherwise be perceived. If the two events occur too close together — say within 50 msec of each other — then the second can completely obliterate the first. Because masking occurs before the brain has time even to decide that something has taken place, the viewer will be completely unaware of a visual event that would otherwise be seen quite clearly. Seeing is a relatively slow process.

On the other hand, because information in sensory store will not persist more than about a second under most conditions, we cannot see more simply by looking longer at one spot. The eyes must be constantly active to replenish the fading stock of visual information in sensory store. A person who stares is not seeing more, but rather is having trouble deciding what was looked at in the first place. Because the contents of sensory store decay rapidly and cannot be replenished from an eye that remains fixed in the same position, the eyes of anyone alert to the visual environment tend to be constantly on the move, even though the brain attends to only the first few moments of every new look. What the brain actually sees of the world around it is constantly subject to interruption.

Seeing Is Episodic

Our eyes are continually in movement — with our knowledge and without it. If we pause to think about it, we know that our eyes are scanning a page of text, or glancing around a room, or following a moving object. These are the movements we can see if we watch another person's face. These movements are rarely random — we would be quickly alarmed if our own eyes or someone else's began rolling around uncontrollably — but instead the eyes move systematically to where there is the most information that we are likely to need. The movements of the eye are controlled by the brain, and by examining what the brain tells the eye to do, we can get a basis for understanding what kind of information the brain is looking for.

But first, we shall consider quite a different kind of eye movement, one not apparently under the direct control of the brain, nor one that is noticeable either in ourselves or others, but which nonetheless can help to underline a point about the constructive nature of vision. Regardless of whether we are glancing around the environment, following a moving object or maintaining a single fixation, the eyeball is in a constant state of very fast movement. This movement, or *tremor*, occurs at the rate of 50 oscillations a second. We do not notice the tremor in other people, partly because it is so fast, but also because the movement covers only a very short distance; it is more a vibration about a central position than a movement from one place to another. But although the movement is normally unnoticeable, it does have a significant role in the visual process; the tremor ensures that more than one group of retinal cells are involved in even a single glance. The tremor provides another illustration of the now familiar point that, if the perceptual experience were a simple reproduction of whatever fell upon the retina, then all we should ever see would be a giddy blur.

The constant tremor of the eye is essential for vision — cancel it and our perception of the world disappears almost immediately. The cancellation is accomplished by a neat experimental procedure called "stabilizing the image" on the retina (Pritchard, 1961; Heckenmueller, 1965). To stabilize the image, the information coming to the eye is made to oscillate at the same rate and over the same distance as the movement of the eye itself. The scene can be reflected through a small mirror mounted directly on the eyeball so that the image always falls on the same position on the retina, no matter what the eye is doing. The consequence of stabilizing the image on the retina is not that the viewer suddenly perceives a super-sharp picture of the world; on the contrary, perception disappears.

The image does not seem to disappear instantaneously, nor does it fade slowly like a movie scene. Instead, entire parts drop away in a very systematic fashion. If the outline of a face has been presented, meaningful parts will vanish, one by one, first perhaps the hair, then an ear, then perhaps the eyes, the nose, until the only thing remaining may be, like the Cheshire cat, the smile. Geometrical figures break up in a similarly orderly way, losing extremities first, or one side after another. The word *BEAT* might disintegrate by the loss of its initial letter, leaving *EAT,* and then by dissolution to *AT* and *A.* By itself, the letter *B* might lose one loop to become *P* and then another to leave *I.* The phenomenon should not be interpreted to mean that the cells of the retina themselves respond to — and then lose — whole words and letters or forms; rather, it shows that the brain holds on to a disappearing image in the most meaningful way possible. Presumably the overworked retinal cells, deprived of the momentary respite the tremor can give them, become fatigued and send less and less information back to the brain, while the brain continues to construct as much of a percept as it can from the diminishing material that it receives.

Other kinds of eye movement need not detain us. There is a kind of slow drift, a tendency of the eye to wander from the point of focus, which is probably not very important because the eye has picked up all the useful information it is going to get during the first few milliseconds. There are "pursuit" movements that the eye makes when it follows a moving object. The only time that the eye can move smoothly and continuously from one position to another is in the course of a pursuit movement. Looking a person up and down with a single sweep of the eyes occurs only in fiction.

The eye movement that is really of concern in reading is, in fact, a rapid, irregular, spasmodic, but surprisingly accurate jump from one position to another. It is perhaps a little inappropriate to call such an important movement a jump, so it is dignified by the far more elegant-sounding French word *saccade* (which translated into English, however, means "jerk").

Fixations and Regressions

A saccade is by no means a special characteristic of reading, but rather the way we normally sample our visual environment for the information about the world. We are very skilled in making saccadic movements of the eye. Guided by information received in its periphery, the eye can move very rapidly and accurately from one side of the visual field to the other, from left to right, up and down, even though we may be unaware of the point or object upon which we will focus before the movement begins. Every time the eye pauses in this erratic progression, a *fixation* is said to occur.

In reading, fixations are generally regarded as proceeding from left to right across the page, although, of course, our eye movements must take us from the top of the page toward the bottom and from right to left as we proceed from one line to the next. Really skilled readers often do not read "from left to right" at all — they may not make more than one fixation a line and may skip lines in reading down the page. We shall consider in a later chapter how such a method of reading can be possible. All readers, good and poor, make another kind of movement that is just another saccade but that has got itself something of a bad name — a *regression*. A regression is simply a saccade that goes in the opposite direction from the line of type — from right to left along a line, or from one line to an earlier one. All readers produce regressions — and for skilled readers a regression may be just as productive an eye movement as a saccade in a forward, or progressive, direction.

During the saccade, while the eye is moving from one position to another, very little is seen at all. The leaping eye is functionally blind. Information is picked up between saccades when the eye is relatively still — during fixations. The qualification "relatively" still has to be made because the eye is never absolutely stationary — there are always tremors and drifts. But neither of these types of movement seems to interrupt the important business of picking up information. The sole purpose of a saccade, in whatever direction, is to move the eye from one position to another to pick up more information. It seems possible to pick up information only once during a fixation — for the few hundredths of a second at the beginning, when information is being loaded into the sensory store. After that time, the back-room parts of the visual system are busy, perhaps for the next quarter of a second, processing the information.

Saccades are fast as well as precise. The larger saccades are faster than the small ones, but it still takes more time to move the eye a long distance than a short one. The movement of the eyes through 100 degrees, say from the extreme left to the extreme right of the visual field, takes about 100 msec — a tenth of a second. A movement of only a twentieth of that distance — about two or three words at a normal reading distance — might take 50 msec.[2] But the fact that a saccade can be made in 50 msec does not mean that we can take in new information by moving the eye 20 times a second. The limit on the rate at which we can usefully move from one fixation to another is set by the time required by the brain to make sense of every new input. That is why there can be little "improvement" in the rate at which fixations are made during reading. You cannot accelerate reading by whipping the eyes along faster.

The number of fixations varies both with the skill of the reader and the difficulty of the passage being read, but not to any remarkable extent. In fact, fixation rate settles down by about Grade 4. There is a slight tendency for skilled readers to change fixations faster than unskilled readers, but the difference is only about one extra fixation a second; adults may average four while the child just starting to read changes fixation three times a second. For any reader, skilled or un-skilled, reading a difficult passage may cut about one fixation a second off the fastest reading rate.

There is also not a dramatic difference between children and adults in the matter of regressions. Children do tend to make more

---

[2]There are some interesting analogies to be drawn between eye movements and hand movements. The top speed of movement for eye and hand are roughly similar, and like the eye, the hand moves faster when it moves over a greater distance. The hand performs the same kind of activity as the eye. It moves precisely and selectively to the most useful position, and it starts "picking up" only when it has arrived. But although the hands of children may move almost as fast and accurately as those of adults, they cannot always be used so efficiently. Children lack the experience of the adult and may not know so precisely what they are reaching for.

regressions than fluent readers, but not so many more, perhaps one for every four progressive fixations compared with one in six for the adult. Once again, the rate of occurrence is determined as much by the difficulty of the passage as by the skill of the reader. Faced with a moderately difficult passage, skilled readers will produce as many regressions as beginning readers with a passage that they find relatively easy. Readers who do not make any regressions are probably reading too slowly — they are not taking enough chances. When children make a lot of regressions, it is a signal that they are having difficulty, not a cause of difficulty. The number of regressions that readers make is an indication of the difficulty of the passage they are trying to read.

In short, the duration of fixations and the number of regressions are not reliable guides for distinguishing between good and poor readers. What does distinguish the fluent from the less-skilled reader is the number of letters or words — or the amount of meaning — that can be identified in a single fixation. As a result, a more meaningful way to evaluate the eye movements of a poor reader and a skilled one is to count the number of fixations required to read a hundred words. Skilled readers need far fewer than the beginners because they are able to pick up more information on every fixation. A skilled reader at the "college graduate" level might pick up enough information to identify words at an average rate of over one a fixation (including regressions) or about 90 fixations per 100 words. The beginner might have to look twice for every word, or 200 fixations per 100 words. The beginner tends to have tunnel vision.

IMPLICATIONS FOR READING

I said at the beginning of this chapter that discussion of the visual system would lead to three important implications for reading and for learning to read — that reading must be fast, that it must be selective, and that it depends upon nonvisual information. By now the basic arguments underlying these implications may be becoming self-evident, but for emphasis I shall elaborate upon them briefly.

Reading Must Be Fast

I mean, of course, that the brain must always move ahead quickly, to avoid becoming bogged down in the visual detail of the text to the extent that tunnel vision might result. I do not suggest that the eyes should be speeded up. As I said earlier, reading cannot be improved by accelerating the eyeballs. There is a limit to the rate at which the brain can make sense of visual information from the eyes, and simply increasing the rate at which fixations are made would have the consequence of further overwhelming the brain rather than facilitating its decisions.

In fact, the customary reading rate of three or four fixations a second would appear to be an optimum. At a slower rate the contents of sensory store may begin to fade and the reader might be in the position of staring at nothing. At a faster rate than four fixations a second, masking can intrude so that the reader loses information before it is properly analysed.

The "slow reading" that must be avoided is the over-attention to detail that keeps the reader on the brink of tunnel vision. Trying to read text a few letters or even a whole word at a time keeps a reader functioning at the level of nonsense and precludes any hope of comprehension. The aim should be to read as much text as possible with every fixation to maintain meaningfulness. Classroom advice to slow down in case of difficulty, to be careful and examine every word closely, can easily lead to complete bewilderment.

There is no one best reading rate; that depends on the difficulty of the passage and the skill of the reader. The best rate also varies with the task itself — on whether the reader is trying to identify every word, for example in order to read aloud, or whether the reading is "for meaning" only. The rate must be different if extensive memorization is being attempted, because rote learning cannot be accomplished quickly. Word-perfect reading aloud and extensive deliberate memorization often require that a passage should be read more than once. A reader is unlikely to comprehend while reading *slower* than 200 words a minute, because a lesser rate would imply that words were being read as isolated units rather than as meaningful sequences. As we shall see in the next chapter, limitations of memory prevent sense being built up from isolated words.

Thus, while comprehension demands relatively fast reading, memorization slows the reader down. As a consequence, comprehension may be impaired and memorization become pointless in any case. If the brain already has a good idea of what is on the page, then slower reading is more tolerable and more time can be spared for memorization. But heavy memory burdens should be avoided when one is learning to read or not familiar with the language or subject matter.

Reading Must Be Selective

The brain just does not have the time to attend to all the information in the print and can be easily inundated by visual information. Nor is memory able to cope with all the information that might be available from the page. The secret of reading efficiently is not to read indiscriminately but to *sample* the text. The brain must be parsimonious, making maximum use of what it knows already and analyzing the minimum of visual information required to verify or modify what it can already predict about the text. All this may sound very complicated, but in fact it is something that every experienced reader can do automatically, and almost certainly you are doing now if you can make any sense of what you read. But like many other aspects of fluent reading, selectivity in picking up and analysing samples of the available visual information is a skill that comes only with experience in reading. Once again the initiative for how the eyes function rests with the brain.

The brain tells the eyes when it has got all the visual information it requires from a fixation and directs the eyes very precisely where to move next. The saccade will be either a progressive or regressive movement, depending on whether the next information that the brain requires is further ahead or further back in the page. The brain always "knows" where to direct the eye, in reading as in other aspects of vision, provided the brain itself knows what it needs to find out. Trying to control eye movements in reading can be like trying to steer a horse by its tail. If the eyes do not go to what we think is an appropriate place in reading, it is probably because the brain does not know where to put them, not that the reader has insufficient acuity for transferring gaze to the right place at the right time.

Reading Depends upon Nonvisual Information

Everything I have said so far should underline this final point. When I assert that reading should be fast, I do not mean recklessly so. A reader must be able to use nonvisual information to avoid being swamped by visual information from the eyes. When I said that a reader should only sample the visual information, I did not want to imply that the eyes could go randomly from one part of the page to another. Rather, the reader should attend to just those parts of the text that contain the most important information. And this again is a matter of making maximum use of what is known already.

To recapitulate, nonvisual information is information we already have in our brain that is relevant to the language and to the subject matter of what we happen to be reading, together with some additional bits of knowledge concerned with quite specific things about writing such as the way spelling patterns are formed. Nonvisual information is anything that can reduce the number of alternatives the brain must consider as we read. If we know that one noun cannot immediately follow another without at least a punctuation mark, then our alternatives are reduced. If we know that only a restricted range of technical terms are likely to crop up in a particular context, then again our uncertainty is reduced. Even the knowledge that certain sequences of letters are unlikely to occur in English words — for example that initial H will not be followed by another consonant — will enable a reader to eliminate many alternatives and see much more at any one time. But meaning is the most important nonvisual information of all.

The skilled reader employs no more *visual information* to comprehend four words in a single glance than the beginning reader who requires two fixations to identify a single word. All the additional information that skilled readers require is contributed by what they know already. When fluent readers encounter a passage that is difficult to read — because it is poorly written or crammed with new information — the number of fixations (including regressions) that they make increases, and reading speed goes down. Because of the additional uncertainty in the situation, they are forced to use more visual information to try to comprehend what they read.

The relative ability to use nonvisual information has consequences in all aspects of vision. Experts — whether in reading, art, chess, or engineering — may be able to comprehend an entire situation at a single glance while the greater uncertainty of novices handicaps them with tunnel vision. When readers in a tachistoscopic experiment are presented with words in a language they do not comprehend, they are able to identify only a few letters. The fact that the words make sense to someone who knows the language is completely irrelevant; to the uninformed readers the letters are essentially random, and inability to see very much will result.[3] The implication for anyone involved in teaching reading should be obvious. Whenever readers cannot make sense of what they are expected to read — because the material bears no relevance to any prior knowledge they might have — then reading will become more difficult and learning to read impossible.

---

[3]There are similar limitations on the amount of incoming information that can be handled by all sensory systems. For example, it is possible to have a distinct hearing loss when trying to understand speech for which there is a lack of "nonacoustic information" — which to all intents and purposes is the same as nonvisual information in reading. Thus we raise our voices when attempting to converse in an unfamiliar language — and children may often be deaf in the classroom although they appear to have no hearing problems outside.

SUMMARY

Reading is not instantaneous; the brain cannot process all the visual information in a page of print. The eyes move in **saccades,** pausing at **fixations** to select visual information, usually progressing in a forward direction but, when needed, in **regressions.** Slow reading interferes with comprehension. Reading is accelerated not by increasing the fixation rate but by reducing dependency on visual information, mainly through making use of meaning.

Notes to Chapter 3 begin on page 202.

CHAPTER 4

BOTTLENECKS
OF
MEMORY

Why should tunnel vision be such a crippling handicap
for readers, whatever their experience and ability? If
a beginning reader can see only a few letters at a
time — say the first half of a word such as

ELEP . . . . — why cannot these letters be remembered for the fraction of a second that the child requires to make a new fixation and see the rest of the word . . . . *HANT*? But unfortunately, memory has its own limitations and cannot be called upon to exceed its own capacity when the visual system is overworked. Fluent reading demands not only parsimony in the use of visual information but also restraint in the burdens placed upon memory. In both cases there are limits upon how much incoming information can be handled. Overloading memory does not make reading easier and can contribute to making reading impossible.

There are a number of paradoxes about the role of memory in reading. The more we try to memorize, the less we are likely to recall. The more we try to memorize, the less we are even likely to comprehend, which not only makes recall more difficult — it makes recall pointless. Who wants to remember nonsense? On the other hand, the more we comprehend, the more memory will take care of itself.

An implication of these paradoxes is that nonvisual information — or what is already in memory — is far more important in reading than trying to hold new information in memory. To repeat a theme which by now should be familiar, the use of nonvisual information in reading is critical (although the importance and functions of nonvisual information are never taught to readers and rarely even acknowledged).

To unravel the paradoxes of memory requires an examination of the way in which memory works — an important topic that deserves a brief chapter to itself.

THREE ASPECTS OF MEMORY

To begin, terms like "memory", "memorization", and "remember" need to be clarified a little. We use the word "memory" in a variety of ways, sometimes to refer to how well we can put new information into our minds, sometimes to how well we can retain it there, and sometimes to how well we can get the information out again. In this chapter we shall consider four specific functions or "operating characteristics" of memory: *input* (or how information goes in), *capacity* (how much can be held), *persistence* (how long it can be held) and *retrieval* (getting it out again). We shall also consider what would appear to be several kinds of memory, since memory does not always appear to be the same process when examined in different ways. Psychologists in fact often distinguish three kinds or aspects of memory, depending on the time that elapses between the original input of information and the

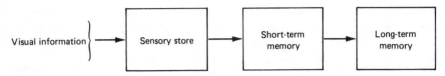

FIGURE 4.1   A typical flow diagram for memory

test to see what can be retrieved. The first aspect, termed *sensory store,* is related to information from its arrival at a receptor organ, such as the eye, until the brain has made its perceptual decision, for example, the identification of several letters or words. The second aspect, usually called *short-term memory,* involves the brief time we can maintain attention to information immediately after its identification, for example, remembering an unfamiliar telephone number as we dial it. Finally, there is *long-term memory,* which is everything we know about the world, our total amount of nonvisual information.

These three aspects of memory are often depicted in textbook "flow diagrams" as if they are separate parts of the brain or successive stages in the process of memorization, as indicated in Figure 4.1. But such a diagram should not be taken too literally. I am not sure that it is most appropriate to refer to different "kinds" of memory, so I shall use the more neutral term "aspects". There is no evidence that different memories exist in different places in the brain, nor that one memory starts functioning when the other leaves off, as the diagram might suggest. It is definitely misleading to imply that information passes in just one direction from short-term to long-term memory, and to ignore the fact that there is always *selectivity* about the amount of incoming information that is processed and its manner of processing.

However, a discussion must begin somewhere and proceed in some kind of sequence, so for convenience I shall discuss the three aspects of memory in the left-to-right order. Later in the chapter I shall offer an alternative diagram for memory.

Sensory Store

The first aspect of memory can be quickly disposed of, because it has already been encountered in the discussion of the visual system in Chapter 3. Sensory store is a theoretical necessity rather than a known part of the brain. Some function or process has to be conceptualized to account for the persistence of visual information after it is received and transmitted by the eye, at the beginning of each fixation, while the brain is working on it. The operating characteristics of sensory store are quickly stated — input is very fast (the first few milliseconds of a fixation), capacity is at least large enough to hold visual information equivalent to 25 letters (although the brain may not be fast enough to identify anywhere near that number), persistence is very brief (about a second under optimal conditions, but normally erased before that time by another fixation), and retrieval depends on how fast the brain can process the information.

Sensory store is of theoretical interest but has little significance for reading instruction because there is nothing that can or need be done about it. Sensory store cannot be overloaded nor can its capacity be increased by exercise. There is no evidence that children's sensory stores are less adequate than adults'. What needs to be remembered is that the brain must make sense of the contents of sensory store, but that the contents do not persist very long. As a result, there is little point in speeding up fixations (which will simply erase sensory store faster) nor in slowing them down (which will result in blank stares). What makes the difference in reading is the effectiveness of the brain in using what it already knows (nonvisual information) to make sense of the incoming information (visual information) briefly held in sensory store.

Short-Term Memory

Can you repeat the sentence you are reading at this moment, without taking a second look at it? Whatever you can do to repeat what you have just read is a demonstration of the function of short-term memory. Short-term memory is "working memory", a "buffer memory", where you retain in the forefront of your mind whatever it is you are attending to at a particular moment. As far as language is concerned, the contents of short-term memory are usually the last few words you have read or listened to, or whatever thoughts you had in your mind instead. Sometimes short-term memory is occupied by what you are about to say or write, by an address you are looking for or a telephone number you want to call. Short-term memory is whatever is holding your attention. And short-term memory is of central importance in reading. It is where you lodge the traces of what you have just read while you go on to make sense of the next few words. It is where you try to retain facts that you want to commit to rote memorization.

Short-term memory would appear to have both strengths and weaknesses, in everyone, just by virtue of the way it functions. On the credit side, there does not appear to be any undue delay in getting information into short-term memory. In fact if someone asks you to call a certain telephone number, your best strategy is to get on your way to dial the number, not to stand around trying to commit the number to memory. Similarly, there does not appear to be any particular problem about retrieving information from short-term memory. If information is in short-term memory you can get it out again at once. Indeed, if you cannot immediately retrieve the information, say the telephone number, then you might just as well go back and ask for it again. Either you have retained the number in short-term memory, in which case it is accessible without delay, or it is gone for good. Short-term memory is what we happen to be attending to at the moment, and if our attention is diverted to something else, the original content is lost.

But if short-term memory seems a reasonably efficient device as far as input and output operations are concerned, in other respects it has its limitations. Short-term memory cannot contain very much information at any one time — little more than half-a-dozen items, in fact. A sequence of seven unrelated digits is about as much as anyone can retain. It is as if a benevolent providence had provided humanity with just sufficient short-term memory capacity to make telephone calls and then had failed to prophesy area codes. For if we try to hold more than six or seven items in short-term memory, then something will be lost. If someone distracts us when we are on our way to make that telephone call, perhaps by asking us the time of day or the location of a room, then some or all of the telephone number will be forgotten and there will be absolutely no point in standing around cudgelling our brains for the number to come back. We shall just have to return and ascertain the number once again. For as much as we try to overload short-term memory, that much of its contents will be lost.

All this is the reason why short-term memory cannot be used to overcome the condition of tunnel vision. The child who has seen only *ELEP* . . . . just cannot hold those letters in short-term memory, read another four or five letters, and get them all organized in a way that makes sense. As the fragmented information from one fixation goes into short-term memory, the fragmented information from the previous fixation is likely to be pushed out. This is not the same phenomenon as the "masking" or erasure of sensory store — it is possible to hold a few items in short-term memory over a number of fixations. But holding such items in the forefront of our attention simply prevents very much more going in and has the obvious result of making reading much more difficult. Not much reading can be done if half your attention is preoccupied with earlier bits of letters and words that you are still trying to make sense of.

The second limitation of short-term memory involves its persistence. Information just does not stay around in short-term memory very long. It is impossible to state an exact amount of time for the duration of information in short-term memory, for the simple reason that its longevity depends on what you do with it. Ignore something in short-term memory for less than a second, and it will be gone. To retain it, you must keep giving it your attention. *Rehearsal* is the technical term often employed. To keep that telephone number in your head, you keep repeating it; it cannot be allowed to elude your attention. Theoretically, information can be kept in short-term memory indefinitely but only if constantly rehearsed, a procedure that is generally impractical because it prevents you from thinking about anything else. Since we can rarely devote much attention to anything apart from what we happen to be doing at a particular moment, and since life tends to be full of distraction in any case, it would therefore seem a reasonable assertion that the persistence of information in short-term memory is generally very brief, even if we cannot put a precise limit to it. Information held in short-term memory must be processed as expeditiously as possible. Retaining information for longer than a fixation or two, for example, pre-empts attention that is required for the task on hand in reading and promotes a further loss of comprehension. The more a reader fills short-term memory with unrelated letters, bits of words, and other meaningless items, the more the letters and bits of words which the reader is currently trying to understand are likely to prove nonsense as well.

Long-Term Memory

Of course, memory is far more than whatever we happen to be thinking about at the moment. There is a vast amount that we know all the time, ranging from names and telephone numbers to all the complex interrelationships that we can perceive and predict among objects and events in the world around us, and only a minute part of all this information is the focus of our attention at any one time. The information that persists in our minds quite independently of rehearsal or conscious knowledge is long-term memory, our continuous knowledge of the world. Long-term memory has some distinct advantages over short-term memory, especially with regard to its relative capacity. Nevertheless long-term memory cannot be used as a dump for any overflow of information from short-term memory, for long-term memory also has its limitations.

Let us begin with the positive side. Where short-term memory is restricted in its capacity to barely half-a-dozen items, the capacity of long-term memory would appear to be infinite. No limit has been discovered to the amount of information that can be lodged in long-term memory. Nothing has to be lost or moved aside in long-term memory to accommodate something new. We never have to forget an old friend's name to make room for the name of a new acquaintance.

Similarly, there is no apparent limit to the persistence of information in long-term memory. No question of rehearsal here. Memories we may not even be aware that we had, recollections of a childhood incident, for example, can quite unexpectedly revivify themselves, triggered perhaps by a few nostalgic bars of music, an old photograph, or even a certain taste or smell.

But as everyone knows, the fact that there seems to be no ultimate limit to the capacity or persistence of long-term memory does not mean that its contents are constantly accessible. It is here that some failings of long-term memory begin to become apparent. Retrieval from long-term memory is by no means as immediate and effortless as retrieval from short-term memory.

Indeed, the processes of retention and retrieval seem quite different. Short-term memory is like a set of half-a-dozen small boxes each of which can contain one separate item of information, by definition immediately accessible to attention because it is attention that holds them in short-term memory in the first place. But long-term memory is more like a network of knowledge, an organized system in which each item of information is related in some way or another to everything else. And whether or not we can retrieve information from long-term memory depends on how the desired information is organized. The secret of recall from long-term memory is to tap one of the interrelationships.

Sometimes the effort to get a hold of something in long-term memory can be most frustrating. We know something is there but cannot find a way to it. An illustration is provided by the "tip-of-the-tongue" phenomenon (Brown and McNeill, 1966). We know someone's name begins with an *S* and has three syllables — and we are sure it is not Sanderson or Somerset or Sylvester. Suddenly the name appears in the set of alternatives that our mind is running through, or perhaps when someone else mentions the name, and then we recognize it at once. It was in long-term memory all the time, but not immediately accessible.

Success at retrieving information from long-term memory depends on the clues we can find to gain access to it and on how well it was organized into long-term memory in the first place. Basically, everything depends on the sense that the information made when we originally put it into memory. It is pointless to try to put an overflow of unrelated pieces of information from short-term memory into long-term memory, and rote learning is so often unproductive. It is not just that nonsense which goes in will be nonsense when it comes out, but that it is extremely difficult to get nonsense out at all.

But there is another reason why it is not feasible to accommodate an overflow from short-term memory in long-term memory, concerned with the rate at which long-term memory can accept new information. In contrast to the practically immediate input of half-a-dozen items into short-term memory, committing something to long-term memory is extremely and surprisingly slow. To put one item into long-term memory takes five seconds — and in that five seconds there is little attention left over for anything else at all. The telephone number which will tax short-term memory to its capacity is at least accepted as quickly as it is read or heard, but to hold the same number in long-term memory, so that it can be dialed the next day, will require a good half minute of concentration, five seconds for each digit.

Committing information to long-term memory is not something that can be attempted recklessly in reading to overcome limitations of visual information processing or of short-term memory. Quite the reverse, attempting to cram information into long-term memory will have the effect of interfering with comprehension. Beginning readers with tunnel vision, who cannot hold in short-term memory more than the few letters they see in a single fixation, are even more confounded if they try to put isolated letters or bits of words into long-term memory.

Fluent readers can find reading impossible if they overburden long-term memory, even if they are trying to read material which they would find completely comprehensible if they relaxed and were content to enjoy it. This problem can be acute for students trying to read a novel or a Shakespearean play and at the same time trying to commit to memory the unfamiliar names of all the characters and every trivial detail or event. Memorization interferes with comprehension by monopolizing attention and reducing intelligibility. Most readers have encountered the perverse textbook that is incomprehensible the day before the examination — when we are trying to retain every fact — yet transparently comprehensible the day after — when all we are reading for is to discover what we missed. If you are having difficulty comprehending what you are reading right now, it may be because you are trying too hard to memorize. On the other hand — as I shall try to demonstrate in a number of ways — comprehension takes care of memorization. If you comprehend what you read or hear, then long-term memory will reorganize itself so efficiently and effortlessly that you will not be aware that you are learning at all.

Long-term memory is in fact extremely efficient, even in terms of selecting and assimilating new information. But only if the process of acquiring and organizing new information is directed by what we know already. Once again we find that it is what we know already that tips the balance, that makes reading possible. It is time to look at how prior knowledge helps to overcome the limitations of both short-term and long-term memory.

OVERCOMING MEMORY LIMITATIONS

There are some paradoxes to be resolved. The experimental evidence is that we can hold no more than half-a-dozen random letters in short-term memory, yet it is usually not difficult to repeat a sentence of a dozen words or more that we have just read or heard for the first time. It appears that we can put no more than one letter or digit into long-term memory every five seconds, yet we can commonly recall many of the larger themes and significant details that we have read in a novel or seen in a film.

To explain these discrepancies it is necessary to clarify some rather loose language that I have been using. I have been talking about retaining half-a-dozen "things" or "items of information" in short-term memory, and putting just one "item of information" into long-term memory. What are these "things" or "items"? The answer is that it depends on what you already know and the sense you are making of what you are reading or listening to. These "things" or "items" are units that exist in long-term memory already.

If you are looking for letters — or if you can only find letters in what you are looking at — then you can hold half-a-dozen letters in short-term memory. But if you are looking for words then short-term memory will hold half-a-dozen words, the equivalent of four or five times as many letters.

It is a question of what you already know. Short-term memory is filled by a seven-digit telephone number, which also requires half a minute to put into long-term memory. But not if the number happens to be 123-4567 because that is a sequence that you already know. The number 1234567 will occupy just one part of short-term memory and will enter long-term memory within a few seconds because, in a sense, it is there already. Can you hold the letters *THEELEPELTJE* in short-term memory? Only if you recognize them as a word, which you will do if you can read Dutch. To put the same sequence of letters into long-term memory would require a good minute of concentration — and even then it is unlikely that you would be able to recall them all tomorrow — unless you already know the word, in which case you will commit it to memory as rapidly as the English word *teaspoon,* which is what the Dutch word happens to mean.

Psychologists refer to this process of storing the largest meaning-ful unit in short-term memory as *chunking*, which is a conveniently picturesque term but also I think a bit misleading. The term suggests that at the beginning we first attend to the small fragments of infor-mation (individual letters or digits) which we subsequently organize into larger units for efficiency in memory. But I think we are looking for the larger units all the time. When we move on to consider more specifically the processes of reading, I shall show that written words can be identified without any reference to letters, and meaning with-out reference to specific words. It is not that we perceive letters which we then — if we can — chunk into words, but that we can perceive words or meaning in the first place and never bother the visual system or memory with letters. The "items" that we commit to memory are the largest meaningful units we can find. In other words, what we put into short-term memory is determined by the largest units that we have available in long-term memory. It is, what we know and are looking for that determines the contents of short-term memory, which is the reason I want to present an alternative diagram of mem-ory to that of Figure 4.1. In Figure 4.2, short-term memory is shown as part of long-term memory — the part that controls what we happen to be looking for in the incoming information. Short-term memory is not an ante-chamber of long-term memory, but that part of long-term memory that we use to attend to, and make sense of, a current situa-tion.

The arrow between short-term memory and sensory store is double-ended to acknowledge that the brain is *selective* about the vi-sual information that it attends to, and the arrows between short-term and long-term memory are double-ended to represent their continual interaction.

One final elaboration must be made. We can hold in short-term memory a few letters, or a few words. But we can also put into short-

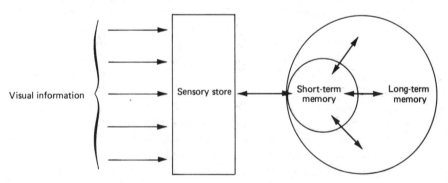

FIGURE 4.2   An alternative diagram for memory

term memory something far more mysterious — we can hold there large rich chunks of meaning. It is impossible to put a number to this — units of meaning cannot be counted the way we can count letters or words. But just as we can hold the letters contained in words in memory far more efficiently than letters that are unrelated to each other, so we can hold meaningful sequences of words in memory far more efficiently than we can hold individual unrelated words. The same applies to long-term memory; we can put an entire "meaning" away in just a few seconds — without any conscious awareness that we are doing so — even though that meaning might have been embedded in a dozen words or more. And by definition, any "meaning" that we put into long-term memory is going to be far easier to retain and retrieve because meaningfulness implies that the input is related to what we already know and makes sense to us.

We must get used to the notion that meaning does not depend on specific words. This crucial point will be elaborated many times in later sections of this book. When we retain a meaningful sequence of words in memory — either short-term or long-term — we are not primarily storing the words at all, but rather the meaning that we attribute to them. "Meaning" is the largest and most efficient unit of analysis that we can bring to bear from what we know already to what we are trying to read (or hear) and understand. For the moment, I shall offer just one illustration of the fact that not only do we look for meaning, rather than specific words, when we comprehend speech or print, but also that this is the most natural thing to do.

I have said that we can hold a dozen or more words in short-term memory if they are in a meaningful sequence, whereas six or seven is the limit for words that make no collective sense, say, the same sequence of words in reverse. Try memorizing: *memory term short in words more or dozen a hold can we.* But in fact it is not the sequence of a dozen or so words that we are holding in short-term memory, but rather their meaning. Often, if you ask a person to repeat a sentence, you will get back the right meaning but not exactly the same words. The person who remembers is not so much recalling the same words as reconstructing the sentence from the meaning that was remembered. We do not in fact attend to words; we attend to meanings. So a substantial "mistake" might be made in repeating exact words — the word *automobile* might be recalled as the word *car,* for example — but there is rarely the substitution of a tiny word that makes a big difference to meaning, such as *not.* We shall see, incidentally, that "errors" of this kind, that preserve meaning, are committed by fluent readers and also by children learning to read who are in the process of becoming good readers. Reading involves looking for meaning, not specific words.

Children do not need to be taught to use memory efficiently — to avoid overloading short-term memory and to refrain from forcing pointless detail into long-term memory. The way their brains are constructed prevents them from doing that. But reading instruction may make these natural efficiencies impossible. Anxiety while learning to read can force children into inefficient uses of memory. Reading, and therefore learning to read, depends on what you already know, on what you can make sense of. Reading teachers help to avoid overloading pupils' memories when they ensure that the material the children are expected to read makes sense to them, and that they are not required — either by the material or by the instruction — to engage in extensive and pointless memorization.

SUMMARY

Short-term memory and **long-term memory** both have their limitations, but these are handicaps only to readers who can make little sense of what they are doing in the first place. When a reader can make sense of the text and does not strain to memorize, there is not even awareness of the bottlenecks of memory.

Notes to Chapter 4 begin on page 207.

CHAPTER 5

KNOWLEDGE AND COMPREHENSION

This book is not concerned with an abstraction called "reading" but with two very real and practical considerations: how we comprehend when we read and how we learn to read in the first place. Here is a provisional definition of comprehension: relating what we attend to in the world around us — the visual information of print in the case of reading — to what we already have in our heads. And here is a provisional definition of learning: modifying what we already have in our heads as a consequence of attending to the world around us. We learn to read, and we learn through reading, by adding to what we know already. If we are to develop and make use of these two provisional definitions, and go on to discuss reading in a meaningful way, then we must first consider what it is that "we already have in our heads".

I have employed two quite different terms to refer to the knowledge that we carry around all the time. I spoke in the first chapter about "nonvisual information", the knowledge we have stored behind the eyes that enables the brain to make sense of the visual information that comes through the eyes while reading. And in the last chapter I talked about long-term memory, our permanent source of information about the world. These are not two distinct parts or aspects of the brain. The nonvisual information that we depend on to understand written language (like the "nonacoustic information" that we need to understand speech) must be long-term memory, our only source of prior knowledge about language and the world. In more general contexts this source of prior knowledge is also referred to by psychologists by a third term — *cognitive structure.* This is a particularly apt term since "cognitive" means knowledge and "structure" implies an organization, and that indeed is what we have in our heads, an organization of knowledge.

Certainly it would be simplistic to suggest that what we carry around in our heads is just "memories". The brain is not an audiovisual souvenir album filled with an assortment of snapshots and tape recordings of bits of the past. At the very least we would have to say that the brain contains memories-with-a-meaning; our memories are related to everything else that we know. Cognitive structure is much more like a summary of our past experience. I do not want to remember that on 16 July I sat on a chair, and that on 17 July I sat on a chair, and on 18 July I sat on a chair. I want to remember that chairs are for sitting on, a summary of my experience. We remember specific events only when they are exceptions to our summary rules or when they have some particularly dramatic or powerful or emotional significance. And even then our memories, when we "recall" them, turn out to be highly colored by our present intentions and perspectives about the world (Bartlett, 1932). Specific memories that cannot be related to our summary, to our present general understanding, will make little sense, which may be the reason we can recall so little of our childhood.

But it would also be an oversimplification to suggest that our heads are filled with an accumulation of facts and rules. The brain is not like a library or encyclopedia where useful information and procedures are filed away under appropriate headings for possible future reference. And certainly the human brain is not like a bank in which nuggets of instruction are deposited by our teachers and our textbooks. Instead, the system of knowledge in our heads is organized into an intricate and internally consistent working model of the world, built up through our interactions with the world and integrated into a coherent whole. We know far more than we were ever taught.

THE THEORY OF THE WORLD IN OUR HEADS

What we have in our heads is a *theory* of what the world is like, a theory that is the basis of all our perceptions and understanding of the world, the root of all learning, the source of all hopes and fears, motives and expectancies, reasoning and creativity. And this theory is all we have. If we can make sense of the world at all, it is by interpreting our interactions with the world in the light of our theory. The theory is our shield against bewilderment.

As I look around my world, I distinguish a multiplicity of meaningful objects that have all kinds of complicated relations to each other and to me. But neither these objects nor their interrelations are self-evident. A chair does not announce itself to me as a chair; I have to recognize it as such. Chairs are a part of my theory. I recognize a chair when my brain decides that a chair is what I am looking at. A chair does not tell me that I can sit on it, or put my coat or books or feet on it, or stand on it to reach a high shelf, or wedge it against a door that I do not wish to be opened. All this is also part of my theory. I can only make sense of the world in terms of what I know already. All of the order and complexity that I perceive in the world around me must reflect an order and complexity in my own mind. Anything I cannot relate to the theory of the world in my head will not make sense to me. I shall be bewildered.

The fact that bewilderment is an unusual state for most of us despite the complexity of our lives is a clear indication that our theory of the world in the head is very efficient. The reason we are usually not aware of the theory is that it works so well. Just as a fish takes water for granted until deprived of it, so we become aware of our dependence on the theory in our head only when it proves inadequate, and the world fails to make sense. That we can occasionally be bewildered only serves to demonstrate how efficiently our theory usually functions. When were you last bewildered by something that you heard or read? Our theory of the world seems ready even to make sense of almost everything we are likely to experience in spoken and written language — a powerful theory indeed.

And yet, when was the last time you saw a bewildered baby? Infants have theories of the world too, not as complex as those of adults, but then children have not had as much time to make their theories complex. But children's theories seem to work very well for their needs. Even the smallest children seem able most of the time to make sense of their world in their own terms; they rarely appear confused or uncertain. The first time many children run into a situation that they cannot possibly relate to anything they know already is when they arrive at school, a time when they may be consistently bewildered or if they are confronted with events that make no sense. We often deny children credit for knowing very much. But, in fact, most of our knowledge of the world — of the kind of objects it contains and the way they can be related — and most of our knowledge of language, is in our heads before we arrive at school. At five or six the framework is there, and the rest is mainly a matter of filling in the details.

For the remainder of this chapter I shall talk a little more about how this theory in the head is organized, and then discuss how it is used so that we can comprehend the world. In Chapter 6 I shall talk about a most important part of the theory of most human beings, that part concerned with language, and then go on to consider language comprehension. In Chapter 7 I shall discuss how the theory of the world is the basis of learning. Then we will be able to get on with the detailed business of examining comprehension and learning in reading.

It may perhaps seem that I am putting these important topics in the wrong order, that comprehension is a consequence of learning which should therefore come first. Certainly it would appear that learning is considered to come before comprehension in school — children must learn in order to understand. But I want to show that learning is more a result of comprehension than its cause. When we eventually get to considering reading in detail I intend to argue that, for a child, learning to read is literally a matter of "understanding reading".

But to do all this I must first explain the nature of comprehension, which will require a short discussion of the way in which our theory of the world is organized, and some detailed consideration of how we put that theory to use.

THE STRUCTURE OF KNOWLEDGE

The system of knowledge that is the theory of the world in our heads has a structure just like any other theory or system of organizing information, such as a library. Information systems have three basic components — a set of categories, some rules for specifying membership of the categories, and a network of interrelations among the categories — and I shall briefly examine each component in turn.

Categories

To categorize means to treat some objects or events as the same, yet as different from other objects or events. All human beings categorize, instinctively, starting at birth. There is nothing remarkable about this innate propensity to categorize, since living organisms could not survive if they did not in fact treat some objects or events as the same, yet as different from other objects and events.

No living organism could survive if it treated everything in its experience as the same; there would be no basis for differentiation and therefore no basis for learning. There would be no possibility of being systematic. Just as a librarian cannot treat all books as the same when putting them on the shelves, so all human beings must differentiate throughout their lives. In our culture at least, everyone is expected to be able to distinguish dogs from cats, tables from chairs, and the letter *A* from the letter *B*.

But similarly, no living organism could survive if it treated everything in its experience as different. If there is no basis for similarity there is still no basis for learning. Thus the librarian must treat some books as the same in some senses — so that all chemistry books are stacked in the same area — even though these books may differ in size, color, and author's name. In the same way everyone, in our culture at least, is expected to ignore many differences in order to treat all dogs as the same, all cats as the same, and many different shapes like A, *A* , *Q*, *a*, *a* as the letter "a".

In other words, the basis of survival and of learning is the ability to ignore many potential differences so that certain objects[1] will be treated as the same, yet as different from other objects. All objects that belong to one category are treated as the same, yet as different from objects belonging to other categories.

---

[1]From this point on, I shall refrain from the cumbersome practice of talking all the time about "objects or events". But every reference to "objects" applies in general to "events" as well.

The categories that we all observe, which are part of our theories of the world, are visually quite arbitrary; they are not generally imposed on us by the world itself. The world does not force us to categorize animals into dogs and cats and so forth — we could divide them up in other ways, for example treating all green-eyed animals as the same, in contrast to those with other eye colors, or differentiating those over fifteen inches in height from those under fifteen inches. The librarian could very neatly organize books on the basis of the color of their covers, or their size, or the number of pages. But we cannot usually invent categories for ourselves — hence the qualification "in our culture at least" in previous paragraphs. The reason we divide animals on a cat and dog basis and not on the basis of size or eye color is that the categories we have are part of our culture. In part, to share a culture means to share the same categorical basis for organizing experience. Language reflects the way a culture organizes experience, which is why many of the words in our language are a clue to the categories in our shared theories of the world. We have the words "dog" and "cat" but not a word for animals with green eyes or less than fifteen inches in height. When we have to learn new categories, the existence of a name in the language tends often to be the first clue that a category exists.

Not that words are essential prerequisites for the establishment of categories. Quite the reverse — categories can exist for which we have no names. I can easily distinguish certain mottled brown and grey birds that come to my garden every morning, but I do not know a name for them. To know a name without an understanding of the category that it labels is meaningless. In fact, the existence of a category is a prerequisite for learning how to use words, since words label categories rather than specific objects. What we call a dog is any individual animal that we put in the category with the name "dog".

The category system that is part of our theory of the world in our heads is essential for making sense of the world. Anything we do that we cannot relate to a category will not make sense; we shall be bewildered. Our categories, in other words, are the basis of our perception of the world. As I have explained, perception can be regarded as a decision-making process. The brain "sees" what it decides it is looking at, which means the category to which visual information is allocated. If I see a chair in front of me, then I must have a category for chairs in my theory of the world and have decided that what I am looking at is an example of that category. If I can see the word *cat* when I read, then I must have a category for that word quite independent of my knowledge of its name or possible meanings, just as I must have categories for the letters *c*, *a*, and *t* if I can distinguish those in the word. Interestingly, we cannot see things in more than one category at a time; it is not possible to see the letters "c", "a", and "t" *and* the word "cat" simultaneously in the visual information *cat,* which is one reason why children may find learning to read more difficult if they have to concentrate on the individual letters in words. Usually you only see what you are looking for, and you are quite unaware of other possible meanings or interpretations. If I ask you to read the address 4I0 LION STREET you will probably not notice that the numerals I0 in 4I0 are exactly the same visual information as the letters I0 in LION. When you look for the category of numbers you see numbers and when you look for the category of letters you see letters. Even now that you are aware of what I am doing, you cannot look at I0 and see both letters and numbers simultaneously, any more than you can see the faces and the vase simultaneously in Figure 5.1. The brain can only make decisions about one category at a time when processing the same visual information (although we could see the faces and vase simultaneously if they did not have a common contour). Unless there is one category to which incoming information can be related, the brain can make no decision at all; the world will not make sense. The brain, like every other executive, needs categories in order to make decisions.

Rules for Category Membership

But categories in themselves are not enough. The category "chemistry books" is useless if a librarian has no way of recognizing a chemistry book when confronted by one, just as a child can make no use of the information that there are cats and dogs in the world without some notion of how to distinguish one from the other. A child who can recite the alphabet has established a set of 26 categories but may not be able to recognize a single letter. For every category that we employ there must be at least one way of recognizing members of that category. Every category must have at least one set of rules, a

FIGURE 5.1   Ambiguous visual information

specification, that determines whether an object (or an event) belongs in that category. Sometimes a single category may have more than one set of rules — we can distinguish an object as an onion by its appearance, feel, smell, and taste. We can recognize the letter "a" in a number of different guises. But just as we must have a category for every object we can distinguish in the world, so we must have at least one set of rules — called *distinctive features* — for allocating that object to the particular category. These are not usually rules that we can put into words, any more than we can open a window into our minds and inspect the categories we have there. Knowledge of this kind is called *implicit* — we only know we have the categories or the rules by the fact that we can make use of them.

The question of what constitutes the rules that differentiate the various categories that we employ in reading and language generally will demand a good deal of attention in later chapters — especially when we see that "teaching" is often little more than telling children that a category exists, leaving them to discover for themselves what the rules are.

Category Interrelations

Rules permit the categories in a system to be used, but they do not ensure that the system makes sense. A library does not make sense simply because all the chemistry books are stacked together in one place and all the poetry books in another. What makes a library a system is the way in which the various categories are related to each other, and this is the way the system in our brains makes sense as well.

I cannot attempt to list all the different interrelations among the categories in the theory of the world in our heads. To do so would be to attempt to document the complexity of the world as we perceive it. As I said when I discussed the content of our minds from the point of view of memory, everything that we know is directly or indirectly related to everything else, and any attempt to illustrate these relationships risks becoming interminable.

For example, consider again an onion. We know what that particular object is called — in more than one language perhaps — and also the names of several kinds of onion. All these are relations of the particular object to language. We also know what an onion looks, feels, smells, and tastes like, again perhaps in more than one way. We know where an onion comes from — how it is grown — and we probably have a good idea about how it gets to the place where we know we can buy one. We know roughly what we have to pay to buy one. We know how an onion can be used in cooking, and probably its other uses as well. We may know half-a-dozen different ways of cooking onions (with different names), and we certainly know a number of things that can be eaten with onions. We know a number of instruments for dealing with onions — knives, graters, and blenders, for example. We not only know what we can do with onions, we also know what onions can do to us, both raw and cooked. We know people who love onions and people who hate them; people who can cook them and people who cannot. We may even know something about the role of onions in history. One enormous ramification of our knowledge of onions is related to the fact that we can call them by more than one name. An onion can also be called a vegetable, which means that everything we know about vegetables in general, applies to onions in particular. Indeed, every time we relate an onion to something else — to a knife, a frying pan, or a particular person — then we discover that what we know about onions is part of what we know about knives, frying pans, and people. There is no end.

Many interrelations are part of the system of language that is such an important part of our theory of the world. One complex set of interrelations is called *syntax*, which is the way elements of language are related to each other. Another set of interrelations is called *semantics*, which is the way language is related to the rest of our theory of the world. Both of these important topics will be considered in the next chapter, which will be devoted to language and in particular to language comprehension.

But just as our knowledge of language is based on our knowledge of the world, so our ability to comprehend language is based on our ability to comprehend the world. The final section of the present chapter will illustrate how we use our theory of the world to comprehend the world.

PREDICTION AND COMPREHENSION

Cognitive structure, the theory of the world in our heads, may so far have seemed rather a static place, not much different in essence from an encyclopedia. But the theory of the world in our heads is *dynamic*, and not just in the sense that it is constantly being added to and changed, particularly during that lively period of intense learning and growth we call childhood. Time and change are an essential part of the way we perceive the world — how otherwise could we understand language, music, or even a football match? — and also of the way we operate upon the world. Our skills are the part of our theory of the world that enables us to interact with the world, to take the initiative in our transactions with our environment. And every skill involves delicate temporal organization. Our theory of the world is indeed dynamic.

Besides, we can do even more with the theory in our heads than make sense of the world and interact with it. We can live in the theory of the world itself. Within this theory we can exercise our imagination to invent and create, to test the possible solutions to problems and examine the consequences of possible behaviors. We can explore new worlds of our own and can be led into other worlds by writers and artists. But the aspect of imagination with which we shall be most concerned is more mundane, though at first encounter it may sound quite exotic. We can use the theory of the world in our heads *to predict the future.* This ability to predict is both pervasive and profound, because it is the basis of our comprehension of the world.

The Pervasiveness of Prediction

Everyone predicts — including children — all the time. Our lives would be impossible, we would be reluctant even to leave our beds in the morning, if we had no expectation about what the day will bring. We would never go through a door if we had no idea of what might be on the other side. And all our expectations, our predictions, can be derived from only one source, the theory of the world in our heads.

We are generally unaware of our constant state of anticipation for the simple reason once again that our theory of the world works so well. Our theory is so efficient that when our predictions fail, we are surprised. We do not go through life predicting that anything might happen — indeed, that would be contrary to prediction, and in that case nothing could surprise us. The fact that something always could rhinoceros take us by surprise — like the word *rhinoceros* a few words ago — is evidence that indeed we always predict but that our predictions are usually accurate. It is always possible that we could be surprised, yet our predictions are usually so appropriate that surprise is a very rare occurrence. When was the last time you were surprised?

We drive through a town we have never visited before, and nothing we see surprises us. There is nothing surprising about the buses and cars and pedestrians in the main street; they are predictable. But we do not predict that we might see anything — we would be surprised to see camels or submarines in the main street. Not that there is anything very surprising or unpredictable about camels or submarines in themselves — we would not be surprised to see camels if we were visiting a zoo or to see submarines at a naval base. In other words, our predictions are very specific to situations. We do not predict that anything will happen, nor do we predict that something is *bound* to happen if it is only *likely* to happen (we are no more surprised by the absence of a bus than we are by the presence of one), and we predict that many things are unlikely to happen. Our predictions are remarkably accurate — and so are those of children. It is rare to see a child who is surprised.

The Need for Prediction

Why should we predict? Why should we not expect anything all the time, and thus free ourselves from any possibility of surprise? I can think of three reasons. The first reason is that our position in the world in which we live changes constantly, and we are usually far more concerned with what is likely to happen in the near and distant future than we are with what is actually happening right now. An important difference between a skilled driver and a learner is that the skilled driver is able to project the car into the future while the learner's mind is more closely anchored to where the car is now — when it is usually too late to avoid accidents. The same difference tends to distinguish skilled readers from beginners, or from anyone having difficulty with a particular piece of reading. In fluent reading the eye is always ahead of the brain's decisions, checking for possible obstacles to a particular understanding. Readers concerned with the word directly in front of their nose will have trouble predicting — and they will have trouble comprehending.

The second reason for prediction is that there is too much ambiguity in the world, too many ways of interpreting just about anything that confronts us. Unless we exclude some alternatives in advance, we are likely to be overwhelmed with possibilities. Of the many things I know about onions, I do not want to be concerned with the fact that they are dug from the ground, or bring my cousin George out in spots, if all I want is some garnish for a hamburger. What I see is related to what I am looking for, not to all possible interpretations. Words have many meanings — *table* can be several kinds of verb as well as several kinds of noun — but there is only one meaning that I am concerned with, that I predict, if someone tells me to put my books on the table. All the everyday words of our language have many meanings and often several grammatical functions — *table, chair, house, shoe, time, walk, open, narrow* — but by predicting the range of possibilities that a word is likely to be, we are just not aware of the potential ambiguities.

The final reason for prediction is that there would otherwise be far too many alternatives from which to choose. As we have seen, the brain requires time to make its decisions about what the eyes are looking at, and the time that it requires depends on the number of alternatives. We take longer to decide that we are looking at the letter *A* when it could be any one of the twenty-six letters of the alphabet than when we know that it is a vowel or that it is either *A* or *B*. It takes much longer to identify a word in isolation compared with a word in a meaningful sentence. The fewer the alternatives, the quicker the recognition. If there are too many alternatives confronting the eyes, then it is much harder to see or to comprehend. Tunnel vision is a consequence of being unable to predict.

Prediction is not reckless guessing, nor is it a matter of taking a chance by betting on the most likely outcome. We do not go through life saying "Round the next corner I shall see a bus" or "The next word I read will be *rhinoceros.*" We predict by disregarding the unlikely. Here is a formal definition: *Prediction is the prior elimination of unlikely alternatives.* We use our theory of the world to tell us the most possible occurrences, and leave the brain to decide among those remaining alternatives until our uncertainty is reduced to zero. And we are so good at predicting only the most likely alternatives that we are rarely surprised.

Put more informally, prediction is a matter of asking specific questions. We do not ask "What is that object over there?" but "Can we put our books on it?" or whatever we want to do. We do not look at a page of print with no expectation about what we shall read next, instead we ask "What is the hero going to do; where is the villain going to hide; and will there be an explosion when liquid A is mixed with powder B?" And provided the answer lies within the expected range of alternatives — which it usually does if we are reading with comprehension — then we are not aware of any doubt or ambiguity. We are neither bewildered nor surprised.

The Relativity of Comprehension

Now at last I can say what I mean by "comprehension". Prediction means asking questions — and comprehension means getting these questions answered. As we read, as we listen to a speaker, as we go through life, we are constantly asking questions; and as long as these questions are answered, and our uncertainty is reduced, then we comprehend. The person who does not comprehend how to repair a radio is the one who cannot answer such questions as "Which of these wires goes where?" The person who does not comprehend the speaker of a foreign language is the one who cannot answer questions like "What is he trying to tell me?" And the person who does not comprehend a book or newspaper article is the one who cannot find the answers to questions concerning what the next part of the print might be about.

Such a definition of comprehension is rather different from the way in which the word is often used in school. So-called comprehension tests in school are usually given after a book has been read, and, as a consequence, are more like tests of long-term memory. (And since the effort to memorize can drastically interfere with comprehension, the test may finish up by destroying what it sets out to measure.) Comprehension is not a quantity, it is a state — a state of having no unanswered questions. If I say that I comprehended a certain book, it does not make sense to give me a test and argue that I did not understand it. A score on a test certainly would not convince me that I had really understood a book or a speaker if my feeling is that I did not. If my eyes glaze over while you talk or my brow furrows deeply as I read, these are reasonable hints that all is not well with my comprehension. But the ultimate test must lie within the individual.

The very notion that comprehension is relative, that it depends on the questions that an individual happens to ask, is not one that all educators find easy to accept. Some want to argue that you may not have understood a book even if you have no unanswered questions at the end. They will ask, "But did you understand that the spy's failure to steal the secret plans was really a symbol of man's ineluctable helplessness in the face of manifest destiny?" And if you say, "No, I just thought it was a jolly good story", they will tell you that you did not *really* comprehend what the story was about. But basically what they are saying is that you were not asking the kind of question they think you should have asked while reading the book, and that is another matter altogether.

SUMMARY

Nonvisual information, long-term memory, and prior knowledge are alternative terms for describing **cognitive structure,** the theory of the world in the brain that is the source of all **comprehension.** The basis of comprehension is **prediction,** or the prior elimination of unlikely alternatives. By minimizing uncertainty in advance, prediction relieves the visual system and memory of overload in reading. Predictions are questions that we ask the world, and comprehension is receiving answers. If we cannot predict, we are confused. If our predictions fail, we are surprised. And if we have nothing to predict because we have no uncertainty, we are bored.

Notes to Chapter 5 begin on page 210.

CHAPTER **6**

LANGUAGE
spoken
and
written

Language constitutes a substantial part of any human being's theory of the world and obviously plays a central role in reading. The present chapter will be concerned with language from a number of perspectives, including the relationships between the sounds (and printed marks) of language and their meaning, between productive aspects of language (talking and writing) and receptive aspects (listening and reading), and between spoken and written language. The chapter will also refer briefly to grammar, and to the relationship between language and thought.

All of these aspects of language are relevant to an understanding of reading; yet all are complex areas of study in their own right. Obviously it will not be possible to study any topics to the same theoretical depth as the professional linguist or psychologist — but fortunately such detail is also not necessary. The handful of basic insights that a student of reading must grasp are relatively easy to explain and to demonstrate. These insights, however, are not always part of the general awareness of educators in the field of reading; they are widely disregarded in many instructional programs and materials and in a good deal of reading research, so that they may appear to be new and even unfamiliar ideas. For example, one basic but neglected insight is that actual instances of language — the statements that people utter or write — do not convey meaning in any simple fashion. Meaning is not contained within the sounds of speech or the printed marks of writing, conveniently waiting to be discovered or decoded, but rather must be provided by the listener or reader. As a consequence, an understanding of reading requires a more complex theory of comprehension than one that simplistically assumes that meaning will take care of itself provided a reader can identify individual words correctly. Most of this chapter will be concerned with the fundamental issue of how language is comprehended.

TWO ASPECTS OF LANGUAGE

Surface Structure and Deep Structure

There are two quite different ways of talking about language, whether spoken or written. On the one hand, you can talk about its physical aspect, about characteristics that can be measured, such as the loudness or duration or pitch of the sounds of speech, or the number, size, or contrast of the printed marks of writing. All of these observable characteristics of language that exist in the world around us may be called *surface structure*. They are the part of language accessible to the brain through the ears and eyes. "Surface structure" is a useful term because it is not restricted to a particular form of language, either spoken or written. Surface structure is the "visual information" of written language — the source of information that is lost to the reader when the lights go out — but it is also the part of spoken language — the part that is lost when a telephone connection is broken.

On the other hand, there is a part of language that can neither be directly observed nor measured, and that is meaning. In contrast to surface structure, the meaning of language, whether spoken or written, can be referred to as *deep structure*. The term is apt. Meanings do not lie at the surface of language but far more profoundly in the minds of the users of language: in the mind of the speaker or writer and in the mind of the listener or reader.

These two different aspects of language, the physical surface structure and the meaningful deep structure, are in fact completely independent, in the sense that it is quite possible to talk about one without reference to the other. We can say that someone is talking loudly or softly, or fast or slowly, without reference to what is being said. We can say that a line of print is five inches wide, or has eight distinct symbols to the inch, without fear that someone will contradict us by saying that we have not understood the meaning of the text. But conversely, meaning is not directly affected by the form of the surface structure. If we are told that Paris will host the next Olympic Games, we cannot reply that it depends on whether the speaker's source of information was spoken or written. Though it may be occasionally overlooked, the truth of an utterance is not related to its loudness or the number of repetitions.

All of this may seem very obvious, trite even, but in fact the distinction between the surface structure and the deep structure of language is crucial for an understanding of reading for one simple reason: the two aspects of language are separated by a chasm. Surface and deep structures are not opposite sides of the same coin; they are not mirror reflections of each other. They are not directly and unambiguously related. Put into technical terms, *there is not a one-to-one correspondence between the surface structure of language and meaning.* In more general terms, meaning lies beyond the mere sounds or printed marks of language, and cannot be derived from surface structure by any simple or mechanistic process.

One way of exemplifying this absence of a one-to-one relationship between the two aspects of language is by showing that differences can occur in surface structure that make no difference to meaning, and that there can be differences in meaning that are not represented in surface structure (Miller, 1965). For example, here are some radically different surface structures that do not correspond to radical differences in meaning: (1) *The cat is chasing a bird;* (2) *a bird is chased by the cat;* (3) *a warm-blooded feathered vertebrate is pursued by the domesticated*

feline quadruped; (4) *le chat chasse un oiseau.* Four quite different sequences of marks on paper; but all represent (in general terms at
least) the same meaning. When we try to say what words mean, all we
can do is offer other words (a synonym or a paraphrase) that reflect
the same meaning. The actual meaning always lies beyond words. It
makes sense to say that *bachelor* means (or more accurately, conveys
the same meaning as) *unmarried man,* but it does not make sense to ask
what the meaning is that *bachelor* and *unmarried man* have in common.
Alternative verbal definitions or descriptions simply compound the
problem. They are additional surface structures.

On the other hand, it is not difficult to find individual surface
structures which have at least two possible meanings or interpretations. For example: *flying planes can be dangerous; visiting professors may
be tedious; the shooting of the principals was terrible; the chickens were too hot
to eat; she runs through the spray and waves; he enjoys talking with old men
and women (all women?); Cleopatra was rarely prone to talk (and Mark
Anthony was not inclined to argue).*

The examples I have just quoted represent a particular kind of
ambiguity, namely puns. But often puns are difficult to comprehend
at once — you may not have seen the alternative meanings in all of the
above examples immediately — and there lies an important theoretical issue: why are we so rarely aware of the potential ambiguity of
language? I propose to show that it is not just puns but every possible
sequence of words in our language, and just about every individual
word for that matter, that is a source of potential misinterpretation.
To understand why we are so rarely aware of the multiple meanings
that might be attributed to surface structures of our language, we
must look at a more basic question. If there is this chasm between
surface structure and deep structure, how then is language comprehended in the first place? The question is of considerable relevance to reading, because if meaning is not immediately and unambiguously given by the surface structure of speech, then there is no
point in expecting a reader to "decode" written language to speech in
order for comprehension to occur. Speech itself needs to be comprehended, and print cannot be read aloud in a comprehensible way
unless it is comprehended in the first place. Written language does
not require decoding to sound in order to be comprehended; the
manner in which we bring meaning to print is just as direct as the
manner in which we understand speech. The basic processes of language comprehension are the same for all surface structures.

The argument is so important that it warrants summarization in a
diagram. Spoken language is comprehended not by "decoding"
sounds, but by bringing meaning to them, as indicated by the
double-ended arrow on the left of Figure 6.1. Reading aloud is not a

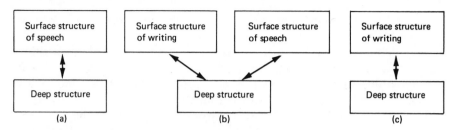

FIGURE 6.1   (a) The comprehension of speech; (b) reading aloud; (c) reading silently

matter of decoding from the surface structure of print to the surface structure of speech, but must also be mediated through meaning (center of Figure 6.1). And for silent reading (right of Figure 6.1) any attempt to understand through subvocal speech is unnecessary as well as disabling, since meaning can be brought to print directly. Oral reading is more complex and difficult than silent reading. All these are points that I shall elaborate upon in subsequent chapters on word and meaning identification in reading.

The Trouble with Words

How then is language understood, whether spoken or written? The answer is not that we put together the meaning of individual words and thereby understand entire sentences. For a start, it seems very doubtful whether words can be said to exist in spoken language at all. Certainly scientific instruments cannot isolate the beginning and ending of many sounds — or even words — that we hear as quite separate. The actual flow of speech is relatively continuous and smoothly changing, and the segmentation into distinct sounds and words is largely something that listeners contribute. You can get some indication of this by uttering the two words "west end" and repeating them while listening very carefully to what you are saying. You will probably find that if you introduce any pause at all in the utterance, it will be between the /s/ and the /t/ — that actually you are saying "wes tend" rather than "west end". Of course, English speakers would never think that you really said "wes tend". But only because they speak the language and are able to work out — and hear — the sounds you *thought* you were producing. The fact that you need to *know* a language in order to be able to *hear* it properly becomes apparent when you listen to a foreign language. Not only can you not distinguish what the distinctive sounds of the language are, but you cannot even distinguish the number of words in an utterance. Believe it or not, foreign speakers — and children — have exactly the same trouble with English. They hear *bank rate* as *bang crate* and *law and order* as *Laura Norder*.

The very existence of words may be an artifact of the writing system. At least in writing we can provide a definition of a word — as something with a white space on either side. Children learning to talk either produce groups of words that they use as one long word — "allgone", "drinkamilk", "gowalk" — or else single words that they use as entire sentences — "drink", "tired", "no". Beginning readers often cannot say how many words are in a sentence, either spoken or written. They need to be readers to understand the question.

Another reason why it is difficult to argue that the meanings of sentences are made up of the meanings of words is that it would appear that words often get meaning as a virtue of occurring in sentences. In fact, it is very difficult to see what meaning a word in isolation can have. Even nouns, which might seem the easiest class of words to account for, present difficulties. It is certainly far from true that every object has one name and every word, one meaning. Every object has more than one name. The family pet, for example can be called a canine, a dog, a boxer, Rover, an animal, and a variety of other titles including, of course, "family pet" and "that slavering brute". What is the "real name" of the animal? There is not one. The appropriate name for the speaker to use depends on the listener and the extent of the listener's uncertainty. In talking to a member of the family, the name "Rover" is adequate, or simply "the dog"; on other occasions no single word would be adequate and the name would have to be qualified as "that brown dog over there" or "the large boxer". Everything depends on the knowledge of the receiver and the alternatives from among which Rover has to be distinguished. The same animal will be described in different ways to the same person depending on the characteristics of other dogs that are around. What then does a word like "dog" mean? The dictionary tells us that it is "any of a large and varied group of domesticated animals related to the fox, wolf, and jackal". But that surely is not the meaning of "dog" in the sentence "Beware of the dog", let alone such expressions as hot dog, top dog, putting on the dog, dirty dog, dog tired, or going to the dogs.

As I pointed out in the previous chapter all the common words of our language have a multiplicity of meanings, with the most common words being the most ambiguous. To test this assertion, just look up a few words in the dictionary. Words that come most immediately to mind — the everyday words like *table, chair, shoe, sock, horse, dog, field, file, take, look, go, run, raise, narrow* are the ones that require many inches and even columns of "definition," while less familiar words like *osmosis, gossamer,* or *tergiversation* are disposed of in a crisp line or two.

The most common words of our language, the prepositions, have so many different senses that they are sometimes maligned as having "function" rather than "content". But it makes a difference whether something is in the box rather than on the box; prepositions have meanings — in great number. The linguist Fries (1952) for example discovered in the Oxford Dictionary no fewer than thirty-nine separate senses for *at* and *by*, forty each for *in* and *with*, and sixty-three for *of*. You would surely have no difficulty in understanding the statement *I found the book by Charles Dickens by the tree by chance; I shall return it by mail by Friday* — but it would be very difficult for you to tell me the meaning (or meanings) of the word "by" on all or any of its five occurrences. Prepositions in context seem full of meaning, but in isolation it is impossible to say what the meaning might be. That is why it is so difficult to translate prepositions from one language to another.

It is not necessary to pursue the argument about the nature of words, or their meaning, because it is quite clear that sentences are not understood by trying to put together meanings of individual words. *The man ate the fish* and *The fish ate the man* contain exactly the same words, yet they have quite different meanings. A *Maltese cross* is not the same as a *cross Maltese,* any more than a *Venetian blind* is a *blind Venetian.* A house that is *pretty ugly* is not exactly ugly, but is certainly not pretty. Obviously, the words in all these examples do not combine in any simple fashion to form the meaning of the whole sentence; in fact, the meaning of many of the individual words in the sentence would appear to be quite different from the meaning we might say they have in isolation.

Perhaps then word order is the key — the word *cross* has one meaning before *Maltese* and another meaning after. But words in the same position can represent different meanings — compare the first words of *Man the boats* and *Man the hunter* — while words in different positions in a sentence may reflect the same meaning. Words that often seem to have a similar meaning, such as *look, view* and *see,* may suddenly acquire quite different meanings without any variation in position, as in *overlook, overview,* and *oversee,* while words that may seem opposite in meaning, such as *up* and *down,* may occasionally lose their distinctiveness, as in *slow up* and *slow down.*

A common explanation is that grammar makes the difference, indeed the entire theory of Chomsky (1957, 1975), is that syntax (word order) is the bridge between the surface structure of language and its deep structure. But the problem with this point of view is that often it is impossible to say what a word's grammatical function is before the sentence in which it occurs is understood. Grammar, in other words, does not reveal meaning; meaning must precede grammatical analysis. Consider again the familiar words that I have been citing like *man, table, chair, shoe, sock, horse, dog, field, take, go,* and so forth; these are all words that not only have a multiplicity of meanings but also a variety of grammatical functions. To ask anyone to identify such words when they are written in isolation is rather nonsensical since they can commonly be both noun and adjective, or noun and verb, or adjective and verb, or perhaps all three. How do we understand a simple statement like *open the empty bottle?* Not by taking into account the fact that *open* is a verb and *empty* an adjective; because in the equally comprehensible sentence *empty the open bottle,* the two words switch grammatical roles without any difference in surface structure. This complicated ambiguity of language is the reason that computers cannot intelligently translate language or make abstracts, even when programmed with a "dictionary" and a "grammar" (Oettinger, 1969). Computers lack the knowledge of the world that is required to make sense of language. Thus a computer is befuddled by over a dozen different possible meanings of a simple expression like *time flies.* Is *time* a noun, or a verb (as in *time the racehorses*) or an adjective (like the word *fruit* in *fruit flies*)? Is *flies* a noun or a verb? Such a computer is said to have interpreted *out of sight, out of mind* as *invisible and insane.*

Not only is it possible to state the grammatical function of individual words outside of a meaningful context, it can also be impossible to state the grammatical structure of entire sentences without prior understanding of their meaning. Most English teachers would automatically parse *the onions are planted by the farmer* as a passive sentence, since it contains the three grammatical markers of the passive form — the auxiliary *are,* the participle ending *-ed* and the preposition *by.* By certain transformational rules the sentence can be converted into the active form: *the farmer plants the onions.* But the sentence *the onions are planted by the tree* is not a passive sentence, although its surface structure would appear to contain the appropriate three grammatical markers. The second sentence cannot be transformed into *the tree plants the onions* — but not for any grammatical reason. Meaning determines the grammatical structure of these sentences, not the surface structure markers. In fact, *the onions are planted by the farmer* need not be a passive sentence, since it is just as ambiguous grammatically as *she was seated by the minister;* the grammar depends upon the meaning.

In other words — and this must be the answer to the question at the beginning of this section — there is only one way in which language can be understood, that print can be comprehended, and that is by having meaning brought to it.

Comprehension through Prediction

The assertion that language is understood by having meaning brought to it obviously cannot be taken to imply that any particular utterances or sentences can mean anything. Usually, there would be some broad general agreement about the main implications of statements, at least when they are made in real world situations. If someone in an elevator remarks "It is raining outside," not many people would want to claim that it could mean that the streets are dry. And by the same argument, the meanings that listeners and readers bring to language cannot be wild guesses; the usual broad general agreement about implications makes the reckless attribution of meaning unlikely as well. If most people seem to be in agreement about the kind of meaning that can be attributed to a particular sequence of words, then some explanation must be found why such agreement exists.

The explanation that can be offered is not unfamiliar. Language tends to be understood in the same way on specific occasions for the same reason that it is understood on any occasion at all — because listeners or readers must have a pretty good idea about the meaning that was intended in the first place. To be more precise, meaning is brought to language through prediction, which you will remember from the previous chapter means the prior elimination of unlikely alternatives. Prediction does not mean staking everything on one wild guess (which would indeed run the risk of frequent error), nor does it mean that the precise meaning is known in advance (which would of course make attention to language unnecessary in the first place). Prediction simply means that the uncertainty of the listener or reader is limited to a few probable alternatives, and provided that information can be found in the surface structure of the utterance to dispose of the remaining uncertainty — to indicate which predicted alternative is appropriate — then comprehension takes place.

Prediction is the reason that the brain is not normally overwhelmed by the possible number of alternatives in language; there are actually only very few alternatives in our minds at any time that we are comprehending what is being said. And prediction is the reason we are so rarely aware of ambiguity: We expect what the writer or speaker is likely to say and just do not contemplate alternative interpretations. We interpret *The thieves decided to head for the bank* in one way if we know they were sitting in a car and in another way if they were swimming in a river. When language is comprehended, in other words, the receiver is usually no more aware of possible ambiguity than the producer. Speakers and writers are presumed to have at least a general idea of what they intend to say and are thus unlikely to consider alternative interpretations of the language they produce. The same applies to listeners or readers. The first interpretation that comes to us is the one that makes the most sense to us at the particular time, and alternative and less likely interpretations will not be considered unless subsequent interpretations fail to be consistent or to make sense, in which case we realize our probable error and try to recapitulate. One interpretation usually satisfies us, provided it makes sense, so we do not waste time looking for a second; this is the reason that puns are so very hard to see, and also why puns are mildly irritating. We do not expect to find more than one meaning for the same sequence of words.

As I indicated in the previous chapter, there is nothing very remarkable or particularly clever about this process of prediction; it goes on all the time. Prediction enables us to make sense of all the events in our daily lives. And we are no more aware of our predictions when we read than we are at any other time for the simple reason that our predictions are usually so good. We are rarely surprised because our predictions rarely let us down, even when we read a book for the first time.

What exactly do we predict when we read? The fundamental answer is meaning, although of course we look at words or letters (or more precisely the *distinctive features* of words or letters) that will confirm or disconfirm particular meanings. But a number of more detailed and specific predictions may be made and tested simultaneously — and constantly modified — as we make our way through the actual text. Every specific prediction, however, no matter how detailed and transient, will be derived from our more general expectations about where the text as a whole might be leading.

In later chapters I shall explain how the meaning that we might be able to bring to sequences of words modifies the predictions that we might make about specific words and thereby enables us to identify words on less visual information, if word identification is required at all. The phenomenon has already been demonstrated in the "tunnel vision" experiments that I described in Chapter 3. We use our prior knowledge of how letters go together in words, and how words go together in meaningful and grammatical sequences, to eliminate unlikely alternatives, and thus reduce our dependence upon visual information. The predictions of course come from nonvisual information, our prior knowledge of the subject matter and of language. It is in fact through prediction that our nonvisual information can be deployed so that we can gain maximum advantage from the limited amount of incoming visual information that the brain is able to cope with. The better idea we have of what we are looking for, the fewer distinctive features we need to discriminate.

The *surface structure* of written language is the *visual information* that intermittently presents itself to the brain through the eyes. The meanings that we bring to language are already located within the brain. They lie at the *deep structure* level as part of the *nonvisual information* that is the basis of comprehension. Inability to make any sense of language is the reflection of a complete absence of relevant nonvisual information.

Some Practical Implications

The preceding discussion should make it clear that it is misleading if not inaccurate to regard reading as a matter of "following the text" or to say that a listener "follows" the meaning of a speaker. Language is understood by keeping ahead of the incoming detail that the brain is striving to handle. By having some expectation of what the speaker or writer is likely to say, by making use of what we already know, we protect ourselves against being overwhelmed by information overload. We avoid the confusion of ambiguity and succeed in bridging the gap between the surface structure of the text and the writer's intention.

It is easy to demonstrate how the brain keeps ahead of the words that we identify as we read. Ask a friend to turn out the light while you read aloud, so that you are deprived of visual information, and you will find that your voice is able to continue "reading" another four or five words. Your eyes were a second or more — perhaps three or four fixations — ahead of the point your voice had reached when the lights went out. This phenomenon is known as the *eye-voice span,* a term that is rather misleading because it might suggest that the brain needs more than a second to organize in speech the sounds of the particular word it is looking at. But this is incorrect. The brain does not need a second to identify a word; the difference in time is not so much a reflection of how far the brain is behind the eye as of how far the brain is ahead of the voice. The brain uses the eyes to scout ahead so that it can make decisions about meaning, and thus about individual words, in advance. Indeed, the eye-voice span exists only when we can make sense of what we read. If we read nonsense — *dog lazy the over jumps fox quick the* rather than *The quick brown fox jumps over the lazy dog* — then brain, eye, and voice tend to converge on the same point, and the eye-voice span disappears. The span, in fact, reflects rather precisely the sense that we make of text, since it tends to extend to the end of a meaningful phrase. The four or five word span is merely an average. If the lights go out just as we are about to read . . . *and drove off into the night* we are likely to continue aloud as far as *off* or as far as *night,* but not stop at *into* or *the.*

It is because the reader must keep ahead of the text that it is so hard for children to learn to read from material that does not make sense to them, or which is so disconnected and fragmentary that prediction is impossible. Reading is similarly much more difficult for children who have been taught that they should get the words right rather than try to make sense of what is being read. Not only is "getting the words right" very much harder and slower unless meaning is brought to the text in the first place, but identifying each successive word on the line one after the other will not, in itself, give meaning. Reading is not a matter of decoding to the surface structure of speech; the sounds will not make sense of their own accord.

The difficulty of many high school "problem readers" is not that they have not tried over the years to learn how to sound out words correctly, nor that they are careless about getting every word right, but rather that they read one word at a time as if meaning should be the last concern. They try to read under the assumption that if they get the words right, then meaning will take care of itself, while, in fact, this is the reverse of the way in which sense is made of reading.

WRITTEN LANGUAGE AND SPOKEN LANGUAGE

Obviously, spoken language and written language are not the same. It is not difficult to detect when a speaker reads from a text prepared for publication or when a passage that we read is the unedited transcription of a spontaneous talk. Speech and print are not different *languages* — they share a common vocabulary and the same grammatical forms — but they are likely to contain different distributions of each. It should not be considered surprising or anomalous that differences exist between spoken and written language; they are generally used for quite different purposes and addressed to quite different audiences. The grammar and vocabulary of spoken language itself are likely to vary depending on the purpose for which speech is used and the relationships between the people using it.

It is curious that the differences between written language and speech are often taken to reflect a defect in writing. Most people seem to assume — and probably rightly so — that spoken English is a reasonably efficient system. They may complain about the way various individuals *use* the language, but the language itself seems above criticism. We rarely hear suggestions that English would be a better spoken language if it had a few sounds more or less in it, or if one or two grammatical structures were added or eliminated. Indeed, signs that the language is changing may be the signal for considerable outrage in the newspapers.

Written language, on the other hand, is frequently the subject of calls for improvement, ranging from spelling reform to its total abolition in beginning reading texts in favor of written-down speech. I want to suggest, however, that written language is different from spoken language for the good reason that spoken language has adapted itself to being heard while written language is more appropriately read.

To understand why such a specialized adaptation might have come about, it is necessary to examine the different demands the two language forms make upon their recipients. There is, for example, the obvious fact that the spoken word dies the moment it is uttered and can only be recaptured if held in the listener's fallible memory or as the result of a good deal of mutual inconvenience as the listener asks the speaker to recapitulate. Even tape recording, to my mind, does little to mitigate the essential transience of speech in contrast to the facile way in which the eye can move backwards and forwards through written text. The reader attends to several words at a time, selects what those words will be, the order in which they will be dealt with, and the amount of time that will be spent on them. In other words, spoken language may make considerable demands on short-term memory which written language does not.

On the other hand, written language might seem to place a far greater burden on long-term memory — on what we already know about language and the world — than does our everyday speech. To bring meaning to spoken language, very often, all we need do is consider the circumstances in which an utterance is made. Much of our everyday spoken language is directly related to the immediate situation in which it is uttered. We may pay very little attention to the actual words the speaker is using, to anything that happened yesterday or to anything that might happen tomorrow. The relevance of the utterance is as ephemeral as the words themselves — "Pass the jam, please" — and requires putting information into long-term memory as little as it requires drawing information out from long-term memory. Written language, by contrast, generally depends on nothing but what we can and do remember. Rarely can we look around the room to make sense of what we have just read.

This matter of clues to meaning must be elaborated upon to consider a different kind of demand that written language places on the reader, related, this time, not to memory but to the far more fundamental question of how we make sense of language in the first place.

The question is how language is verified; how can we confirm that the information we are receiving is likely to be the truth, that it makes sense, or that indeed we are understanding it correctly? What is the source of the predictions that can cut through all the ambiguity inherent in language so that we make the most reasonable and reliable interpretation? For the kind of everyday spoken language I have been talking about, the answer is simple: Look around. Even if the topic of concern is not completely clarified by what our senses can tell us of present circumstances, any uncertainty we have can probably be removed by what we know already of the speaker's nature, interests, and likely intentions. But the language of texts offers no such shortcuts. There is only one final recourse if we are not sure of what we have read, and that is to return to the text itself. For verification, for disambiguation, and to avoid error, a difficult and possibly unique kind of skill is required. That is the skill of evaluating an argument, of looking for internal consistencies, of complex abstract thought. As I said earlier, both the source and the test of many of the changing predictions that are necessary for the comprehension of written language must lie in the text itself, informed by the more general expectations that readers bring from their prior knowledge. The text determines what the actual alternatives might be and whether they have been successfully predicted.

The particular requirements of written language have so impressed some theorists (Havelock, 1976; Goody and Watts, 1972; Olson, 1977) that they have argued that writing has introduced a whole new mode of thought to our basic human repertoire of intellectual skills. It might be objected that not all our spoken language is of the "everyday", situationally verifiable kind that I have been discussing. Some of our spoken language can be as abstract, argumentative, and unrelated to the circumstances in which it is comprehended, as an article in a scientific journal. But Olson (1977) claims that our ability to produce and understand such spoken language is in fact a byproduct of our being literate. It is only because of our experience in reading that we can make sense of this kind of spoken language, which, in its form, is more like writing than everyday speech.

If prediction is the basis for the comprehension of written language, then obviously an important part of the nonvisual information of readers must be familiarity with the conventions and unique characteristics of the different forms that written language takes. The more one knows about written language, the easier it will be to read, and thus to learn to read. All this is part of the reason that I shall argue not only that reading is learned through reading but that learning to read begins with being read to.

SUMMARY

The sounds of speech and the visual information of print are **surface structures** of language and do not represent meaning directly. Meaning is part of the **deep structure** of language and must be contributed by listeners and readers. Reading is not "decoding to sound". Written language and spoken language are not the same, although the same process of **prediction** underlies the comprehension of both.

Notes to Chapter 6 begin on page 211.

CHAPTER 7

LEARNING ABOUT THE WORLD AND ABOUT LANGUAGE

This chapter, which introduces the topic of learning, is the last of the "general" chapters before we become involved with specific issues in a detailed analysis of reading. The chapter will not be deeply concerned with learning to read; this topic will be postponed until after the detailed consideration of reading. But the chapter will be concerned with the *process* by which children learn to read, because this learning process is the same as that by which children earlier achieve their mastery of spoken language and, even earlier, begin learning about the world in general through their first elaborations of a theory of the world.

In fact, the present chapter provides an appropriate link between the preceding general chapters about comprehension and the following specific chapters about reading because it will attempt to show that the basis of all learning, including learning how to read, is comprehension. Children learn by relating their understanding of the new to what they know already, in the process modifying or elaborating their prior knowledge. I shall also try to demonstrate that learning is a continuous and completely natural process, so much so that it is not necessary to propose separate processes of motivation and reinforcement to sustain and consolidate learning (nor should it be necessary for teachers to regard motivation and reinforcement as separate concerns that can be grafted onto reading instruction). Children may not always find it easy or even necessary to learn what we try to teach them, but they find the state of not learning anything at all intolerable.

CONSTRUCTING A THEORY OF THE WORLD

In Chapter 5 I discussed the complex yet precise and accurate theory of the world that we all have lodged in our brains. Obviously, we were not born with such a theory. The ability to construct a theory of the world and to predict from it may be innate, but the actual contents of the theory, the specific detail underlying the order and structure that we come to perceive in the world, is not part of our birthright. But equally obviously, very little of our theory can be attributed to instruction. Only a small part of what we know is actually *taught* to us. Teachers and other adults are given altogether too much credit for what we learn as children.

Consider for example what it is that we know that enables us to tell the difference between cats and dogs. What were we taught that has given us this skill? It is impossible to say. Just try to write a description of cats and dogs that would enable a being from outer space — or even a child who has never seen cats and dogs before — to tell the difference. Anything you might want to say about some dogs, that they have long tails or pointed ears or furry coats, will apply to some cats and not to other dogs. The fact is that the difference between cats and dogs is *implicit* in our heads, knowledge that cannot be put into words. Nor can we communicate this knowledge by pointing to a particular part of cats and dogs and saying, "That is where the difference lies."

Differences obviously exist between cats and dogs, but you cannot find and do not need language to distinguish them. Children without language can tell the difference between cats and dogs. Cats and dogs can tell the difference between cats and dogs. But if we cannot say what this difference is, how can we teach it to children? What we do, of course, is point out to children examples of the two kinds of animal. We say, "That is a cat" or "There goes a dog." But pointing out examples does not teach children anything; it merely confronts them with the problem. In effect, we say "There is something I call a cat. Now you find out why." The "teacher" poses the problem and leaves the child to discover the solution.

The same argument applies to just about everything we can distinguish in the world, to all the letters of the alphabet, to numbers, chairs and tables, houses, foodstuffs, flowers, trees, utensils, and toys, to every kind of animal, bird, and fish, to every face, every car and plane and ship, thousands upon thousands of objects that we can recognize not only by sight but by other senses as well. And when did anyone tell us the rules? How often has anyone told us "Chairs can be recognized because they have four legs and a seat and possibly a back and arms"? (You can see how inadequate a description that would be.) Instead, somebody once said, "There is a chair" and left us to decide not only how to recognize chairs on other occasions but also to discover what exactly the word "chair" means, how chairs are related to everything else in the world.

With reading we do not even need someone to pose the problem in the first place. Reading at the same time presents both the problem and the possibility of its solution. Just by virtue of being a reader, every one of us has acquired a sight vocabulary of at least fifty thousand words, words that we can identify on sight the way we recognize familiar faces and houses and trees. How did we acquire this enormous talent? Fifty thousand flashcards? Fifty thousand times a teacher wrote a word on a board and told us what it was? Fifty thousand times we blended together the sound of a word through phonics? We have learned to recognize words by reading.

Not only can we recognize fifty thousand words on sight — and also, of course, by sound — we can usually make sense of all of these words. Where have all the meanings come from? Fifty thousand trips to the dictionary? Fifty thousand lessons? We have learned language through using language, by speaking it, reading it, and making sense of it. What we know about language is largely implicit, just like our knowledge of cats and dogs. So little of our knowledge of language is actually taught, we underestimate how much of language we have learned.

Our language is full of rules that we were never taught. You would think it odd if I wrote *I have a small wooden blue sailing boat* or *a blue wooden small sailing boat*. There is only one way to say what I want to say — *I have a small blue wooden sailing boat* — and just about every English speaker over the age of five would agree. There is a rule for how we do this, but it is not a rule that most of us can put into words. It is not a rule that we were taught.

I am not saying that there is nothing we are taught. We may be taught the rules of certain games just as we may be shown how to hold a fishing rod (although most of our skills come from practice rather than direct instruction). Certainly we are taught that two times two is four and that Paris is the capital of France. But everything we are taught must be related to what we already know if it is to make sense. And most of our theory of the world, including most of our knowledge of language, whether spoken or written, is not the kind of knowledge that can be put into words; it is more like the implicit cat-and-dog kind of knowledge. Knowledge which no one can put into words is not knowledge that can be communicated by direct instruction.

How, then, do we acquire and develop the theory of the world we have in our heads? How does it become so complex and precise and efficient? There seems to be only one answer: *by conducting experiments.*

Learning by Experiment

Children learn by testing hypotheses and evaluating feedback. For example, a child might hypothesize that the difference between cats and dogs is that cats have pointed ears. The child can then test this hypothesis in experiments, by saying, "There is a cat" or "What a nice cat" or "Hi cat" when any animal with pointed ears passes by, and "There is a dog" (or "That's not a cat") for any animal without pointed ears. Relevant feedback is any reaction that tells the child whether the hypothesis is justified or not. If someone says something like, "Yes, there's a pretty cat" or accepts the child's statement by making no overt response at all, then the child has received feedback that the hypothesis has worked, on this occasion at least. The child's theory can be tentatively modified to include a rule that cats are animals with pointed ears. But if the feedback is negative, if someone says to the child, "No, that's a dog" or even something as rude as, "Think again, stupid," then the child knows that the hypothesis has failed. Another hypothesis must be selected and tested. Clearly more than one experiment will be required; it will take a lot of experience with cats and dogs before a child can be reasonably certain of having uncovered the true differences between them (whatever the differences may be). But the principle is always the same: stay with your theory for as long as it works; modify your theory, look for another hypothesis, whenever it fails.

Note that it is essential for the child to understand the problem in the first place. Children will not learn to recognize cats simply by being shown cats; they will not know what to look for. Both cats and dogs must be seen in order for hypotheses about their relevant differences to arise. Children learn each letter of the alphabet by seeing them all; they must see what the alternatives are.

There is an intimate connection between comprehension and learning. The children's experiments never go beyond their theories; they must comprehend what they are doing all the time they are learning. Anything that bewilders a child will be ignored; there is nothing to be learned there. It is not nonsense that stimulates children to learn but the possibility of making sense; that is why children grow up speaking language and not imitating the noise of the air conditioner. Children do not learn by being denied access to problems. A child learning to talk must be immersed in spoken language, and it is far better that a beginning reader having difficulties should be helped to read than be deprived of reading.

This process of hypotheses testing goes on instinctively, below the level of awareness. If we were aware of the hypotheses we test, then we could say what it is that enables us to tell the difference between cats and dogs. We are no more conscious of the hypotheses that underlie learning than we are of the predictions that underlie comprehension or of the theory of the world itself. Indeed, there is basically no difference between comprehension and learning; hypotheses are simply tentative predictions.

LEARNING ABOUT LANGUAGE

When does all this experimentation take place? I think that for young children there is only one answer: they are testing hypotheses all the time. Their predictions are always tentative. This assertion is best illustrated with respect to the topic with which we are most concerned, namely language.

Bringing Meaning to Speech

Consider for example the relatively well-researched procedures by which infants gradually master rules that enable them to produce grammatical utterances in the language spoken around them (Brown, 1973; McNeill, 1970). No one could spell out these rules with sufficient precision to attempt to teach them to a child, nor is there any indication that children could produce comprehensible utterances as a result of being given instruction in these rules. Instead, infants "invent grammar". They hypothesize rules for the formation of utterances as and when they require them, and test the adequacy of these hypotheses by putting them to use to represent a meaning. And infants progressively modify these hypothesized rules in the light of the feedback which they receive from the speakers of the language to whom their utterances are addressed. Adults not only correct infants' language; they provide relevant models by elaborating in adult language the meaning that infants try to express in their own tentative way. The critical focus of this interaction is on the meaning that is shared; the adult must be able to comprehend what the infant is talking about. Adults do not know the rules by which infants form their early utterances, but they can make sense of these utterances by their prior understanding of the infants and of the situations in which the utterances are made. As a consequence, the infants can get on with the problem of working out how the surface structure and deep structure are related.

Children who have just begun to talk frequently make statements that are completely obvious. A child looking out of a window with you will say something like "See big plane" although you may even have pointed the plane out in the first place. Why then should the child bother to make the statement? The answer is because the child is learning, conducting an experiment. In fact, a child could be conducting no fewer than three different experiments at the same time in that one simple situation.

The child could be testing the hypothesis that the object you can both clearly see in the sky *is* a plane, that it is not a bird or cloud or something else as yet unidentified. When you say, "Yes, I see it", you are confirming that the object is a plane: positive feedback. Even silence is interpreted as positive feedback, since the child would expect you to make a correction if the hypothesis were in error. The second hypothesis that the child might be testing concerns the sounds of the language, that the name "plane" is the right name for the object, rather than "pwane", "prane", or whatever else the child might say. Once again the child can assume that if you do not take the opportunity to make a correction, then there is nothing to be corrected. A test has been successfully conducted. The third hypothesis that the child may be testing is linguistic, whether "See big plane" is a grammatically acceptable and meaningful sentence in adult language. The feedback comes when the adult says, "Yes, I can see the big plane." The child learns to produce sentences in your language by using tentative sentences for which you both already know the meaning, *in a situation which you both comprehend.*

The same principle of making sense of language by understanding the situation in which it is used applies in the other direction as children learn to *comprehend* adult speech. At the beginning of language learning, infants must be able to understand what adults say before they can understand adult language. Does that statement sound paradoxical? What I mean is that children do not come to understand sentences like "Would you like a drink of juice?" or even the meaning of single words like "juice", by figuring out the language or by having someone tell them the rules. Children learn because initially they can hypothesize the meaning of a statement from the situation in which it is uttered. An adult is usually carrying or pointing to a drink of juice when a sentence like "Would you like a drink of juice?" is spoken. From such situations a child can hypothesize what might happen the next time someone mentions "juice". The situation provides the meaning and the utterance provides the evidence; that is all a child needs to construct hypotheses that can be tested on future occasions. Children do not learn language to make sense of words and sentences; they make sense of words and sentences to learn language (Macnamara, 1972).

There is an interesting role for the eyes to play in these first experiments with language. Newson and Newson (1975) have noted that the sharing of meaning is facilitated by a convergence of gaze. When a parent offers an infant a drink of juice, they are probably looking not at each other but at the cup that the adult is offering. When a parent says, "Ah, there's a diaper pin" to a baby who does not understand a word of speech, the gaze of parent and baby are likely to converge on the diaper pin. By bringing a possible meaning to the utterance the infant can hypothesize a relationship between the two, and thus test, confirm, or modify provisional rules about this relationship — a highly efficient procedure that will work only if the infant can make sense of the purpose of adult language.

I know of no research on how much language children might learn simply by observation. But if a baby can hypothesize and test a potential meaning when offered a cup of juice, I see no reason why the child could not test a similar hypothesis by overhearing one adult offer another a cup of coffee, provided the entire incident can also be seen. The child could again compare probable meaning with utterance. There are obvious limits to the number of language interchanges in which infants are directly involved, and which in any case may be in the pseudo "baby talk" of adults which cannot be of much use to children trying to learn adult language. It might at least seem possible that most infants overhear far more language than is actually addressed to them, though again there is no research on the issue. And by and large much of this overheard domestic language would be meaningful; it would have functions and outcomes that are both predictable and testable.

Bringing Meaning to Print

Put in another way, the basic insight that must enable a child to make sense of speech is that its sounds are not random, they are not arbitrarily substitutable. By this I mean that the sounds of speech make a difference. An adult cannot produce the sounds "There's a truck" when the intended meaning is "Let's go for a walk."

A similar insight that differences have a purpose, that they are meaningful and not arbitrary, must also be the basis for learning to understand print. Children must have the insight that print is meaningful because that is what reading is — making sense of print. For as long as children see no sense in print, for as long as they see it as arbitrary or nonsensical, they will find no reason to attend to print. They will not learn by trying to relate letters to sounds, partly because written language does not work that way and partly because it is not something that makes sense to them.

Again, research has so far little to offer in the way of relevant data, but it might seem a reasonable hypothesis that the majority of children are as much immersed in written language as they are in speech. I am not referring to school, nor to those overrated books that are supposed to surround and somehow inspire some privileged children to literacy. I refer instead to the wealth of print to be found on every product in the bathroom, on every jar and package in the kitchen, in the television guide (and in television commercials), in comics, catalogs, advertising fliers, telephone directories, on street signs, store fronts, gas stations, billboards, at fast-food outlets, supermarkets, and department stores. And all of this print is meaningful; it makes a difference. We no more predict cereal in a package labeled *detergent* than we expect candy in a store advertising *cleaning* or a concert in a television program announced as *football*.

For those not blind to it (which experienced readers are inclined to be), our visual world is frequently festooned with print, most of it (check in your supermarket) literally right in front of our eyes. The question is whether children who cannot yet read pay very much attention to it. I have told of a three-and-a-half-year-old boy who obviously could not read the words *luggage* and *footwear* on signs in a department store (because he got both of them wrong) but who nevertheless asserted that the first said "cases" and the second said "shoes" (Smith, 1976). Here was one child who could bring meaning to print long before he could read the actual print, and who therefore had acquired the insight that differences in print are meaningful.

There is only one way in which such an insight might be achieved, and that is when a child is being read to or observes print being responded to in a meaningful way. At this point, I am not referring to the reading of books or stories, but to the occasions when a child is told "That sign says 'Stop' ", "That word on the door is 'Boys' ", or "This is the jar for cookies." Television commercials may do the same for a child — they not only announce the product's name, desirability, and uniqueness in spoken and written language, but they even demonstrate the product at work. The point in all of these cases is that no substitution could be made; the choice of print is not arbitrary like the pattern on the wallpaper, but intimately related to the situations in which it appears, just like the spoken language of the home. And just as with the spoken language of the home, there is a great deal a child might learn just through observation — by hypothesizing a likely meaning and seeing if the hypothesis is confirmed. Children can test hypotheses about the meaning of the printed word *toys* in a store, not because anyone reads it to them, but on the basis of whether the sign does in fact indicate the location of the toy department. There is a consistency between the print and its environment. The print that normally surrounds children is potentially meaningful, and thus provides an effective basis for learning. It is usually possible to hypothesize and test what such printed words mean — or at least what they are likely to mean — by the context in which they occur.

Continuous Text

When we come to consider continuous text — the written language of books and of other extended materials such as letters and newspaper articles — we find that the same principles of consistency and non-substitutability apply, but now the constraints lie in the language of the text itself, rather than in the physical context of the surrounding situation. No one — not even the author — can arbitrarily substitute one word for another in a text because the choice of words is severely limited by what the author is trying to say and the language being used to say it. Each word that I write now must be consistent with the meaning that I am trying to express.

These constraints that limit an author's choice of words are guides to a reader or to a child learning to read. Each word in meaningful text is largely predictable from the words around it. In fact every other word can be eliminated from most reasonably intelligible print without seriously affecting comprehension (Miller, 1956). This is another illustration of *redundancy* in written language; a reader's comprehension of the whole can contribute to comprehension of the parts, and even to the learning of words that are unfamiliar. We not only learn to read by reading; we simultaneously build up our competence in language generally. A child can just as easily hypothesize the identity and even the intended meaning of the word *toys* when it occurs in a paragraph as when it is printed on a sign over a department in a store, except that now the clues are in the text itself.

But as I explained in the previous chapter, the written language of texts is not the same as the spoken language of the child's out-of-school environment. If a child is to comprehend and learn from written language — if prediction and hypothesis testing are to be possible — then the child must be familiar with written language. A knowledge of the particular form of written language must be part of the child's nonvisual information.

It does not matter that we cannot say with any precision what exactly are the differences between spoken and written language. We cannot say what the rules of spoken language are, yet children learn to make sense of speech. Provided children can make sense of written language, there is no convincing evidence that they must fail to learn the rules of that either. The general requirements of immersion in the problem, the possibility of making sense, a plentiful experience, and the opportunity to get feedback to test hypotheses would seem to be just as easily met with written language as with speech. In fact, written language might seem to have several advantages as far as hypothesis testing is concerned, provided the child can make sense of it in the first place, since a number of tests can be conducted on the same material — a second hypothesis tried if the first one fails. And by virtue of its internal consistency the text itself can provide relevant feedback about the correctness of hypotheses. When you are reading something you comprehend, you can usually tell if you make a mistake that makes a difference for the very reason that the mistake makes a difference. At some point the text is unlikely to make sense, and you will be able to go back to find out why.

However, none of this will be of any value to children learning to read if the language from which they are expected to learn is not, in fact, "written language", or if they are not familiar with the particular conventions of written language, or do not have the fundamental insight that written language and speech are not in any case the same. These are problems that we shall have to look at in more detail when we come to consider reading instruction.

THREE ASPECTS OF LEARNING

Learning, I have said, is the modification or elaboration of what is already known, of cognitive structure, the theory of the world in the head. What exactly is modified or elaborated? It çan be any of the three components of the theory: the category system, the rules for relating objects or events to categories (sets of distinctive features), or the complex network of interrelations among categories.

Children are constantly required to establish new categories in their cognitive structure and to discover the rules that limit the allocation of events to that category. They have to learn that not all animals are cats and dogs but that some animals are. Children learning to sight-recognize the printed word *cat* have to establish a visual category for that word, just as they must have a category for actual cats, distinguished from other categories for dogs, and so forth. Skilled readers develop categories for every letter of the alphabet and also for every word that can be identified on sight, together, possibly, with lists for frequently occurring syllabic groups of letters. This process of learning to establish categories involves hypothesizing what are the significant differences — the only reason to establish a new category is to make a new differentiation in our experience, and the learning problem is to find the significant differences that should define the category.

Each category that we distinguish must be specified by at least one set of distinctive features. Every time children succeed in learning to recognize something new, they must have established a new set of distinctive features. But usually they go further and establish *alternative* sets of features for specifying the same categories. They learn that an *a*, *a*, or even an *A* should be categorized as a letter "a" just as many different-looking animals must be categorized as a cat. Any set of features that will serve to categorize an object I shall term a *criterial set*, and I shall refer to alternative sets for the same category as *functionally equivalent*. As children learn, they discover more and more ways in which to make the decision that a particular object or event should be categorized in a certain way. The number of functionally equivalent criterial sets gets larger. Learning is also involved in the ability to make use of less and less featural information to comprehend text. We shall run into many examples of the use of functionally equivalent criterial sets of features in our discussion of the processes of reading. We shall find that most skilled readers can identify words that have had large parts (many features) obliterated, such as H̸A̸P̸P̸I̸N̸E̸S̸S̸ and can make sense of text that has even more features obliterated. All this is possible because we have learned to make optimal use of the information that is available, both visually and from our acquired knowledge of the language.

Finally, children constantly learn new interrelationships among categories, developing their ability to make sense of language and the world. Understanding how words go together in meaningful language makes prediction possible and, therefore, comprehension. As I have tried to show, these interrelationships, the syntactic and semantic rules of language, are also not taught. But a child can learn new interrelationships by the same process of hypothesis-testing. Comprehension is the basis of a child's learning to read, but reading, in turn, contributes to a child's growing ability to comprehend by permitting elaboration of the complex structure of categories, feature lists, and interrelationships that constitute every child's theory of the world.

LEARNING ALL THE TIME

Learning is a continual and effortless process, as natural as breathing. A child does not have to be especially motivated or rewarded for learning; in fact the thrust is so natural that being deprived of the opportunity to learn is aversive. Children will struggle to get out of situations where there is nothing to learn, just as they will struggle to escape from situations where breathing is difficult. Inability to learn is suffocating.

There is no need to worry that children who are not constantly driven and cajoled will "take the easy way out" and not learn. Young children who read the same book twenty times, even though they know the words by heart, are not avoiding more "challenging" material in order to avoid learning; they are still learning. It may not be until they know just about every word in a book that they can get on with some of the more complex aspects of reading, such as testing hypotheses about meaning and learning to use as little visual information as possible.

Children will not stay in any situation in which there is nothing for them to learn. Everyone is equipped with a very efficient device that prevents our wasting time in situations where there is nothing to learn. That device is called *boredom,* and boredom is something all children want to escape. A child who is bored in class is not demonstrating illwill or inability or even sheer cussedness; boredom should convey just one very clear message for the teacher: there is nothing in the particular situation for the child to learn.

Unfortunately, there are two reasons why there might be nothing for a child to learn in a particular situation, and hence two reasons for boredom, that arise from quite different sources. One reason why children might have nothing to learn is very simple — they know it already. Children will not attend to anything they know already. Nature has equipped them not to waste their time in this way. But children will also suffer and exhibit the same symptoms of boredom, not only because they know something already, but because they cannot make sense of what they are expected to learn. Teachers might see quite clearly that a certain exercise will improve a child's useful knowledge or skills, but unless the child can see some sense in the exercise, the instruction is a waste of time.

The Risk and Rewards of Learning

There is one other reason why children might turn their faces against learning, and that is its risk. In order to learn you must take a chance. When you test a hypothesis, there must be a possibility of being wrong. If you are certain of being right, there can be nothing to learn because you know it already. And provided there is a possibility of being wrong, you learn whether you are right or not. If you have a hypothesis about what constitutes a cat, it makes no difference then whether you say "cat" and are right or say "dog" and are wrong. In fact, you often get the most useful information when you are wrong because you may be right for the wrong reason, but when you are wrong you know you have made a mistake.

Many children become reluctant to learn because they are afraid of making a mistake. If the previous statement seems even slightly improbable, consider the relative credit children are given in and out of school for being "correct" and for being "wrong".

There should be no need for special inducements to motivate a child to learn. Children are motivated to learn whenever there is something they do not understand, provided they feel there is a chance that they can learn. They learn language, basically, because it is part of the world around them; because they see other people using it, it makes sense. Irrelevant inducements — sometimes called extrinsic reinforcement — become necessary only when a child is confronted with something that does not make sense. And forcing a child to attend to nonsense is a pointless enterprise in any case. Bewilderment is aversive.

Nor does learning need to be extrinsically rewarded. The final exquisite virtue of learning is that it provides its own reward. Learning is satisfying, as everyone knows. Deprivation of learning opportunities is boring, and failure to learn is frustrating. If a child needs "reinforcement" for learning, then there is only one conclusion to be drawn: that the child does not see any sense in attempting the learning in the first place.

SUMMARY

Most of what we know about language and the world is not formally taught. Instead, children develop their theory of the world and competence in language by testing **hypotheses,** experimenting with tentative modifications and elaborations of what they know already. Thus, the basis of learning is comprehension. Children are able to learn to make sense of print when the physical situation in which it occurs or the text itself provides clues to meaning. To make sense of text, however, children also need to be familiar with the differences between spoken and written language.

Notes to Chapter 7 begin on page 219.

CHAPTER 8

LETTER
IDENTIFICATION

The easiest route through complicated terrain may not
be the most direct. Now that we are beginning an
analysis of reading, an indirect approach will be
adopted. The point we are heading for is that fluent

99

reading does not normally require the identification of individual letters or words, but the most convenient route to that point begins with a discussion of letter identification. Letter identification focuses on an aspect of reading where the issue can be concisely stated and specified: what is the process by which individuals who know the alphabet can discriminate and name any one of the 26 alternatives that is actually presented to them?

Unlike the reading of words, the question does not arise whether letters are read a bit at a time or all at once. Individual letters cannot be "sounded out" like words; their appearance has a purely arbitrary relationship to the way they are pronounced. And there can be little question about their meaning; we "comprehend" a letter when we can say its name, and that is that.

Yet despite this simplification, letter and word identification are alike in one important aspect, they both involve the discrimination and categorization of visual information. Later we shall see that the process by which letters are identified may be of special relevance to an understanding of the identification of words.

Before we move ahead, a digression may be in order to explain the somewhat arbitrary use of the terms "identification" and "recognition" as labels for the process by which a letter or word (or meaning) is discriminated and allocated to a particular cognitive category. Dictionary definitions of the two words are tortuous but it is clear that they are not, strictly speaking, synonymous. "Identification" involves a decision that an object now confronted should be put into a particular category. There is no implication that the object being identified should have been met before. "Recognition," on the other hand, literally means that the object now confronted has been seen before, although identification may not be involved. We *recognize* people when we know we have seen them before, whether or not we can put a name to them. We *identify* people when we put a name to them, whether or not we have met them before.

Experimental psychologists and reading specialists usually talk about letter and word *recognition,* but the use of the term seems doubly inappropriate. First, they would hardly consider a word to be recognized unless its name could be given; they would not consider that a child recognized a word if all the child could say about it was "That's the very same squiggle I couldn't read yesterday." Second, the skilled reader can very often attach a name to visual information that he has never met before. As a rather extreme case, do you "recognize" or "identify" the visual information *rEaDiNg* as the word "reading"? You almost certainly have never seen the word written that way before. The weight of evidence would seem to favor "identification," and the term is therefore used for formal purposes such as chapter headings. But having made a point of the distinction, we need not be dogmatic about it; "identify", "recognize", "categorize", "name", and even "read" will, in general, continue to be used interchangeably; it is the process we are concerned with at the moment, not the flexible way in which language is used.

It is, in fact, not strictly correct to refer to the visual information that the brain strives to identify on particular occasions as "letters"; this implies that the perceptual decision has already been made. Whether a particular mark on the page should be characterized as a letter depends upon the intention of the perceiver (whether the reader or the writer). As we have seen, *10* may be identified as two letters or two numbers. Prior to an identification decision, the visual information that is *10* is merely a pattern of contrasting ink marks on paper, more precisely referred to as a *visual configuration*, a *visual array*, or even a *visual stimulus*.

THEORIES OF PATTERN RECOGNITION

Letter identification is a special problem within the broader theoretical area of "pattern recognition" — the process by which any two visual configurations are "cognized" to be the same. The process of recognition is of classical philosophical concern because it has been realized for over two thousand years that no two events are ever exactly the same; the world is always in flux, and we never see an object twice in exactly the same form, from the same angle, in the same light, or with the same eye. A topic of very general interest to psychology is what exactly determines whether two objects or events shall be considered to be equivalent. The equivalence decision clearly rests with the perceiver and not in any property of the visual array. Are *J* and *ʝ* the same? Many might say yes, but a printer would say no. Are two automobiles of the same year, model, and color identical? Possibly to everyone except their owners. *It is the perceiver, not the object, that determines equivalence.* We organize our lives and our knowledge by deciding that some things should be treated as equivalent — these are the things that we put into the same category — and some as different. Those differences between objects or events that help us to place them in category systems may be called by a variety of names, such as "defining attributes" or "criterial attributes" or "criterial properties"; in essence, they are the differences that we choose to make *significant.* The differences that we choose to ignore, the ones that do not influence our decision, are often not noticed at all. Obviously it is more efficient to pay attention only to significant differences, particularly in view of the limited information-processing capacity of the human brain. It is, therefore, hardly surprising that we may overlook differences that we are not looking for in the first place, like the sudden absence of our friend's beard, or the pattern of his tie, or the misspelling in the newspaper headline. Human beings owe their preeminent position in the intellectual hierarchy of living organisms not so much to their ability to perceive the world in many different ways as their capacity to perceive things as the same according to criteria that they themselves establish, selectively ignoring what might be termed "differences that do not make a difference". The intellectual giant is not the one who recognizes every individual animal in the zoological gardens, but the one who can look past the individual differences and group them into "equivalent" species and families on a more abstract and systematic basis.

The process that determines how particular letters or words are treated as equivalent has become a focus of theoretical attention because of its particular application to computer technology. There is an obvious economic as well as theoretical interest in designing computers that might be able to read. The construction of a computer with any fluent degree of reading ability is currently impossible for a number of reasons, one of which is that not enough is known about language to give a computer the necessary basic information. Language can be understood only if there is an underlying understanding of the topic to which the language happens to refer, and the ability of computers to "understand" any topic is very limited indeed. But it has not proved possible to provide a computer with rules for identifying letters, let alone words or meanings, at least not with anything like the facility with which humans can identify them. If we consider the problems of pattern recognition from the computer point of view, we may get some insights into what must be involved in the human skill.

There are two basic ways in which a computer might be constructed to recognize patterns, whether numbers, letters, words, texts, photographs, fingerprints, voiceprints, signatures, diagrams, maps, or real objects. The two ways are essentially those that appear to be open theoretically to account for the recognition of patterns by humans. The alternatives may be called *template matching* and *feature analysis;* and the best way to describe them is to imagine trying to build a computer capable of reading the 26 letters of the alphabet.

For both our models, for the template matching and the feature analytic devices, the ground rules have to be the same. We shall consider the computer to be equipped with exactly the same input and output mechanisms. At the input end is an optical system, a light-sensitive electronic "eye" to examine visual information and "ask questions" about the arrangement of light and shade, and at the output end is a set of 26 responses, namely the possibility of printing out (or even "speaking" with auxiliary equipment) each of the letters of the alphabet. The aim, of course, is to construct a system between the input and output mechanisms to insure that when the visual array *E* is presented at the input end, "E" will be indicated by the output.

Template Matching

For a template-matching device, a series of internal representations must be constructed to be, in effect, a reference library for the letters that the device is required to identify. We might start with one internal representation, or "template", for each letter of the alphabet. Each template is directly connected with the appropriate response, while between the eye and the templates we shall put a "comparator" or matching mechanism capable of comparing any input letter with all of the set of templates. Any letter that comes into the computer's field of view will be internalized and compared with each of the templates, at least until a match is made. Upon "matching" the input with a template, the computer will perform the response associated with that particular template and the identification will be complete.

There are obvious limitations to such a system. If the computer is given a template for the representation A, what will it do if confronted with A or A not to mention A or even A or A? Of course, some flexibility can be built into the system. Inputs can be "normalized" to iron out some of the variability; they can be scaled down to a standard size, adjusted into a particular orientation, have crooked lines straightened, small gaps filled, and minor excrescences removed; in short, a number of things can be done to increase the probability that the computer will not respond "I don't know" but will instead match an input to a template. But, unfortunately, the greater the likelihood that the computer will make a match, the greater the probability that it will make a mistake. This is the "signal detection" problem of Chapter 2. A computer that can "normalize" A to make it look like the template A will be likely to do the same with A and A. The only remedy will be to keep adding templates to try to accommodate all the different styles and types of lettering the device might meet. Even then, such a computer will be unable to make use of all the supporting knowledge that human beings have; it will be quite capable of reading the word HOT as AOT because it does not have any "common sense" to apply in the elimination of alternatives.

The critical limitations of template-matching systems, for both computer and human, lie in their relative inefficiency and costliness. A single set of templates, one for each category, is highly restricted in the number of inputs that it can match, but every increase in the number of templates adds considerably to the size, expense, and complexity of the system. The template-matching model does work — in fact, the only existing practical system for character recognition by computers is based on this technique — but the system copes with the diversity of input representations by cheating its way around the problem. Instead of providing the computer with templates to meet many different styles of character, it makes sure the computer eye meets only one style, like the "bankers' numbers" ⑤⸚⑵⑩⑭ that are printed on our checks.

Feature Analysis

The alternative method of pattern perception, feature analysis, dispenses with internal representations completely. There is no question of attempting to match the input with anything, but instead a series of tests is made on the input. The results of each test eliminate a number of alternatives until, finally, all uncertainty is reduced and identification is achieved. The "features" are properties of the visual array that are subjected to tests to determine which alternative responses should be eliminated. Decisions about which alternatives each test shall eliminate are made by the perceivers (or computer programmers) themselves.

To clarify the explanation, let us again imagine constructing a computer for the identification of letters, this time using feature analysis. Remember, the problem is essentially one of using rules to decide into which of a limited number of categories might a very large number of alternative events be placed. In other words this is a matter of establishing equivalences.

At the receptor end of the system, where the computer has its light-sensitive optical scanner, we shall establish a set of "feature analyzers". A feature analyzer is a specialized kind of detector that looks for — is sensitive to — just one kind of feature in the visual information, and which passes just one kind of report back. For the sake of illustration, we might imagine that each analyzer looks for a particular "distinctive feature" by asking a question; one analyzer asks "Is the configuration curved?" (like C or O); another asks "Is it closed?" (like O or P); a third asks "Is it symmetrical?" (like A or W), and a fourth asks "Is there an intersection?" (as in T or K). Every analyzer is, in fact, a test, and the message it sends back is binary — either "yes" or "no", signal or no signal. Without looking too closely at the question of what constitutes a distinctive feature, we can say it is a property of visual information that can be used to differentiate some visual configurations from others. By definition, a distinctive feature must be common to more than one object or event, otherwise it could not be used to put more than one into the same category. But, on the other hand, if the feature were present in all objects or events, then we could not use it to segregate them into different categories; it would not be "distinctive". In other words, a feature, if detected, permits the elimination of some of the alternative categories into which a stimulus might be allocated.

As an example, a "no" answer to the test "Is the configuration curved?" would eliminate rounded letters such as *a, b, c, d,* but not other letters such as *i, k, l, v, w, x, z.* A "yes" answer to "Is it closed?" would eliminate open letters such as *c, f, w,* but not *b, d,* or *o.* The question about symmetry would distinguish letters like *m, o, w,* and *v,* from *d, f, k, r.* Different questions eliminate different alternatives, and relatively few tests would be required to distinguish among 26 alternatives in an alphabet. In fact, if all tests eliminated about half of the alternatives, and there was no test that overlapped with any other, only five questions would be needed to identify any letter. (The logic of the previous statement is set out in the discussion of information theory in the Notes.) No one would actually suggest that as few as five tests are employed to distinguish among 26 letters, but it is reasonable to assume that there need be many fewer tests than categories — that is one of the great economic advantages of a feature analytic system.

With an input bank of say ten or a dozen feature analyzers built into the letter-identification device, a link has to be provided to the 26 responses or output categories; "decision rules" must be devised so that the results of the individual tests are integrated and associated with the appropriate letter names. The most convenient way to set up the rules is to establish a feature list for each category, that is, for each of the 26 letters. The construction of the feature lists is the same for every category, namely a listing of the analyzers that were set up to examine the visual configuration. The feature list for every category also indicates whether each particular analyzer should send back a "yes" or "no" signal for that category. For the category *c,* for example, the feature list should specify a "yes" for the "curved?" analyzer, a "no" for the "closed?" analyzer, a "no" for the "symmetrical?" analyzer, and so forth. Feature lists for a couple of the categories might be conceptualized as looking like Figure 8.1. (The "+" sign indicates "yes.") Obviously, every category would be associated with a different feature list pattern, each pattern providing a specification for a single category.

The actual wiring of the letter-identification device presents no problems — every feature analyzer is connected to every category

Table 1   Feature Lists for Letters

	Category "A"		Category "B"	
Test	1	−	Test 1	+
	2	+	2	+
	3	+	3	−
	4	+	4	+
	5	−	5	+
	6	+	6	−
	7	−	7	−
	8	−	8	−
	9	+	9	+
	10	−	10	+

FIGURE 8.1   Feature lists for letters

that lists a "yes" signal from it, and we arrange that a categorizing decision (an "identification") is made only when "yes" signals are received for all the analyzers listed positively on a category's feature list.

And that, in a simplified and schematic form, is a feature-analytic letter-identification device. The system is powerful, in the sense that it will do a lot of work with a minimum of effort. Unlike the template model, which to be versatile requires many templates for every decision that it might make together with complex normalizing devices, the feature-analytic device demands only a very small number of analyzers compared with the number of decisions it makes. Theoretically, such a device could decide among over a million alternatives with only "20 questions."

Functional Equivalence and Criterial Sets

A considerable advantage of the feature-analytic model over template matching is that the former has very much less trouble in adjusting to inputs that ought to be allocated to the same category but which vary in size or orientation or detail, for example A, **A** , **X** , **A** , and **ʎ** . The types of tests that feature analyzers apply are far better able to cope with distortion and "noise" than any device that requires an approximate match. But far more important, very little is added in the way of complexity or cost to provide one or more alternative feature lists for every category. With such a flexibility, the system can easily allocate not only the examples already given, but also forms as divergent as **α** and **ə** to the category "A". The set of alternative feature lists for a single letter response might then look something like Figure 8.2. The only adjustment that need be made to the battery of analyzers is in wiring additional connections between them and the categories where the feature lists require positive tests, so that an identification will be made on any occasion when the specifications of any of the alternative lists are satisfied.

Table   2   Functionally Equivalent Feature Lists

Category "A"

Test			
1	−	+	+
2	+	+	+
3	+	−	−
4	+	−	+
5	−	+	−
6	+	−	+
7	−	−	+
8	−	+	−
9	+	+	−
10	−	−	+

FIGURE 8.2   Functionally equivalent feature lists

I shall call any set of features that meet the specifications of a particular category a *criterial set*. With the type of feature-analytic device being outlined, more than one criterial set of features may exist for any one category. Obviously, the more criterial sets that exist for a given device, the more efficient that device will be in making accurate identifications.

It will also be useful to give a special name to the alternative criterial sets of features that specify the same category — we shall say that they are *functionally equivalent*. A , *a* and **a** are functionally equivalent for our imagined device because they are all treated as being the same as far as the category "A" is concerned. Of course, the configurations are not functionally equivalent if they are to be distinguished on a basis other than their membership of the alphabet; a printer, for example, might want them categorized into type styles. But as I pointed out earlier, it is the prerogative of the perceiver, not a characteristic of the visual information, to decide which differences shall be significant — which sets of features shall be criterial — in the establishment of equivalences. Functional equivalence can be determined by any systematic or arbitrary method that the pattern recognizer follows. All that is required to establish functional equivalence for quite disparate visual configurations is alternative feature lists for the same category.

Another powerful aspect of the feature-analytic model of pattern recognition is that it can work on a flexible and probabilistic basis. If a single feature list specifies the outcomes of ten analyzer tests for the categorical identification of a letter of the alphabet, a considerable amount of redundant information must be involved. Redundancy, as I have noted in Chapter 2, exists when the same information is available from more than one source, or when more information is available than is required to reduce the actual amount of uncertainty. Ten analyzer tests could provide enough information to select from over a thousand equally probable alternatives, and if there are only 26 alternatives, information from five of those tests could be dispensed with, and there might still be enough data to make the appropriate identification. Even if analyzer information were insufficient to enable an absolutely certain selection between two or three remaining alternatives, it might still be possible to decide which of the alternatives is more likely, given the particular pattern of features that is discriminated. By not demanding that *all* the specifications of a particular feature list be satisfied before a category identification is made, the system can greatly increase its repertoire of functionally equivalent criterial sets of features. Such an increase significantly enhances the efficiency of the device at a cost of little extra complexity.

The fact that different criterial sets can be established within a single feature list provides an advantage that was alluded to in the previous paragraph — a feature-analytic system can make use of *redundancy*. Let us say that the system already "knows" from some other source of information that the configuration it is presented with is a vowel; it has perhaps already identified the letters *THR*. . . and it has been programmed with some basic knowledge of the spelling patterns of English. The device can then exclude from consideration for the fourth letter all those feature lists that specify consonant categories, leaving considerably reduced criterial sets for selection among the remaining alternatives. (Three tests might easily distinguish among five or six vowels.)

A final powerful advantage of the feature-analytic model has also already been implied; it is a device that can easily *learn*. Every time a new feature list or criterial set is established is an instance of learning. All that the device requires in order to learn is *feedback* from the environment. It establishes, or rejects, a new feature list for a particular category (or category for a particular feature list) by "hypothesizing" a relationship between a feature list and a category and testing whether that relationship is, in fact, appropriate.

You may have noticed that as soon as learning processes are discussed, the feature-analytic description slips easily into such information-processing language as "thinking" and "learning". It is evident that the more efficient and sophisticated we make our imaginary letter-identifying device, the more we are likely to talk about its realization in human rather than computer form. It is time for the analogy to be discarded and to adopt a more specific focus on the human pattern recognizer.

The Human Letter Identifier

The analogy is discarded; I intend to use feature analysis as a model for the process by which letters are identified by readers. We learn to identify the letters of the alphabet by establishing feature lists for the required 26 categories, each of which is interrelated to a single name "A," "B," "C," and so forth. The visual system is equipped with analyzers that respond to those features in the visual environment that are distinctive for alphabetic discriminations (and many other visual discriminations as well). The results of the analyzer tests are integrated and directed to the appropriate feature lists so that letter identifications can occur. The human visual perceptual system is biologically competent to demonstrate all the most powerful aspects of the feature-analytic model outlined in the last section — to establish manifold criterial sets of features with functional equivalence, to function probabilistically, to make use of redundancy, and to learn by testing hypotheses and receiving feedback.

Two aspects of letter identification can be distinguished. The first aspect is the allocation of visual configurations to various cognitive categories — the discrimination of various configurations as different, as not functionally equivalent. The greater part of perceptual learning involves finding out what exactly are the distinctive features by which various configurations should be categorized as different from each other, and what are the sets of features that are criterial for particular categories. The second aspect of letter identification is the establishment of the categories themselves and especially the allocation of category names to them, such as "A," "B," "C". These are precisely the two aspects of object or concept learning discussed with reference to the "cat-and-dog problem" in Chapter 7.

To distinguish the two aspects of letter identification, we must ask how new categories might be established and associated with a particular response, such as the name of a letter of the alphabet. The first point to be made is that the association of a name with a category is neither necessary nor primary in the discrimination process. It is quite possible to segregate visual configurations into different categories without having a name for them. We can see that A and $\&$ are different, and know they should be treated differently, even though we may not have a category name, or even a specific category, for $\&$. In fact, we cannot allocate a name to $\&$ unless first we acquire some rules for discriminating it from A and from every other visual configuration with which it should not be given functional equivalence. We shall not learn a name for $\&$ if we cannot distinguish that particular visual configuration from A. The motivation for the establishment of a new category may come from either direction: either a configuration such as $\&$ cannot be related to any existing category, or a new name such as "ampersand" cannot be related to an existing category. The intermediate steps that tie the entire system together are the establishment of the first feature lists and criterial sets for the category so that the appropriate feature tests and the category name can be related.

Not only is the relating of a name to a category not primary; it is not difficult. The complicated part of learning to make an identification is not in remembering the name of a particular category but in discovering the criterial sets of features for that category. As I pointed out in Chapter 7, children at the age when they are often learning to read are also learning hundreds of new names for objects every year — names of friends and public figures and automobiles and animals — as well as the names of letters and words. And remember the method by which children succeed in learning names. The instructor usually points to an object and says "That is an 'X'," in effect, leaving the child with the problem. The instructor rarely tries to explain the equivalence rules for putting various objects into the category that is to be called "X"; it is left for the child to work out what the significant differences must be. The complicated part of learning is the establishment of functional equivalences for the categories with which names are associated.

The reason that "learning names" is frequently thought to be difficult is that the intermediate steps are ignored and it is assumed that a name is applied directly to a particular visual configuration. Of course, children may find it difficult to respond with the right name for the letters *b* or *d* (or for the words *house* and *mouse,* or for an actual dog or cat) but this is not because they cannot put the name to the configuration — that is not the way the visual system works. Their basic problem is to find out how two alternatives are significantly different. Once they can make the discrimination, so that the appropriate functional equivalences are observed, the allocation of the correct verbal label is a relatively easy problem because the label is related directly to the category.

The Letter Identifier in Action

We have come to the final question of the present chapter: is there evidence to support the feature analytic model of the human visual system? Some of the physiological evidence has already been indicated. There is no one-to-one correspondence between the visual information impinging on the eye and anything that goes on behind the eyeball. The eye does not send "images" back to the brain; the stammering pattern of neural impulses is a representation of discrete features detected by the eye, not the transfer of a "picture". In the brain itself, there is no way of storing a set of templates or even acquiring them in the first place. The brain does not deal in veridical representations; it organizes knowledge and behavior by shunting abstract information through its complex neural networks. It is true that one aspect of the brain's output, our subjective experience of the world, is generated in the form of "percepts" that might be regarded as pictures, but this experience is the consequence of the brain's activity, not something the brain "stores" and compares with inputs. Our visual experience is the product of the perceptual system, not part of the process.

Now we shall examine evidence for the feature-analytic model from two kinds of letter-identification experiments. (Details are given in the Notes at the end of the book.) The basic assumption to be tested is that letters are actually conglomerates of features, of which there are perhaps a dozen different kinds. The only way in which letters can differ physically from each other is in the presence or absence of each of these features. Letters that have several features in common will be very similar, while letters that are constructed of quite different feature combinations will be quite dissimilar in appearance. How does one assess "similarity"? Letters are similar — they are presumed to share many features — if they are frequently confused with each other. And letters that are rarely confused with each other are assumed to have very few features in common.

Of course, we do not very often confuse letters, and when we do the character of the error is usually influenced by nonvisual factors. We might, for example, think that the fourth letter in the sequence *REQF* . . . is a *U* not because *F* and *U* are visually similar but because we normally expect a *U* to follow *Q*. However, large numbers of visual letter confusions can be generated by experimental techniques in which the stimulus letter is so "impoverished" that viewers cannot see it clearly, although they are forced to make a guess about what the letter probably is. In other words, the experimental subjects must make letter-identification decisions on minimal visual information. The experimental assumption is that viewers who cannot see the stimulus clearly must lack some vital information and thus be unable to make some feature tests. And if they are unable to make certain feature tests, then the tests they are able to make will not reduce all uncertainty about the 26 alternative responses. Viewers will still be left in doubt about a few possibilities that can be differentiated only by the tests that they have been unable to perform.

The actual method of impoverishing the stimulus is not important. The presentation may be a tachistoscopic brief presentation, or it may involve a stimulus that has very little contrast with its surroundings, projected by a lamp at a very low intensity, or printed on a page under several layers of tissue paper, or hidden behind a lot of visual noise, like *A*. As soon as viewers start making "errors", one can assume that they are not getting all the information that they need to make an identification. They are deciding on something less than a criterial set of features.

On the face of it, there are only two possibilities if viewers are forced to identify a letter on insufficient information; either their guesses will be completely random, or they will respond in some systematic way. If guesses are random, there can be no prediction of what the answer will be; they will be just as likely to respond with any of the 26 letters of the alphabet, whatever the letter that is presented. If we examine the record of "confusions", the occasions when a letter is reported incorrectly, we should find that each of the other 25 letters is represented about equally often. But if responses are systematic, there are two possibilities, both of which limit considerably the number of confusions likely to occur. One possibility, which is not very interesting, is that the viewers will always say the same thing if they cannot distinguish a letter; one might say "That's a 'k'," for example, whenever there is uncertainty. Fortunately, such a bias is easy to detect. The other and more interesting possibility is that the viewers will select only from those alternative responses that remain after the features that can be discriminated in the presentation have been taken into account. In such a circumstance, it is to be expected that the confusions will "cluster"; instead of 25 types of confusion, one for all the possible erroneous responses, there will be only a few types.

The evidence can be summarized in a few words: Letter confusions fall into tightly packed clusters, and over two-thirds of the confusions for most letters can be accounted for by three or four confusion types. If a subject makes a mistake in identifying a letter, the nature of the erroneous response is highly predictable. Typical confusion clusters can be very suggestive about the kind of information the eye must be looking for in discriminating letters. Some typical confusion clusters are (*a, e, n, o, u*), (*t, f, i*), and (*h, m, n*) (Dunn-Rankin, 1968).

The specific conclusion to be drawn from the kind of experiment just described is that letters are indeed composed of a relatively small number of features. Letters that are easily confused, like *a* and *e*, or *t* and *f*, must have a number of features in common, while those that are rarely confused, like *o* and *w*, or *d* and *y*, must have few if any features in common. The general conclusion that may be drawn is that the visual system is indeed feature analytic. Letter identification is accomplished by the eye examining the visual environment for featural information that will eliminate all alternatives except one, thus permitting an accurate identification to be made.

There is a second line of experimental evidence supporting the view that letters are arrangements of smaller elements, and this is related to the fact that recognition is faster or easier when there are fewer alternatives for what each letter might be. The classic example of such evidence has already been described in the "tunnel vision" discussion of Chapter 3, where it was shown that nonvisual information can be employed to reduce the amount of visual — or distinctive feature — information required to identify letters. There will be other illustrations when we come to consider the identification of words in the next chapter.

WHAT IS A FEATURE?

The entire discussion of letter identification by feature analysis has been conducted without actually specifying what a feature is. The omission has been deliberate, because nobody knows what the distinctive features of letters are. Not enough is known about the structure of the human visual system to say exactly what is the featural information that the system looks for.

Of course, general statements about features can be made. There have been a number of attempts to do this, with statements like "The only difference between *c* and *o* is that *o* is 'closed'; therefore, being closed must be a distinctive feature" or "The only difference between *h* and *n* is the 'ascender' at the top of *h;* therefore, an ascender must be a distinctive feature." This kind of deductive reasoning is quite illuminating, and it is true that one can make predictions about which pairs of letters might be confused on the basis of such analyses. But such features are proposed on the basis of logic, not of evidence, because we really do not know whether, or how, the eye might look for "closedness" or for "ascenders". It can be argued that these hypothesized features are really properties of whole letters — we actually cannot tell whether something is closed or has an ascender until we see the letter as a whole, and it is far from clear how a property of the whole could also be an element out of which the whole is constructed. It is obviously a reasonable assertion that the significant difference between *h* and *n* has something to do with the ascender, but it is an oversimplification to say that the ascender is the actual feature.

Another good reason for avoiding the specific question of what the features are is that one always has to make the qualification "It depends." The significant difference between *A* and *B* is not the same as the significant difference between *a* and *b*. In fact, one cannot predict what letters will be confused in an identification experiment unless one knows the type face that is being used and whether the letters are upper or lower case.

Fortunately, it is not necessary to know exactly what the features are in order to learn something about the identification process or to assist a child in discriminating letters. We can trust the child to locate the information required provided the appropriate informational environment is available. The appropriate informational environment is the opportunity to make comparisons and discover what the significant differences are. Remember, the primary problem of identification is to distinguish the presented configuration from all those to which it might be equivalent but is not; the configuration has to be subjected to feature analysis and put in the appropriate category. Presenting h to children 50 times and telling them it is "h" because it has an ascender will not help them to discriminate the letter. The presentation of h and other letters in pairs and groups, together with the feedback that they are *not* functionally equivalent, is the kind of information required for the visual system and brain to find out very quickly what the distinctive features really are.

SUMMARY

A feature identification model is proposed for letter identification. **Feature lists** are established to permit the allocation of visual information to specific cognitive categories, in the present case for letters. The names of the letters (and their relationships to sounds) are part of the interrelations among categories; they are not directly associated with particular visual configurations. To permit the identification of the same letter when it has different configurations, e.g., A, a and a , **functionally equivalent** feature lists are established. For each feature list there will be a number of alternative **criterial sets** to permit identification decisions on a minimum of visual information, depending on the number and nature of the alternatives.

Notes to Chapter 8 begin on page 224.

CHAPTER 9

WORD IDENTIFICATION

I have just devoted the first chapter specifically about "reading" to letter identification. Now I want to show that word identification does not require the prior identification of letters. The present chapter will be restricted to considering words in isolation, where there is no extrinsic clue to their identity. But the chapter will be another step towards a demonstration that procedures permitting the identification of words without the prior identification of letters will also permit comprehension without the prior identification of words.

THREE THEORIES OF WORD IDENTIFICATION

It is traditionally asserted that there are three theories of word identification: whole-word identification, letter-by-letter identification, and an intermediate position involving the identification of letter clusters, usually "spelling patterns". In effect, these three views represent three attempts to describe the mechanism by which the skilled reader is able to identify words on sight. They are accounts of what a reader needs to know and do in order to be able to say what a word is. One or another of the three views is apparent in practically every current approach to reading instruction.

I shall argue that each of these traditional theories of word recognition leaves more questions unanswered than it resolves. Nevertheless, each of the theories contains a kernel of truth about reading, otherwise it could not have survived to achieve a place in the folklore of the subject. In the following paragraphs I shall look a little more closely at which aspects of reading each theory appears particularly competent to illuminate and which aspects it leaves in the dark.

The *whole-word* view is based on the premise that readers do not stop to identify individual letters (or groups of letters) in the identification of a word. The view asserts that knowledge of the alphabet and of the "sounds of letters" is irrelevant to reading (although there is frequently a failure to indicate whether this stricture applies to fluent reading alone or to learning to read as well). One incontrovertible source of support for the whole-word view has already been alluded to — the fact that a viewer can report from a single tachistoscopic presentation either four or five random letters or a similar number of words. Surely if a word can be identified as easily as a letter, then it must be just as much of a unit as a letter; a word must be recognizable as a whole, rather than as a sequence of letters. Another unimpeachable piece of supporting evidence is that words may be identified when none of their component letters is clearly discriminable. For example, a name may be identifiable on a distant roadside sign, or in a dim light, under conditions that would make each individual letter of that name quite illegible if presented separately. If words can be read when letters are illegible, how can word recognition depend on letter identification? Finally, there is a good deal of evidence that words can be identified as quickly as letters. It has been shown that perception is far from instantaneous, and that successively presented random letters — or random words — cannot be identified faster than five or six a second (Newman, 1966; Kolers and Katzman, 1966). And if entire words can be identified as quickly as letters, how can their identification involve spelling them out letter by letter?

So much for some of the arguments in support of the whole-word point of view; now we can give equal time to the counter-position that, as a theory, it is most inadequate. One fundamental objection is that the view is not a theory at all; it has no "explanatory power" but merely rephrases the question that it pretends to answer. If words are recognized "as wholes", how are the wholes recognized? What do readers look for, and in what way is their prior knowledge of what a word looks like stored? It is no answer to say they have already learned what every word looks like, because that is the basic question: what exactly do readers know if they know what a word looks like? The qualification that words are identified "by their shapes" merely changes the name of the problem from "word identification" to "shape identification". Fluent readers may be able to recognize about 50,000 different words on sight — by what I shall call *immediate word identification*. Does that mean that readers have pictures of 50,000 different shapes stored in their minds, and that every time they come across a word in reading they riff through a pack of 50,000 templates in order to find out which one it is? But in what way would they sort through 50,000 alternatives? Surely not by starting at the beginning and examining each internal representation until they find a match. If we are looking for a book in a library, we do not start at the entrance and examine every volume until we come across the one with a title that matches the title we are looking for. Instead we make use of the fact that books are categorized and shelved in a systematic way; there are "rules" for getting to the book we want. It would appear reasonable to suggest that word identification is also systematic, and that we make use of rules that enable us to make our decision quickly. We can usually find some explanation for any error that we make. We may misread *said* as "sail" or "send" (or even as "reported" in circumstances where the substitution would make sense), but never as "elephant" or "plug" or "predisposition". In other words, we obviously do not select a word from 50,000 alternatives, but rather from a much smaller number. An unelaborated whole-word point of view cannot account for this prior elimination of alternatives.

Besides, we have already discovered that 50,000 internal representations of shapes would be far from adequate to enable us to identify 50,000 different words. Even if we could identify *HAT* by looking up an internal representation, how could the same representation enable us to identify *hat* or *hat* or any of the many other ways in which the word may be written?

The letter-by-letter theory, which the whole-word view is supposed to demolish, itself appears to have quite substantial evidence in its favor. We do appear to be sensitive to individual letters in the identification of words. The whole-word point of view would suggest that if viewers were presented with the stimulus *fashixn* tachistoscopically, they would either identify "the whole word" without noticing the *x*, or else fail to recognize the word at all because there would be no "match" with an internal representation. Instead, viewers typically do identify the word but report that there is something wrong with it, not necessarily reporting that there is an *x* instead of an *o*, but offering such explanations as "There's a hair lying over the end of it" (Pillsbury, 1897).

Furthermore, readers are very sensitive to the *predictability* of letter sequences. Letters do not occur haphazardly in any language; in English, for example, combinations like *th, st, br,* and almost any consonant and vowel pair are more likely to occur than combinations like *tf, sr, bm, ae,* or *uo*. The knowledge that readers acquire about these differing probabilities of letter combinations is demonstrated when words containing common letter sequences are more easily identified than those with uncommon sequences. Readers can identify sequences of letters that are *not* English words just as easily as some English words, provided the sequences are "close approximations" to English — which means that they are highly probable letter combinations (Miller, Bruner, and Postman, 1954). The average reader for example hardly falters when presented with sequences like *vernalit* or *mossiant* or *ricaning* — yet how could these be identified "as wholes" when they have never been seen before? A letter-by-letter view might also seem to be somewhat more economical; instead of learning to recognize 50,000 words, one learns to recognize 26 letters and applies a few spelling rules, decoding every word on the spot.

A rather illogical argument is sometimes proposed to support the letter-by-letter view. In its most extreme form, this view seems to imply that since letters in some way spell out the sound of a word, therefore word identification *must* be accomplished by sounding out the individual letters. It would be about as compelling to suggest that we must recognize cars by reading the manufacturer's name on the front or back, simply because the name is always there to be read. Besides, there are impressive arguments that the spelling of words is not a reliable guide to their sound. This question is so complex that "phonics" will be given a chapter to itself. For the moment we are not concerned with whether knowledge of letters can be used to identify words, but rather whether the skilled readers normally and necessarily identify words "that they know" by a letter-by-letter analysis.

The intermediate position — that words are identified through the recognition of clusters of letters — has the advantage of being able to account for the relatively easy identifiability of nonwords such as *vernalit*. It argues that readers become familiar with spelling patterns, such as *ve* and *rn* and even *vern*, which are recognized and put together to form words. The larger the spelling patterns we can recognize, the easier the word identification, according to this view. The view is compatible with our normal experience that when a new word like *zygotic* or *Helsingfors* halts our reading temporarily we do not seem to break it down to the individual letters before trying to put together what its sound must be. But many of the arguments that favor the whole-word position over letter analysis also work against the letter-cluster view. It may be useful, occasionally, to work out what a word is by analysis of letters or syllables, but normal reading does not appear to proceed on this basis; in fact, it would seem impossible. There is no time to "work out" what words are by synthesizing possible sound combinations. Besides, as the letter cluster argument is pushed to its extreme it becomes a whole-word approach since the largest and most reliable spelling patterns are words themselves.

The fact that the three traditional theories of word recognition continue to enjoy a wide acceptance obviously indicates that they rest on a fairly solid foundation of data, despite their shortcomings. No one can conclusively prove them wrong. Each approach, however, has inadequacies that are partly met by an alternative view, which would suggest that they are not mutually exclusive and that no one of them has any real claim to be the closest representation of the truth. In their place we need to find a theory of reading that will not be incompatible with any of the data, but that will also offer an explanation for inadequate aspects of the three traditional views. In short, any serious attempt to understand reading must be able to explain why it might sometimes appear that words are identified as wholes and at other times through the identification of component letters or groups of letters.

A Feature-Analytic Alternative

There is another point of view that would appear to overcome the major weaknesses of the three traditional theories without being incompatible with any of the evidence in their favor. Such a theory proposes that words are indeed identified "as wholes", but that the manner of their identification involves precisely the same procedures as the identification of letters, and in fact makes use of the same kind of visual information.

In the previous chapter, two models for letter identification were examined, feature analysis and template matching. The traditional whole-word theory that words are identified because of the familiarity of their "shape" is essentially a template-matching model, and arguments for its inadequacy have already been presented. The remainder of the present chapter will consider the alternative, a feature-analytic model for word identification. It should be reiterated that the present chapter is concerned only with the *identification of individual words,* of words actually in isolation or effectively so because context is ignored. The identification of words in meaningful sequences — which is of course more representative of most reading situations — will be considered in Chapter 11.

Basically, the feature-analytic model proposes that the only difference between the manner in which letters and words are identified lies in the categories and feature lists that the perceiver employs in the analysis of visual information. In brief, the difference depends on whether the reader is looking for letters or words; the process of looking and deciding is the same. If the reader's objective is to identify letters, then the analysis of the visual configuration is carried out with respect to the feature lists associated with the 26 letter categories, one for each letter of the alphabet. If the objective is to identify words, then there is a similar analysis of features in the visual configuration with respect to the feature lists of a larger number of word categories.

What are the features of words? They obviously must include the features of letters, because words are made up of letters. The arrays of marks on the printed page that can be read as words can also be distinguished as sequences of letters, so the "distinctive features" of letters that constitute a significant difference between one configuration and another must also be distinctive features of words. For example, whatever visual information permits the brain to distinguish between *h* and *n* must also permit it to distinguish between *hot* and *not*. And precisely the same procedures that distinguish between *h* and *n* will accomplish the discrimination between *hot* and *not*. At first glance, many more discriminations and analyses of distinctive features would appear to be required to distinguish among tens of thousands of alternative words compared with only 26 alternative letters, but we shall see that the difference is not so great. In fact no more information — no more featural tests — may be required to identify a word in meaningful text than to identify a single letter in isolation.

If the distinctive features of the visual configurations of letters are the same as those for the visual configurations of words, it might be expected that feature lists for letter and word categories would be similar. However, feature lists for word categories require an additional dimension to those for letters in that the analysis of word configurations involves *the position of features within a sequence.* The following examples, imaginary and quite arbitrary, compare four feature lists — two functionally equivalent lists for *H* and *h* in the letter category "h", and two functionally equivalent lists for the alternative forms *HORSE* and *horse* in the word category "horse". Each "test" represents information that could be received from an analyzer in the visual system about whether a particular feature is or is not present in the configuration being examined, and each + or − indicates whether a feature should or should not be present if the configuration is to be allocated to that particular category (see Figure 9.1).

The number of "positions" in a word feature list indicates the number of times a particular feature could occur in the letter sequence that constitutes the word and obviously corresponds to the number of letters. Similarly, a feature test that will be applied only once for the identification of a letter may be employed several times in the identification of a word, the maximum number of tests depending on the number of letters in the word. A feature list for a word could, therefore, also be regarded as a set of specifications for its component

	Letter Category "H"		Word Category "Horse"									
	H FEATURE LIST	h FEATURE LIST	HORSE FEATURE LIST *Position*					horse FEATURE LIST *Position*				
			1	2	3	4	5	1	2	3	4	5
Tests 1	+	−	+	+	−	+	−	−	+	−	−	+
2	+	+	+	−	−	+	+	+	−	+	+	−
3	−	−	−	+	−	+	−	−	−	+	−	+
4	+	−	+	−	+	+	+	−	+	−	−	−
5	−	+	−	+	+	−	−	+	+	−	+	+
6	−	+	−	+	−	+	+	+	−	+	+	−
7	+	+	+	−	−	−	+	+	−	−	+	+
8	−	−	−	+	−	+	+	−	+	−	−	+
9	−	+	−	−	+	+	−	+	−	+	−	−
10	+	+	+	+	+	−	+	+	+	−	−	+

FIGURE 9.1 Feature lists for letters and words

letters, as in Figure 9.1 where the features for the first position of *horse* are the same as the features for the letter *h*. This congruence between "position" and "letter" lists is inevitable because distinctive features of letters are also distinctive features of words, but it does not follow that letters must be identified in order for words to be identified. The term "position" is employed rather than "letter" to avoid any implication that a word is identified by its letters, rather than by the distribution of features across its entire configuration. A number of arguments will be presented to show that the fact that feature test specifications for positions and letters are identical is irrelevant to word identification.

(It should be added that there could be a few distinctive features of words that are not features of letters — for example, the relative height of different parts of the configuration or its length. As already noted, not enough is known of the visual system to assert what distinctive features actually are. The present discussion is restricted to presenting the view that words can be identified without the intervening identification of letters and does not claim to make precise statements about the actual features of letters or words.)

The feature-analytic view of *letter* identification asserts that because there is redundancy in the structure of letters — because there is more than enough featural information to distinguish among 26 alternatives — not all features of a letter need be discriminated in order to identify a letter. Therefore, a number of alternative *criterial sets* of features may exist within each feature list, information about the features within any criterial set being sufficient for an identification to be made. For example, Tests 1, 3, 4, 5, 7, and 8 or Tests 1, 2, 4, 5, 7, 9, or Tests 2, 3, 4, 6, 7, 9, 10 might constitute a criterial set of the *H* feature list for "*h*". Information about any of these combinations of features would be sufficient to eliminate all the 25 other alternative letters and permit the categorization — the identification — of a particular configuration as "*h*". Similar criterial sets would exist within the *h* feature list for the same category.

It would be expected that criterial sets also exist for *word* identification, except that now they would cover the second dimension and take into account feature combinations extending across the entire word. Criterial sets within the feature list for *HORSE* for example, might include Tests 3, 4, 6, and 9 for Position 1; Tests 3, 7, and 9 for Position 3; Tests 4, 6, 7, and 8 for Position 4; and Tests 4, 6, 7, and 10 for Position 5. Three significant aspects of such a criterial set of features should be noted.

First, in no position are sufficient features tested to permit identification of a letter if that letter were standing in isolation. For example, feature tests 3, 4, 5, and 9 in Position 1 would not constitute a criterial set for the identification of *H* standing alone, although they are sufficient for the first position of *HORSE* (provided certain other features are tested in other positions). The explanation, of course, is that a criterial set for *H* alone would have to contain sufficient information to eliminate the 25 other letters of the alphabet while there are not that many alternatives that could occur in front of the sequence *-ORSE*. The difference between a criterial set for the first position of *Horse* and for the letter *H* in isolation illustrates the point that the "positions" in words should not be regarded as letters; word configurations are tested for featural information that leads directly to word categories, not to intermediate letter categories. Experimental evidence will be cited to show that words can be identified before any of their component letters are discriminable.

Second, the illustrative criterial set of features for *HORSE* does not include any features from the second position. The omission indicates that all of that particular part of the word (the letter *O*) could be blacked out and the word would still be identifiable because only one single letter can occur in that position. The ready identifiability of the sequence H-RSE is an example of the *redundancy* that exists within words, permitting the fluent reader to identify words on far less visual information than may be available in their configurations.

Third, the total number of features required to identify "horse" in the particular criterial set given as an example is far less than would be required to identify the letters *H, O, R, S,* and *E* if they were presented in isolation, or in mixed up order, or to a beginning reader or foreign-language speaker who could not recognize the whole word. Again, this economy is a consequence of redundancy within words.

If you recognize that the first letter of an English word is *T* and the second letter *H*, you do not get — or at least you do not need — as much information from the second letter as you did from the first. Knowing the first letter of a word provides information about the second. The first letter contains sufficient visual information to enable you to discard 25 out of 26 alternatives (assuming for the sake of argument that a word is equally likely to start with any of the letters of the alphabet). The second letter also contains enough visual information, or distinctive features, to distinguish among 26 alternatives because obviously you can distinguish it from all the other letters of the alphabet when it is standing alone. But you do not need featural information to distinguish the second letter from among 26 alternatives because there are not 26 letters that it could be. If the first letter of an English word is *T*, then there is a very high degree of probability that the second letter will be *H, R,* or one of the vowels; the number of possible alternatives for the second letter is fewer than ten. In fact, the more letters that are known of a word, the fewer alternatives there are on the average for what each additional letter could be. And because there is much less uncertainty about each letter, less and less featural information is required for their identification.

Knowledge of the way in which letters are grouped into words may be called *orthographic information*. This information, which is located within the brain of the fluent reader, is an alternative nonvisual source of information to the *featural* or *visual information* that the eyes pick up from the page. To the extent that both of these sources of information reduce the number of alternatives that a particular letter might be, there is redundancy. Such duplication of information is also called *sequential redundancy* because its source lies in the fact that the different parts of a word are not independent; the occurrence of particular alternatives in one part of a sequence limits the range of alternatives that can occur anywhere else in the sequence.

The orthographic redundancy of English is enormous. If all 26 letters of the alphabet could occur without restriction in each position of a five-letter word, there could be nearly twelve million different five-letter words, compared with perhaps ten thousand that actually exist.

Redundancy among Distinctive Features

I have been talking so far about the constraints that one letter places on the occurrence of *letters* in other parts of a word. But precisely the same argument can apply to *features*. Obviously, if we can say that the occurrence of the letter *T* in the first position of a word restricts the possibilities for the second position to *H, R, A, E, I, O, U,* and *Y;* then we can also say that the occurrence of *features* of the letter *T* in the first position limits the possible *features* that can occur in the second position. In fact, we can eliminate the mention of letters and specific positions altogether and say that when certain features occur in one part of a word, there are limits to the kinds of feature combinations that can occur in other parts of the word. A reader implicitly aware of such limitations is able to make use of *sequential redundancy among features,* the overlapping sources of information being the visual information that could eliminate all possible sets of alternative feature combinations and the reader's knowledge that many of the possible alternative sets do not in fact occur.

By virtue of sequential redundancy, the skilled reader can identify words with so little visual information that the identification of letters is completely by-passed. It is not necessary to identify letters in any part of a word in order to identify the entire word. Words may be identified before there is sufficient featural information in any position to permit the identification of a letter standing alone.

Here is a simple illustration of how featural redundancy might permit the identification of a two-letter word before either of the letters could be identified individually. Imagine that sufficient features could be discriminated in the first position of the word so that if we were looking at that position alone our alternatives would be reduced to either *a* or *e* — but that we could not make a final decision between the two. Suppose also that in the second position of the word we could detect sufficient features to reduce the alternatives to *f* or *t*, but not to make a final choice. From the four possibilities that might be constructed, *af, at, ef, et*, only one construction would be acceptable as a word. Because word categories do not exist for the other three possibilities, the configuration would be allocated to the category "at", identified as "at", and so perceived. If there was also a word (a category) "et" in the language, then a decision could not be made, and if "et" existed but not "at", then *et* is what would be seen.

Two qualifications ought to be made regarding the preceding example. Both have been made before but bear reiterating. The first is that we do not know what the features of letters or words actually are, therefore it is not suggested that the particular *af, at, ef, et* situation might actually arise, although there are many ways of demonstrating that we often see what we think must be present rather than what is actually present. The second qualification is that it is not suggested that readers are *aware* of their knowledge of sequential redundancy, any more than they are aware of the decision-making process that is involved in reading or any other form of perception. But in the Notes I shall give some examples to show that the fluent reader must indeed be regarded as possessing such a knowledge of language.

Functional Equivalence for Words

Some remarks remain to be made concerning functional equivalence for word configurations. The notion of criterial sets permits a good deal of flexibility in the operation of a feature-analytic process. With letters, for example, ability to make an identification although information about one or two features may be absent from (or even contrary to) the total specification of a feature list need not prevent the categorization of a configuration. As a result, such diverse configurations as A,ᴧ, A,ᴀ, and such impoverished forms as /ᴀ/ and %ᴀ% might all meet the specifications of one or another of the criterial subsets of the feature list for *A*, and be allocated to the category "a".

When alternative forms reach a particular level of featural dissimilarity, however, such as *a* and *A,* there is the additional possibility available of setting up "functionally equivalent" feature lists for the same category. Within each such feature list a number of alternative criterial sets might exist.

Just as there may be functionally equivalent feature lists for various forms of the same letter, so alternative feature lists for functionally equivalent versions of the same word would be expected. Invented examples have been given of one feature list for *HORSE* and another for *horse.* However, it is not proposed that these two (and other) feature lists for the same word would exist completely independently, but rather that a visual configuration would be allocated to a particular category if tests of its parts satisfied positional specifications on any set of functionally equivalent feature lists. As an oversimplified example, it is not proposed that there must necessarily be a special feature list for the visual configuration *Horse,* because the first position of that configuration is congruent with the beginning of *HORSE* (and many other words) while the remainder is congruent with part of *horse* (and some other words). While tests of the configuration *Horse* will not satisfy a criterial set within the feature lists for *HORSE* or *horse* or any other word, it is only within the two functionally equivalent feature lists for the category "horse" that the configuration meets criterial requirements at both beginning and end. In other words, a configuration may be identified if it is congruent with nonoverlapping parts of two criterial sets of features, provided that these incomplete criterial sets are functionally equivalent for the same category. Such a view would suggest that a quite unfamiliar configuration like *HoRsE* should still be identifiable through meeting the criterial requirements for Positions 1, 3, and 5 for *HORSE* and Positions 2 and 4 for *horse* — and there is evidence that this is the case (Smith, Lott, and Cronnell, 1969).

It must be emphasized that we are still not talking about letters — I am not saying that *H, R,* and *E* are identified from one feature list and *o* and *s* from another. It is still proposed that the identification is being made directly to the category "horse" through the various equivalent feature lists for a word and not through the unrelated feature lists of individual letters.

To summarize, the difference between letter and word identification is simply the category system that is involved — the manner in which featural information is allocated. If the reader is examining an array of visual information in order to identify letters, the visual information will be tested and identifications made on the basis of the feature lists for the 26 letter categories. If the purpose is to identify words, the visual information will be tested with respect to the feature lists for words, and there will be no question of letter identification. It follows from the present argument that it should be impossible to identify a word and its component letters simultaneously, because one cannot use the same information to make two different kinds of decision.

Because letter and word identification involve the same featural information, it is not possible to identify a configuration both as a word and as a sequence of letters at the same time. We can see the configuration *cat* either as the letters *c, a, t* or as the word *cat,* but not as both simultaneously. Similarly, we can see the configuration *read* either as the word pronounced "reed" or as the word pronounced "red" but not as both at once; and *IO* can be seen either as a number or as letters but not as both. We cannot apply the same information to two categories simultaneously, just as we cannot use the same contour as part of two figures simultaneously — the center line of ⟩⟨ can be seen as part of a face on the left or as part of a face on the right, but the two faces can never be seen simultaneously.

It is easily shown that the limitation in the previous cases does not lie in an inability to allocate identical configurations to two different categories — we have little difficulty in seeing *io io* as "ten eye-oh" or the two faces in ⟩⟨ , or even *cat is cat* as "c, a, t is cat," or *read read* as if pronounced "red reed" — as in *I PICKED UP THE NOTE AND READ "READ THIS QUICKLY"* — provided that there is featural information for each of the two categories we are using. The impossibility is to use the *same* information for two purposes simultaneously.

LEARNING TO IDENTIFY WORDS

There are two aspects of learning to identify words which are analogous to the two aspects of learning to identify letters outlined at the end of the last chapter. One aspect is establishing criterial sets of functionally equivalent distinctive features for each category, and the other is associating a name with a category. For letter identification it was asserted that relating the name to the category was not a problem; children learn names for visual configurations all the time. In word identification there may indeed be a problem in relating names to categories, not because children have particular difficulty in remembering the name for a category once they have found out what it is, but in finding out what the name of a category is in the first place. When children are beginning to discover written language, helpful adults usually act as mediators by saying what the printed words are, leaving to the child the more complex task of discovering how to distinguish one word from another. This is precisely the same as the "cat-and-dog" problem. The process of finding out the name of a category may be termed *mediated word identification,* and is the topic of the next chapter. Word identification must be *mediated* when a word cannot be identified on sight by allocation to a category through an existing feature list. By contrast, I refer to word identification as I have discussed it in this chapter as *immediate word identification.* The term "immediate" is used not in the sense of instantaneous, which we know is not the case, but to mean "not mediated", indicating that a word is identified directly from its features. The aspect of learning with which the remainder of this chapter will be concerned is the establishment of appropriate visual feature lists for words.

It will help if we consider a specific instance. A child is about to learn to recognize a particular written name, say *John.* The task confronting the child is to discover the rules for recognizing this event when it occurs again, which means finding out something about the configuration that will distinguish it from other configurations that should not be called "John". I shall assume that the child has already discovered that a reliable distinguishing characteristic for the configuration is not the color of the paper that it is printed on, or the color of the ink, both of which may be reasonable cues for other types of identification but which will sooner or later prove to be inadequate for the allocation of visual information to word categories. I shall also assume that the child at this time is not confronted by *John* in a number of different type styles. The ability to name any or all of the letters of the alphabet has no direct relevance in immediate word identification, although there will be an obvious (although by no means essential) advantage for children if they have learned to distinguish even a few letters, without necessarily being able to name them, because they will have begun to acquire cues about the features that distinguish words.

That is the problem for the child: to discover cues that will distinguish *John* from other configurations. The child may decide that a good cue lies in the length of the word, or the two upright strokes, or the shape of the "fishhook" at the beginning. In selecting a cue that will be the basis for recognition of the word, a child will establish the first tentative "distinctive features" to be looked for in the future when testing whether to allocate a configuration to the category "John".

Exactly what the first distinctive features will be depends on circumstances; it depends on the other words from which the child tries to distinguish the configuration *John.* Until the child comes across another word that is not *John* there is no problem; the child applies the single test and calls every configuration that passes the test "John". But until the child comes across another word that is not *John,* there can be no learning. What brings a child to the beginning of the process of developing feature lists that will serve for *reading* is having to distinguish *John* from all the other configurations with which it is not functionally equivalent. The child will only really be able to identify *John* after learning not to apply that name to every other word configuration that is met. It is when the child is confronted by a configuration that should go into a different category that the soundness of the tentative discrimination is tested, and, of course, it is soon found to be wanting. If the hypothesized distinctive features were related to the length of the word, then the child would respond "John" to the configuration *Fred.* If the hypothesis involved the initial fishhook, the child would say "John" to *Jack* or *June* or *Jeremiah.* The more nonequivalent configurations — the more different "words" — children have to discriminate among, the more they will come to select as distinctive features those that will be appropriate to the eventual task of fluent reading. But until children can understand what they have to distinguish *John* from, they will never acquire an appropriate set of distinctive features for identifying that word.

The preceding statement does *not* mean that children must be able to *name* every other word they meet; not at all. All they have to do is see a representative sample of words that are not *John,* so that they can find out in what respects *John* is different. It does not matter if they cannot discriminate among all the other words (although in learning to identify *John* they will learn something about all other words); the beginning can be the establishment of only two categories: configurations that are "John" and configurations that are not "John". Attempting to teach "one word at a time" — writing a word on a variety of different surfaces and occasions and insisting "This is 'John'; this is 'John' " — will not help children to learn the word because they will never learn how *John* may be distinguished from any other word. The notion that a child can learn to identify a word by the repetitious presentation of just that word is a template theory. Its inappropriateness is obvious as soon as we realize that there is no way in which a child can transfer a picture of what is presented to his eyes into a storehouse in his brain. Children do not need to be told interminably what a word is; they have to be able to see what it is *not.*

Acquaintance with a wide variety of nonequivalent alternatives is everything. Through growing familiarity with the written form of language, children learn not only to discriminate distinctive features, to establish feature lists, and to recognize functional equivalences, they also learn about redundancy. And by acquiring a pool of knowledge about the redundancy of words, they learn to identify words economically, on minimal quantities of visual information; they establish large numbers of alternative criterial sets.

It is perhaps a sobering thought that just about everything that a child learns, as described in the preceding paragraph, is never explicitly taught. Among the many positive things reading teachers can do — providing motivation, direction, learning opportunities, encouragement, feedback — they cannot include the provision of rules by which words are to be recognized. That part of learning must be left to the children themselves.

A POSTSCRIPT ABOUT WORDS

One of the inevitable consequences of examining closely a subject like reading, about which so much is taken for granted, is that it turns out to be far more complicated and less well understood than we thought it to be. An obvious first step in my discussion of word identification might have been to state clearly and precisely how many words the average fluent reader knows: this would give some useful knowledge about the dimensions of the problem. But the trouble with a simple request for a count of the words that a person knows is that the answer depends on what is meant by "word", while in any case there is no way to compute a reliable answer.

Consider first the matter of deciding what we want to call a word. Should *cat* and *cats,* or *walk* and *walked* be regarded as two different words or as two forms of the same word? Dictionaries usually provide entries only for the base or root form of words, refusing to count as different words such variations as plurals, comparatives, adjectival forms, and various verb tenses. If we want to call *cat* and *cats,* or *walk* and *walked* different words (and certainly we would not regard them as functionally equivalent visually), the number of words we know on sight might turn out to be three or four times greater than the number of words the dictionary maker would credit us with. Furthermore, common words have many meanings as in "You can *bank* on the *bank* by the river *bank*." But if the same spelling is to be regarded as (at least) three different words because *bank* has several meanings, should a preposition like "by", which has so many different senses, be counted as forty words or more?

The next problem is to count. Obviously, it is not good enough simply to count the number of words that a person reads or hears or produces during the course of a day, for many words will be used more than once and others will occur not at all. To count the number of *different* words a person produces we have to look carefully in a torrent of very familiar words. But in how big a torrent shall we look? How can we ever be certain that we have given sufficient opportunity for all the words a person knows? Without a doubt, we shall find some new words in every additional sample of a thousand that we record, but surely a law of decreasing returns would apply. After analyzing say 100,000 words from one person, it would seem unlikely that many new ones would be produced. But such is not the case. Very many words with which we are quite familiar occur less than once in every million — and it may take anywhere from two months to two years for a person to produce that number of words. One very extensive analysis of nearly five million words in popular magazines (Thorndike and Lorge, 1944) found over 3000 words that occurred an average of less than once in every million, and almost all of these words would fall under our category of "known". Here is a sample of words that occurred only once in every *five million* words — *earthiness, echelon, echidna, eclair, effluence, egad, egotistic* — one or two may be a little unusual, but by and large they are words that we can recognize.

There is something a little eerie even to think about how we might acquire and retain familiarity with the relatively infrequent words. We meet them perhaps once a year, but it is not often we have to stop and wonder "Haven't I seen you before somewhere?" Obviously, it is not possible to "count" how many different words a person knows, so one has to make an estimate. And many estimates have been offered, varying from 20,000 to over 100,000 depending on the definitions used and assumptions made. This gives one good answer to the question of how many words a person might know — it is impossible to say.

SUMMARY

Words, like letters, can be identified directly from the distinctive features that are the visual information of print. **Immediate word identification** takes place when feature analysis allocates a visual configuration to the feature list of a word category in cognitive structure, without the intermediate step of letter identification. **Criterial sets** of features within **functionally equivalent** feature lists permit the identification of words on minimal information, for example when the reader can employ prior knowledge of the **orthographic redundancy** within words.

Notes to Chapter 9 begin on page 227.

CHAPTER 10

PHONICS
and
mediated
word
identification

The preceding chapter was concerned with *immediate* word identification, with the manner in which visual feature lists are established and used so that words can be recognized on sight, without "decoding to sound" or any

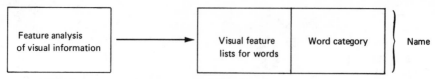

FIGURE 10.1   Immediate word identification

other method of *mediated* word identification. In fact, the previous chapter argued that letter-by-letter identification is unnecessary and even impossible for word identification in normal reading, thus leaving no room for decoding to sound. Immediate word identification is illustrated in Figure 10.1.

But in the preceding chapter I was talking about the identification of words where the "name" of the word — its pronunciation when read aloud — is either known to the reader or otherwise available to the learner. The learner does not need to figure out what the visual configuration "says", but only how it should be recognized on future occasions. I compared this situation with the cat-and-dog learning problem where the child is told that a particular animal is a cat and then left to discover how to recognize one another time.

Suppose, however, that the name of a word is not immediately available to the learner — that there is no one to identify an unfamiliar word, and there are no context cues, perhaps because the word is seen in isolation or as part of a list of unrelated words. Now the learner has a double problem, not only to discover how to recognize the word in the future, but to find out what the word is in the first place. This is the cat-and-dog problem without the learner being told whether the animal is in fact a cat or a dog. In such a situation in reading, a word obviously cannot be identified *immediately;* its identification must be *mediated* by some other means of discovering what it is. The present chapter is about the use of *phonics* — a set of relationships between letters and sounds — and other methods of mediated word identification. The use of phonic rules to mediate word identification is illustrated in Figure 10.2.

In particular this chapter will examine the extent to which knowledge of the sounds associated with letters of the alphabet will help in

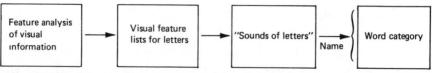

FIGURE 10.2   Mediated word identification: The phonic model

the identification of words. For many, this process of decoding the spelling of words to their sounds is the basis of reading, a view which I do not think is tenable. It is not necessary to "say" what a written word is before we can comprehend its meaning. We no more need to say a written word is "cat" in order to understand it than we need to say that a particular animal is a cat in order to recognize it. Indeed, just as we cannot say that the animal is a cat unless we have already identified it, so the naming of a word normally occurs after the identification of its meaning.

This chapter is still not the whole story of reading, even as far as words are concerned. In both the preceding and the present chapters, the assumption is made that the word a reader is trying to identify already exists in the reader's spoken language vocabulary; its meaning is known. The reader's problem is to identify the word, to discover or recognize its "name", not to learn its meaning. The next chapter will deal with the situation of words that are truly new, where the meaning must be discovered as well as the name or pronunciation.

THE AIMS AND COMPLEXITY OF PHONICS

Mediated word identification is not the most critical part of reading, and phonics is not the only strategy available for mediated word identification. Nevertheless, phonics frequently plays a central role in reading instruction, and it will clear the air if we examine the nature and efficacy of phonics first of all.

Rules and Exceptions

The aim of phonics instruction is to provide readers with rules that will enable them to predict how a written word will sound from the way it is spelled. The value of teaching phonics depends on how many correspondences there are between the letters and sounds of English. A correspondence exists whenever a particular letter (or sometimes a group of letters) represents a particular sound (or absence of sound). Thus *c* is involved in at least three correspondences — with the sound /s/ as in *medicine,* with /k/ as in *medical,* and with no sound at all as in *scientist.* Alternatively, a correspondence exists whenever a particular sound is represented by a particular letter or letters, as /f/ can be represented by *f, ph,* and *gh.* Thus, the total number of "spelling-to-sound" correspondences must be the same as the total number of "sound-to-spelling" correspondences. But by now it is probably no surprise that any question related to language involving a simple "how many" leads to a very complicated and unsatisfactory evasion of an answer. Phonics is no exception.

Everything is wrong about the question. The first problem concerns our expectations about rules. If we expect a rule to mean a correspondence that has no exceptions, then we shall have a difficult task finding any rules in phonics at all. Here is a phonic rule that would appear to have impeccable credentials: Final *e* following a single consonant indicates that the preceding vowel should be long, as in *hat* and *hate*, or *hop* and *hope*. And here are two instant exceptions: *axe* has a single consonant but a short /a/, while *ache* has a double consonant but a long /a/. We have the choice of admitting that a familiar rule is not impervious to exceptions, or else we have to make a rule for the exceptions. One explanation that might be offered is that *x* is really a double consonant, *ks*, and that *ch* is really a single consonant, /k/. But then we are in the rather peculiar position of changing the notion of what constitutes a single letter simply because we have a rule that does not fit all cases. And if we have to say that the definition of what constitutes a letter depends on the pronunciation of a word, how can we say the pronunciation of a word can be predicted from its letters? Besides, what can we say about the silent *e* at the end of *have* or *love*, which is put there only because there is a convention that English words may not end with a *v*? Or the *e* at the end of *house*, which is to indicate that the word is not a plural? Or the *o* in *money* and *women*, which is there because early printers felt that a succession of up-and-down strokes, like *mun* and *wim*, would be too difficult to decipher?

Having made the point that phonic rules will have exceptions, the next problem is to decide what constitutes an exception. Some exceptions occur so frequently and regularly that they would appear to be rules in their own right. It is quite arbitrary how anyone decides to draw the line between rules and exceptions. We have a choice of saying that the sounds of written English can be predicted by relatively few rules, although there will be quite a lot of exceptions, or by a large number of rules with relatively few exceptions. Indeed, if we care to say that some rules have only one application, for example that *acht* is pronounced /ot/ as in "yacht", then we can describe English completely in terms of rules simply because we have legislated exceptions out of existence.

If the concept of a rule seems somewhat arbitrary, the notion of what constitutes a letter is even more idiosyncratic. It is true that in one sense there can be no doubt about what a letter is — it is one of the 26 characters in the alphabet — but any attempt to construct rules of spelling-sound correspondence is doomed from the start if we restrict our terms of reference to individual letters. To start with, there are only 26 letters compared with about 40 different sounds of speech, so many letters at least must do double duty. We shall find, of course, that many letters stand for more than one sound, while many sounds are represented by more than one letter. However, many sounds are not represented by single letters at all — *th, ch, ou, ue,* for example — so that we have to consider some combinations of letters as quite distinct *spelling units* — rather as if *th* were a letter in its own right. It has been asserted, with the help of a computer analysis of over 20,000 words (Venezky, 1967, 1970) that there are 52 "major spelling units" in English, 32 for consonants and 20 for vowels, effectively doubling the size of the alphabet.

The addition of all these extra spelling units, however, does not seem to make the structure of the English writing system very much more orderly. Some of the original letters of the alphabet are quite superfluous. There is nothing that *c* or *q* or *x* can do that could not be done by the other consonants. And many of the additional spelling units that are recognized simply duplicate the work of single letters, such as *ph* for *f*, and *dg* for *j*. There are also compound vowels whose effect duplicates the silent final *e*, like *ea* in *meat* compared with *mete*. Some combinations of letters have a special value only when they occur in particular parts of a word — *gh* may be pronounced as *f* (or as nothing) at the end of a word *(rough, through)* but is pronounced just like a single *g* at the beginning *(ghost* and *gold, ghastly* and *garden)*. Often letters have only a relational function, sacrificing any sound of their own in order to indicate how another letter should be sounded. An obvious example is the silent *e*, another is the *u* that distinguishes the *g* in *guest* from the *g* in *gem*.

So for our basic question of phonics, what we are really asking is how many arbitrarily defined rules can account for an indeterminate number of correspondences between an indefinite set of spelling units and an uncertain number of sounds (the total and quality of which may vary from dialect to dialect).

Some aspects of spelling are simply unpredictable, certainly to a reader with a limited knowledge of word derivations, no matter how one tries to define a spelling unit. An example of a completely unpredictable spelling-to-sound correspondence is *th*, which is pronounced in one way at the beginning of words like *this, than, those, them, then, these* but in another way at the beginning of *think, thank, thatch, thong, theme,* and so on. There is only one way to tell whether *th* should be pronounced as in /this/ or as in /think/, and that is to remember every instance. On the other hand, in many dialects there is no difference between the sounds represented by *w* and *wh*, as in *witch* and *which*, so that in some cases it can be the spelling that is not predictable, not the sound.

Almost all common words are exceptions — *of* requires a rule of its own for the pronunciation of *f*.

The game of finding exceptions is too easy to play. I shall give only one more example to illustrate the kind of difficulty one must run into in trying to construct — or teach — reliable rules of phonic correspondence. How are the letters *ho* pronounced, when they occur at the beginning of a word? And here are eleven possible answers; all, you will notice, quite common words: *hope, hot, hoot, hook, hour, honest, house, honey, hoist, horse, horizon.*

Of course, there are rules (or are some of them merely exceptions?) that can account for many of the pronunciations of *ho*. But there is one very significant implication in all the examples that applies to almost all English words — in order to apply phonic rules, *words must be read from right to left*. The way in which the reader pronounces *ho* depends on what comes after it, and the same applies to the *p* in *ph*, the *a* in *ate*, the *k* in *knot*, the *t* in *-tion*. The exceptions are very very few, like *asp* and *ash* which are pronounced differently if preceded by a *w*, and *f*, pronounced /v/ only if preceded by *o*. The fact that sound "dependencies" in words run from right to left is an obvious difficulty for a beginning reader trying to sound out a word from left to right, or for a theorist who wants to maintain that words are identified on a left-to-right basis.

In summary, English is far from predictable as far as its spelling-sound relationships are concerned. Just how much can be done to predict the pronunciation of a relatively small number of common words with a finite number of rules we shall see in a moment. But before I conclude this catalogue of complications and exceptions, two points should be reiterated. The first point is that phonic rules can only be considered as probabilistic, as guides to the way words might be pronounced, and that there is rarely any indication of when a rule does or does not apply. The rule that specifies how to pronounce *ph* in *telephone* falls down in the face of *haphazard*, or *shepherd*, or *cuphook*. The rule for *oe* in *doe* and *woe* will not work for *shoe*. The only way to distinguish the pronunciation of *sh* in *bishop* and *mishap*, or *th* in *father* and *fathead*, is to know the entire word in advance. The probability of being wrong if you do not know a word at all is very high. Even if individual rules were likely to be right three times out of four, there would still be only one chance in three of avoiding error in a four-letter word.

The second point is that phonic rules look deceptively simple when you know what a word is in the first place. I do not intend to be facetious. Teachers often feel convinced that phonic rules work because letter-sound correspondences seem obvious if a word is known in advance; the alternatives are not considered. And children may seem to apply phonic rules when they can recognize a word in any case — or because the teacher also suggests what the word is — thereby enabling them to identify or recite the phonic correspondences that happen to be appropriate.

The Efficiency of Phonics

One systematic attempt has been made to construct a workable set of phonic rules for English (Berdiansky, Cronnell and Koehler, 1969). The effort had modest aims — to see how far one could go in establishing a set of correspondence rules for the 6092 one- and two-syllable words among 9000 different words in the comprehension vocabularies of six- to nine-year-old children. The words were all taken from books to which the children were normally exposed — they were the words that the children knew and ought to be able to identify if they were to be able to read the material with which they were confronted at school.

The researchers who analyzed the 6092 words found rather more than the 52 "major spelling units" to which I have already referred — they identified 69 "grapheme units" which had to be separately distinguished in their rules. A group of letters were called a "grapheme unit", just like a single letter, whenever their relationship to a sound could not be accounted for by any rules for single letters. Grapheme units included pairs of consonants such as *ch, th;* pairs of vowels such as *ea, oy;* and letters that commonly function together, such as *ck* and *qu*, as well as double consonants like *bb* and *tt*, all of which require some separate phonic explanation. The number of grapheme units should not surprise us. The previously mentioned 52 "major units" were not intended to represent the only spelling units that could occur but only the most frequent ones.

An arbitrary decision was made about what would constitute a rule: it would have to account for a spelling-sound correspondence occurring in at least ten different words. Any distinctive spelling-sound correspondence, and any grapheme unit, that did not occur in at least ten words was considered an "exception". Actually, the researchers made several exceptions among the exceptions. They wanted their rules to account for as many of their words as possible, and so they let several cases through the net when it seemed to them more appropriate to account for a grapheme unit with a rule rather than to stigmatize it as an exception.

The researchers discovered that their 6000 words involved 211 distinct spelling-sound correspondences. This does not mean that 211 different sounds were represented, any more than there were 211 different grapheme units, but rather that the 69 grapheme units were related to 38 sounds in a total of 211 different ways. The results are summarized in Table 10.1.

Eighty-three of the correspondences involved consonant grapheme units, and 128 involved vowel grapheme units, including no fewer than 79 that were associated with the six "primary" single-letter vowels, *a, e, i, o, u, y*. In other words, there was a total of 79 different ways in which single vowels could be pronounced. Of the 211 correspondences, 45 classified as exceptions, about half involving vowels and half consonants. The exclusion of 45 correspondences meant that about ten percent of the 6092 words had to be set aside as "exceptions".

The pronunciation of the remaining words was accounted for by a grand total of 166 rules. Sixty of these rules were concerned with the pronunciation of consonants (which are generally thought to have fairly "regular" pronunciations) and 106 with single or complex vowels.

The research that has just been outlined is important in a number of ways for understanding reading and the teaching of reading. Some conclusions that can be drawn are far-reaching in their implications. The first is very simply that phonics is complicated. Without saying anything at all about whether it is desirable to teach young children a knowledge of phonics, we now have an idea of the magnitude of the endeavor. We now know that if we really expect to give children a

TABLE 10.1   Spelling-sound correspondences among 6092 one- and two-syllable words in the vocabularies of nine-year-old children

	Consonants	Primary Vowels	Secondary Vowels	Total
Spelling-sound correspondences	83	79	49	211
"Rules"	60	73	33	166
"Exceptions"	23	6	16	45
Grapheme units in rules	44	6	19	69

mastery of phonics, then we are not talking about a dozen or so rules. We are talking about 166 rules, which will still not account for hundreds of the words they might expect to meet in their early reading.

It is obvious that the most that can be expected from a knowledge of phonic rules is that they may provide a *clue* to the sound (or "name") of a configuration being examined. Phonics can provide only approximations. Even if readers do happen to know the 73 rules for the pronunciation of the six vowels, they would still have no sure way of telling which rule applied — or even that they were not dealing with an exception.

There is still one issue to be considered concerning the *effectiveness* of phonics. Is the limited degree of efficiency that might be attained worth acquiring? Other factors have to be taken into account related to the *cost* of trying to learn and use phonic rules. There is the possibility that reliance on phonics will involve readers in so much delay that short-term memory will be overloaded, and they will lose the sense of what they are reading. A tendency to rely exclusively on phonic rules may create a handicap for beginning readers whose biggest problem is to develop speed in reading. Our working memories do not have an infinite capacity and reading is not a task that can be accomplished at too leisurely a pace. As we shall see, other sources of information exist for finding out what a word in context might be, especially if the word is in the spoken vocabulary of the reader.

The Cost of "Reform"

The involved relation between the spelling of words and their sound has led to frequent suggestions for modifying the alphabet or for rationalizing the spelling system. To some extent both these intentions share the same misconceptions and difficulties. A number of contemporary linguists would deny that there is anything wrong with the way most words are spelled; they argue that a good deal of information would be lost if spelling were touched. Most of the apparent inconsistencies in spelling have some historical basis; the spelling system may be complex, but it is not arbitrary — it has become what it is for quite systematic reasons. And because spelling is systematic and reflects something of the history of words, much more information is available to the reader than we normally realize. (The fact that we are not *aware* that this information is available does not mean that we do not use it; we have already seen a number of examples of the way in which we have and use a knowledge of the structure and redundancy of our language that we cannot put into words.) Spelling reform might seem to make words easier to pronounce, but only at the cost of other information about the way words are related to each other, so that rationalizing words at the phonological level might make reading more difficult at syntactic and semantic levels. As just one example, consider the "silent *b*" in words like *bomb, bombing, bombed,* which would be an almost certain candidate for extinction if spelling reformers had their way. But the *b* is something more than a pointless appendage; it relates the previous words to others like *bombard, bombardier, bombardment* where the *b* is pronounced. And if you save yourself the trouble of a special rule about why *b* is silent in words like *bomb*, at another level there would be a new problem of explaining why *b* suddenly appears in words like *bombard.* Remove the *g* from *sign* and you must explain where it comes from in *signature.*

Another argument in favor of the present spelling system is that it is the most competent one to handle different dialects, a matter relevant also to those who would want to change the alphabet. Although there is almost universal acceptance of the idea that words should be spelled in the same way by everyone, we do not all pronounce words in the same way. If the spelling of words is to be changed so that they reflect the way they are pronounced, whose dialect will provide the standard? Is a different letter required for every different sound produced in any dialect of English we might encounter? Phonics instruction becomes even more complicated when it is realized that in many classrooms teacher and students do not speak the same dialect and that both may speak a different dialect from the authorities who suggested the particular phonic rules they are trying to follow. The teacher who tries to make children understand a phonic difference between the pronunciation of *caught* and *cot* will have a communication problem if this distinction is not one that the children observe in their own speech. The teacher may not even pronounce the two words differently, so that while the teacher thinks the message to the child is "That word is not *cot;* it is *caught,*" the message coming across is "That word is not *cot;* it is *cot.*"

Spelling and Meaning

The manner in which words are spelled in English is seen as a problem primarily if reading is perceived as a matter of decoding words to sound, which it is not and could not be, and if the primary function of spelling is regarded as the representation of *sounds* of words. But in fact, spelling also represents meaning, and where there is a conflict between pronunciation and meaning it is usually meaning which prevails, as if even the spelling system of written language recognized the priority of meaning. For example, the plural represented by a simple *s* in written language may be pronounced in three different ways in speech — as the /s/ sound on the end of "cats", the /z/ sound on the end of "dogs", and the /iz/ sound on the end of "judges". Would writing be easier to read if the past tense of verbs were not indicated by a consistent -*ed* but rather reflected the pronunciation, so that we had such variations as *walkt* and *landid*. The reason that *medicine* and *medical* are spelled as they are is not because *c* is sometimes arbitrarily pronounced /s/ and sometimes /k/ but because the two words have the same root meaning, represented by *medic*. This commonality of meaning would be lost if the two words were spelled *medisin* and *medikal*. It should be noted, incidentally, that the consistent representation of the various pronunciations of the plural meaning by *s* or the past tense meaning by *ed* rarely cause difficulty to readers, even beginners, provided they are reading for sense. If a child understands a word, the pronunciation will take care of itself, but the effort to produce pronunciation as a prerequisite for meaning is likely to result in neither being achieved.

Of course, spelling is a problem, both in school and out, but it is a problem of *writing*, not of reading. Readers are not normally aware of spelling. They attend to the appearance of words, to their features, not to their individual letters. Knowing how to spell does not make a good reader because reading is not accomplished by the decoding of spelling. Good readers are certainly not necessarily good spellers; we can all read words that we cannot spell. I am not saying that knowledge of spelling is not important, only that it does not have a role in reading, and that undue concern with the way in which words are spelled can only interfere with a child's learning to read.

There is a frequent argument that if spelling and decoding to sound are as irrelevant to reading as the preceding analyses indicate, why should we have an alphabetic written language at all? My view is that the alphabetic system is more of a help to the writer than to the reader. For a variety of reasons, including the memory load required to reproduce every word legibly in all its featural detail, writing is a much harder skill to learn and to practice than reading, at least if the writer is to be conventionally "correct" with respect to such matters as grammar, punctuation, neatness, and so forth. Spelling may be complicated for writers (especially if they have not been taught how spelling reflects meaning as well as sound), but it still makes the task much easier than if writers had to remember and reproduce thousands and thousands of nonalphabetic ideographic forms, like writers of Chinese.

The alphabetic system may have allowed more people to learn to write, but at a cost to readers. The Chinese ideographic system can be read by people from all over China, even though they might speak languages that are mutually unintelligible. If a Cantonese speaker cannot understand what a Mandarin speaker says, they can write their conversation down in the nonalphabetic writing system they both share and be mutually comprehensible. This is something English and French speakers cannot do unless they employ the small part of their own writing systems that is not alphabetic, such as arithmetic symbols like $2 + 3 = 5$.

When we cannot remember or do not know how a word should be written, we have little recourse to anything but what we know about the spelling system. It does not help much in writing to look at the words before and after the one that is giving difficulty. But in reading we have some more effective alternatives before we need call upon phonics for help in identifying a word, and it is to these alternatives that we shall now turn.

STRATEGIES OF MEDIATED WORD IDENTIFICATION

To repeat, the problem with which we are concerned is that of a reader who encounters a word that cannot be recognized on sight, for which a visual feature list must be established, but where the reader does know what the word is to which the feature list will be assigned. The reader's problem is to identify the word by a mediated strategy.

Phonics, as we have seen, is one such strategy. But it is not the only one. An obvious alternative is simply being told what the word is. Before most children come to school, well-intentioned adults say to them "That word is 'John' ," "That word is 'girls' ," "That word is 'cereal' ," just as on other occasions they say "That animal is a cat," in all cases leaving it to the child to solve the more complex problem of working out exactly how to recognize the word or animal in future. But when children get to school this support is frequently taken away from them, at least as far as reading is concerned. Another well-intentioned adult is likely to say to them: "Good news and bad news today, children. The bad news is that no one is ever likely to tell you what a word is again. The good news is that we are going to give you 166 rules and 45 exceptions so that you can work it out for yourselves."

Alternative Identification Strategies

Ask fluent readers what they do when they come across a word they do not recognize, and the most probable answer is that they skip it. Passing over a word is a reasonable first strategy because it is not necessary to understand every word to understand a passage of text, and lingering to try to decipher a word may be more disruptive to comprehension than missing the word altogether. The second preferred strategy is to "guess", which again does not mean a reckless stab in the dark but making use of context to eliminate unlikely alternatives for what the unfamiliar word might be. The final strategy may be trying to work out what the word is from its spelling, but that is not so much likely to be decoding the word to sound with phonics as making use of what is already known about other words. This final strategy might be called "identification by analogy," since all or part of the unknown word is compared with all or part of words that are known.

Examine the same question with a child who is progressing in learning to read and again you are likely to get the same sequence of strategies. The best learners tend to skip unknown words (unless constrained by a teacher to "read carefully" and figure out every word). The second preference, especially if there is no helpful adult around to provide assistance, is to hypothesize what a word might be based on the meaning of the text, and the final choice is to use what is known about similar-looking words. Trying to sound out words without reference to meaning is a characteristic strategy of poor readers; it is not one that leads to fluency in reading.

What is the best method of mediated word identification? The answer depends on the situation a reader is in. Sometimes the best strategy will indeed be to ignore the unfamiliar word altogether, since sufficient meaning may be carried by the surrounding text not only to compensate for lack of understanding of the unknown word, but subsequently to provide critical cues to what the unknown word might be. For a child beginning to learn to read, or confronted by text where many words are unfamiliar, the best situation is probably to have an adult or more competent young reader to turn to, if necessary by reading the entire passage to the child. But if the reader can understand enough of the passage to follow its sense, then a most effective strategy may be identification by analogy, making use of what is already known about reading.

The point is that phonics in itself is almost useless for sounding out words letter by letter, since every letter can represent too many sounds. But uncertainty about the sound of a particular letter diminishes as letters are considered not in isolation but as part of letter-clusters or "spelling patterns". This has led a number of theorists to argue that the basic unit for word recognition should be regarded as the syllable rather than the individual letter. And indeed it is true; the pronunciation of syllables is far less variable than the pronunciation of the individual letters that make up syllables. The trouble is that it would take a reader years to learn to read by memorizing the pronunciation of hundreds of syllables, since syllables in themselves tend to be meaningless — there are relatively few one-syllable words — and the human brain has great difficulty in memorizing, and particularly in recalling, nonsense. What a reader can turn to for a ready-made store of syllable information is *words* that have already been learned. It is far easier for a reader to remember the unique appearance and pronunciation of a whole word like *photograph,* for example, than to remember the alternative pronunciations of meaningless syllables or spelling units like *ph, to, gr* or *gra,* and *gh.* A single word, in other words, can provide the basis for remembering different rules of phonics, as well as the exceptions, since not only do words provide a meaningful way to organize different phonic rules in memory, they also illustrate the phonic rules at work. The ten different ways of pronouncing *ho* cause no difficulty if one already has words like *hot, hoot, hope,* and so forth in one's sight vocabulary.

The basis of the mediated word identification strategy of identification by analogy is looking for cues to a word's pronunciation and meaning from words that look the same. We do not learn to sound out words on the basis of individual letters or letter clusters whose sounds have been learned in isolation, but rather by recognizing sequences of letters that occur in words that are already known. Such a strategy offers an additional advantage to the reader because it does more than indicate possible pronunciations for all or part of unknown words; it can offer suggestions about meaning. As I pointed out earlier, English spelling in general respects meaning more than sound — words that look alike tend to share the same sense. And as I have reiterated throughout this book, the basis of reading and of learning to read is meaning. The advantage of trying to identify unknown words by analogy with words that are known already is not simply that known words would provide an immediately accessible stock of pronunciations for relatively long sequences of letters, but that all or part of known words can provide clues to meaning, which is always a far better clue to pronunciation than just the way in which an unknown word is spelled.

I am not suggesting that fluent readers do not use their knowledge of spelling-sound correspondences to help identify unfamiliar words, or that the existence of such correspondences should be concealed from children learning to read. But there are three fundamental problems with spelling-sound correspondences: the total number of rules and exceptions, the time it takes to apply them in practice, and their general unreliability. The problem of the number of rules can be solved by not trying to learn (or teach) the rules in the abstract, independently of actual words. The easiest way to learn a phonic rule is to learn a few words that exemplify it, which means — another point that will bear some reiteration — that children master phonics as a result of learning to read rather than as a prerequisite for reading. The time problem is overcome by resorting to phonics in actual reading as infrequently as possible.

The problem of the unreliability of phonic generalizations is another matter. Phonic generalizations alone will not permit a reader to decode the majority of words likely to be met in normal reading simply because there are always too many alternatives. This is the reason that producers of phonic workbooks always prefer to work with strictly controlled vocabularies — there is not as much uncertainty of pronunciation with *The fat cat sat on the flat hat* as there is with *Two hungry pigeons flew behind the weary ploughman,* a sentence that makes more sense but defies phonic analysis.

But phonic generalizations can work if all they are required to do is reduce alternatives, without being expected to identify words completely or to decode them to sounds. To give an example, the use of phonics will never succeed in decoding *horse* if the word appears in isolation or is any one of thousands of alternatives. But if the reader knows that the word is either *horse, mule,* or *donkey* then the strategy will work effectively. It is not simply that minimal phonic analysis is required to know that *mule* and *donkey* could not begin with *h*, but that not much more can be expected of phonic rules in any case. This is why I have asserted that phonics is easy — for the teacher and the child — if they know what a word is in the first place. I am not suggesting that the word has to be known absolutely. In that case neither phonics nor any other mediated word identification strategy would be required. But if the reader has a good idea of what the word might be, if there is a predication that includes what the word actually is among the likely alternatives, then the use of phonics will probably eliminate the remaining uncertainty.

Phonic strategies cannot be expected to eliminate all uncertainty when the reader has no idea what the word might be. But if the reader can reduce alternatives in advance — by making use of nonvisual information related both to reading and to the subject matter of the text — then phonics can be made most efficient. One way to reduce uncertainty in advance is to employ the mediating technique of making use of context. Understanding of the text, in general, will reduce the number of alternatives that an unknown word might be. The other way to reduce uncertainty in advance is to employ the alternative mediating technique of identification by analogy, comparing the unknown word with known words that provide hypotheses about possible meanings and pronunciations. The reason that we can so easily read nonwords like *vernalit, mossiant,* and *ricaning* is not because we have in our heads a store of pronunciations for meaningless letter sequences like *vern, iant,* or *ric* but because these close approximations to English are made up of parts of words or even entire words that are immediately recognizable, such as *vernal, lit, moss,* and so forth.

There is no simple answer to any question about the ideal method of mediated word identification. The three alternatives that I have specifically discussed — spelling-to-sound correspondences, prediction from context, and identification by analogy — are all likely to be inadequate when used alone. While all will reduce some uncertainty, none is likely to eliminate all alternatives by itself. But used in conjunction, the strategies complement each other. A reader using phonics will rarely identify an unfamiliar word without making sense of the passage as a whole, using this understanding to eliminate unlikely alternatives in advance. To ignore alternative means of reducing uncertainty is to ignore the redundancy which is a central part of all aspects of language.

And the prior elimination of unlikely alternatives is, after all, what reading is all about, according to the analysis of comprehension that I have offered in Chapter 6. By this analysis, phonics is neither the basis of reading nor a strategy that a reader has to depend on wholly whenever an unfamiliar word is encountered. Rather, the use of phonic rules takes a supplementary and subordinate place in normal meaningful reading, occurring so rarely and effortlessly that the reader is not usually aware of the strategies employed as unfamiliar words are tentatively identified and feature lists established. Phonic rules function almost as a sentinel; they cannot decipher unknown words on their own, but they will protect the reader against making impossible hypotheses.

LEARNING MEDIATED WORD IDENTIFICATION STRATEGIES

In an earlier chapter two critical points were made about learning:

1. The basis of all learning — and especially of language learning — is meaningfulness. It is pointless to expect a child to memorize lists of rules, definitions, even names, if these have no apparent purpose or utility to the child; not only will learning be very difficult, but recall will be almost impossible. Two of the mediated

word identification strategies that I have discussed can fall into the category of meaningless learning, if a child is expected to acquire them outside a context of meaningful reading. It is useless to expect a child to memorize phonic rules, or the pronunciation of syllables or letter clusters, prior to learning how to read. The mediating strategy that I discussed, identification by analogy, can only be fostered after a child has begun to read.

2. Learning is a continuous, effortless and entirely natural process, self-directing and self-reinforcing, when children are in a situation which they basically can make sense of and where there is something new — a problem to be solved — that can be related to what they know already. In other words, the basis of learning is comprehension. Rules that cannot be verbalized about many aspects of the physical world and of spoken language are hypothesized and tested with little awareness on the part of children or adults, and "names" are learned by the thousand. Where a child can understand a relationship, the child can learn the relationship, whether it is the relationship of a name to a word, of a meaning to a word, or of spelling-sound correspondences.

What all this means is that reading is basically a matter of increasing returns; the more that children read, the more they will learn to read. The more they can recognize words, the easier they will be able to understand phonic correspondences, to employ context cues, and to identify new words by analogy. The more that children are able to read — or are helped to read — the more they are likely to discover and extend these strategies for themselves.

By acquiring an extensive "sight vocabulary" of immediately identifiable words, children are able to understand, remember, and utilize phonic rules and other mediated identification strategies. But such a summary statement does not imply that the way to help children read is to give them plenty of experience with flashcards and word lists. The easy way to learn words is not to work with individual words at all but with meaningful passages of text. We are considering only a limited and secondary aspect of reading when we restrict our attention to individual words. As we turn our attention to reading sequences of words that are grammatical and make sense, we shall find that word identification and learning are more easily explained theoretically and more easily accomplished by the child.

The time has come to complete the picture of reading by recognizing that words are rarely read or learned in meaningless isolation. Reading is easiest when it makes sense, and learning to read is also easiest when it makes sense. We are ready to view reading from a broader and more meaningful perspective.

SUMMARY

Mediated word identification is a temporary expedient for identifying unfamiliar words while establishing feature lists to permit immediate identification. Alternative strategies for mediated word identification include asking someone, using contextual cues, analogy with known words and the use of **phonics** (spelling-sound correspondences). Attempting to decode isolated words to sound is unlikely to succeed because of the number, complexity, and unreliability of phonic generalizations. Phonic rules will help to eliminate alternative possibilities only if uncertainty can be reduced by other means, for example, if the unfamiliar words occur in meaningful contexts. Spelling-sound correspondences are not easily or usefully learned before children acquire some familiarity with reading.

Notes to Chapter 10 begin on page 230.

CHAPTER **11**

THE
IDENTIFICATION
OF MEANING

The preceding three chapters have been concerned with the identification of letters and words. They examined feature analysis as a mechanism for identifying letters, and showed how the same feature analytic process could

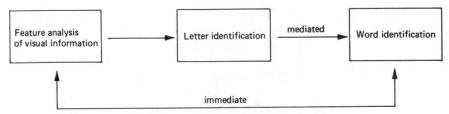

FIGURE 11.1   Immediate and mediated word identification

be employed directly for the identification of words. Word identification does not require the prior identification of letters, at least not the immediate word identification that readers accomplish when a word they are concerned with is familiar to them, a part of their "sight vocabulary". It is only when words cannot be identified immediately that the prior identification of letters becomes relevant at all, and then only to a limited extent depending on the amount of contextual and other information that the reader might have available. The alternatives are summed up in Figure 11.1.

Now I want to show that comprehension, or the identification of meaning, does not require the prior identification of words. Meaning identification can be as immediate as the identification of letters or words. I shall argue that the same feature analytic process that underlies the identification of letters and words is also available for the *immediate* apprehension of meaning from visual information. While *mediated* meaning identification may sometimes be necessary, because for some reason meaning cannot immediately be assigned to the text, attempting to make decisions about possible meaning by the prior identification of individual words is highly inefficient and unlikely to succeed.

In other words, I am asserting that immediate meaning identification is as independent of the identification of individual words as immediate word identification is independent of the identification of individual letters. The alternatives are represented in Figure 11.2.

I shall make the argument in three steps:

1. Showing that immediate meaning identification *is* accomplished;

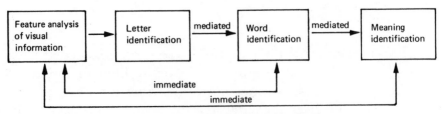

FIGURE 11.2   Immediate and mediated meaning identification

that readers normally can and do identify meaning without or ahead of the identification of individual words.
2. Proposing how immediate meaning identification is accomplished.
3. Discussing how immediate meaning identification is learned.

In a final section I shall briefly discuss mediated word identification, or what a reader does when the direct apprehension of meaning is not possible. (There will also be a further discussion of the role of prediction in comprehension, which is best explained when we get to it.)

USING MEANING IN READING

One demonstration has already been given that readers employ meaning to assist in the identification of individual words rather than laboring to identify words in order to obtain meaning. I am referring to the experiment showing that from a single glance at a line of print — the equivalent of about one second of reading — a reader can identify four or five words if they are in a meaningful sequence like *KNIGHTS RODE HORSES INTO WAR* but scarcely half that amount if the words are unrelated to each other, like *READY JUMP WHEAT POOR BUT*. My explanation in Chapter 3, when I originally described this classic study (Cattell, 1885), was that with meaningful text a reader could recruit nonvisual information to reduce alternatives so that the amount of visual information that the brain can handle in a second would go twice as far, to identify four or five words instead of a couple. The nonvisual information that the reader already possesses can only be meaning, or prior knowledge of the way in which words go together in language that is not only grammatical but makes sense.

It is important to understand that the reader in the situation I have just discussed is making use of meaning from the very beginning; meaningfulness facilitates the identification of every word in the line. The reader does not first identify one or two words by a word identification strategy, as if they had nothing to do with the other words in the line, and then make an educated guess about the rest. Indeed, that same experiment shows that if two words had to be identified to give a clue about the others, then there would be no time left for the others to be identified. Two is the limit for words that have no meaningful relationships. Where a sequence of words does make sense, the identification of every word is facilitated, the first as well as the last, just as individual words can be identified in conditions in which none of their component letters would be individually discriminable. As we shall see, it is all a matter of the prior elimination of unlikely (and impossible) alternatives.

The demonstration I have discussed is historic; it was first conducted and reported nearly a century ago (Cattell, 1885), and has been replicated many times since. But in a sense, the fact that meaning facilitates the identification of individual words is replicated every time we read, because reading would be impossible if we labored along, blindly striving to identify one word after another with no prior insights into what those words might be. Slow reading is not efficient reading because it tends to create tunnel vision, overload short-term memory, and leave the reader floundering in the ambiguity of language. Yet is is impossible to read quickly language that does not make sense, as you can experience for yourself if you try to read the following passage:

Be might words those what into insights prior no with, another after word one identify to striving blindly, along labored we if impossible be would reading because, read we time every replicated is words individual of identification the facilitates meaning that fact the, sense a in but.

The words you have just tried to read are what I hope is a perfectly meaningful English sentence — since I used it myself in the previous paragraph — written backwards. Any difference between the rate and ease with which you could read the backwards and forwards versions of that sentence can only be attributable to whether you were able to make sense of it. (If you had read the backwards passage aloud, incidentally, you probably would have sounded very much like many of the older "problem readers" at school, who struggle to identify words one at a time in a dreary monotone as if each word had nothing to do with any other. Such children seem to believe — and may well have been taught — that meaning should be their last concern; that sense will take care of itself provided they get the words right rather than that meaning facilitates the identification of words.)

Professional readers, for example broadcasters, know the importance of prior understanding of what they are about to read; that is why they like to scan through a script in advance. Looking ahead also helps the silent reading of novels and technical books — we can get a general idea of what will transpire and then go back where necessary to study particular points. The general comprehension comes out of fast reading, while the slow reading that might be necessary for memorization or for reflection upon detail can only be accomplished if comprehension has already been taken care of. Conversely, meaning can interfere with some reading tasks. Proofreaders tend to overlook misprints if they attend to the sense of what they read; they see the spellings and words that should be on the page rather than those that actually are there. Sometimes proofreaders will deliberately read backwards in order to give all their attention to spelling and individual words, but then of course they will overlook anomalies of meaning. Their dilemma highlights the fact that attention to individual words and to meaning are alternative and not successive aspects of reading.

The prior use of meaning ensures that when individual words must be identified, for example in order to read aloud, a minimum of visual information need be used. And as a consequence, mistakes will often occur. If a reader already has a pretty good idea of what a word might be, there is not much point in delaying to make extra certain what the word actually is. As a result it is not unusual for even highly experienced readers to make misreadings that are radically different visually — like reading "said" when the word is actually *announced* or *reported* — but which make no significant difference to the meaning. Beginning readers often show exactly the same tendency, demonstrating that children will strive for sense even when they learn to read (provided the material they are expected to learn from has any possibility of making sense in the first place). The mistakes that are made are sometimes called *miscues* rather than *errors* to avoid the connotation that they are something bad (Goodman, 1969). Such misreadings show that these beginning readers are attempting to read in the way fluent readers do, with sense taking priority over individual word identification. Of course, reading with minimal attention to individual words will sometimes result in misreadings that do make a difference to meaning, but one of the great advantages of reading for meaning in the first place is that one becomes aware of mistakes that make a difference to meaning. An important difference between children who are doing well in reading and those who are not is not that good readers make fewer mistakes, but that they go back and correct the mistakes that make a difference. Children who are not reading for sense have no chance of becoming aware of even important errors.

A unique illustration of the way in which the meaning takes priority over the identification of individual words has been provided by Kolers (1966), who asked bilinguals fluent in both English and French to read aloud from passages of text which made sense but where the actual language changed from English to French every two or three words. For example:

His horse, followed de deux bassets, faisait la terre résonner under its even tread. Des gouttes de verglas stuck to his manteau. Une violente brise was blowing. One side de l'horizon lighted up, and dans la blancheur of the early morning light, il aperçut rabbits hopping at the bord de leur terriers.

The subjects in this experiment could read and understand such passages perfectly well, but when they had done they often could not remember whether particular sequences of words were in English or French. Most significantly, they frequently substituted for a word in one language an appropriate word in the other. They might read "porte" when the word was *door* or "hand" when *main* was given, getting the meaning right but the language wrong. This does not mean that they were not looking at individual words at all — the passage was not that predictable — but that they were looking at words and finding meanings, just as an English speaker might look at *2000* and understand "two thousand" while a French speaker would look at the same print and understand "deux milles".

An important and perhaps difficult point to understand from the preceding discussion is that it is possible to make meaningful decisions about words without saying exactly what the words are. In other words, we can *see* that the written word *door* means door without having to say aloud or to ourselves that the word *is* "door". Written words convey meaning directly; they are not intermediaries for spoken language. An obvious example is provided for English by words which have different spellings for the same sound, like *their* and *there*. It is easy to detect the spelling error in *The children left there books behind* because *there* represents the wrong meaning. The difference between *their* and *there*, and *read* and *reed*, and *so, sew*. and *sow*, is evidently not that the different spellings represent different sounds, because they do not, but that the different appearances of the words indicate different meanings. The visual appearance of each word indicates meaning directly.

The fact that readers can, do, and must read directly for meaning is similarly apparent with a written language like Chinese, which does not correspond to any particular sound system. It would be pointless to argue whether the written symbol 家 represents the Mandarin or the Cantonese word for "house" (or even whether the symbol represents the word "house" or the word "residence" in either spoken language) because it simply represents a *meaning*. My present assertion is that any written language is read as Chinese is read, directly for meaning, and the fact that some written languages are also more or less related to the sound system of a spoken language is quite coincidental as far as the reader is concerned. As I suggested earlier, the alphabet could have originated purely for the convenience of writers. Certainly, there is no evidence that fluent readers identify letters in order to identify familiar words, and English spelling is, at best, a poor guide to the identification of words that are unfamiliar.

My final example that written language indicates meaning directly is rather poignant, since it comes from studies of brain-injured patients. People who are unable to find the exact word have been reported, for example, as reading the isolated word *ill* as "sick", *city* as "town", and *ancient* as "historic" (Marshall and Newcombe, 1966). Or *injure* as "hurt", *quiet* as "listen", and *fly* as "air" (Shallice and Warrington, 1975). In a remarkable "misreading" one patient identified *symphony* as "tea", presumably first visually confusing the written word with *sympathy*.

COMPREHENSION AS THE REDUCTION OF UNCERTAINTY

I have tried to show that meaning can take priority over the identification of individual words in two ways, both for fluent readers and for beginners. In the first case, the meaning of a sequence of words will permit the identification of individual words with relatively less visual information, and even make the precise identification of particular words unnecessary. In the second case, written words represent meaning directly; they make their contribution to the comprehension of a passage of text without the necessity of being identified precisely. Usually both aspects of meaning identification occur simultaneously; we comprehend text using far less visual information than would be required to identify the individual words, and without the necessity of identifying individual words. Both aspects of meaning identification are, in fact, reflections of the same underlying process — the use of minimal visual information to make decisions specific to implicit questions (or predictions) about meaning on the part of the reader.

I am using the rather awkward expression "meaning identification" as a synonym for comprehension in this chapter to underline the fact that the process by which a reader makes sense of text is no different from that by which individual letters or words may be identified in the same text. What is different about comprehension is that readers bring to the text implicit questions about meaning rather than about letters or words. The term meaning identification also helps to emphasize that comprehension is an active process. Meaning does not reside in surface structure. The meaning that readers comprehend from text is always relative to what they already know and to what they want to know. Put in another way, comprehension can be regarded as *the reduction of the reader's uncertainty,* which is a point of view I have already employed in the discussions of letter and word identification.

A passage of text may be perceived in at least three ways: as a sequence of letters from a certain alphabet, as a sequence of words of a particular language, or as a sequence of meanings in a certain domain of knowledge or understanding. But in fact a passage of text is none of these things, or at least it is only these things potentially. Basically written text is a lot of inkmarks on a page, variously characterized as visual information, distinctive features, or surface structure. Whatever readers perceive in text — letters, words, or meanings — depends upon the prior knowledge (nonvisual information) that they happen to bring and the implicit questions they happen to be asking. The actual information that readers find (or at least seek) in the text depends upon their original uncertainty.

Consider, for example, this sentence that you are reading at this moment. The visual information in the sentence can be used to make decisions about letters, for example, to say that the first letter is "c", the second "o", the third "n", and so forth. Alternatively, exactly the same visual information could be used to decide that the first word is "consider"; the second word, "for"; the third word, "example"; and so forth. The reader employs the same visual information, selects from among the same distinctive features, but this time sees words, not letters. What readers see depends upon what they are looking for, on their implicit questions or uncertainty. Finally, exactly the same visual information can be employed to make decisions about meaning in the sentence, in which case neither letters nor words would be seen. It is not so easy to say precisely what is being identified in the case of meaning, but that is due to the conceptual difficulty of saying what meaning is, not because the reader is doing anything intrinsically different. The reader is using the same source of visual information to reduce uncertainty about meaning rather than about letters or words.

As we have already seen, the amount of visual information required to make letter or word identification depends upon the extent of the reader's prior uncertainty, upon the number of alternatives that exist in the reader's mind (and also the degree to which the reader wants to be confident in the decisions to be made). With letters it is easy to say what the maximum number of alternatives is — 26 if we are considering just one particular typeface in upper or lower case in the English alphabet. It is similarly easy to show that the amount of visual information required to identify each letter goes down as the number of alternatives that the letter might be (the reader's uncertainty) is reduced. The fewer alternatives, the faster or easier a letter is identified, because fewer distinctive features need to be discriminated for a decision to be made. It is not so easy to say what the maximum number of alternatives is for words, because that depends upon the range of alternatives that the reader considers in the first place, but again it is not difficult to show that the amount of visual information required to identify a word goes down as the reader's uncertainty is reduced. A word can be identified with fewer distinctive features when it comes from a couple of hundred alternatives than from many thousands. Finally, it is quite impossible to say how many alternative meanings there might be for a passage of text, because that depends entirely on what an individual reader is looking for, but it is obvious that reading is easier and faster when the reader finds the material meaningful than when comprehension is a struggle. The less uncertainty readers have about the meaning of a passage, the less visual information is required to find what they are looking for in the passage.

In each of the preceding cases nonvisual information can be employed to reduce the reader's uncertainty in advance and to limit the amount of visual information that must be processed. The more prior knowledge a reader can bring to bear about the way letters go together in words, the less visual information is required to identify individual letters. Prediction, based on prior knowledge, eliminates unlikely alternatives in advance. Similarly, the more a reader knows about the way words go together in grammatical and meaningful phrases — because of the reader's prior knowledge of the particular language and of the topic being discussed — the less visual information is required to identify individual words. In the latter case, meaning is being used as part of nonvisual information to reduce the amount of visual information required to identify words. An example may be given in the form of a demonstration (based on a study reported by Tulving and Gold, 1963).

First, as a kind of pretest, I shall ask whether you can identify a word, or any of the letters, in the minimal visual information ▬ ▬ ▬ ▬ ▬ ▬ ▬ Now we can proceed with the illustration. Because of the syntactic redundancy of language a sentence like *After dinner let's go to the* ———— is almost certain to end with a noun rather than a verb or adjective or preposition, a piece of grammatical prior knowledge that reduces considerably the number of alternatives that the word in the final position might be. In addition there are semantic (meaning) constraints that go even further in reducing the number of alternatives. In fact, just one word has a much higher probability of being put into the blank position in the sentence than any other — the word "theater". You can discover for yourself that "theater" is the most probable word for that context by canvassing your friends; you will find that the proverbial four-out-of-five think "theater" is the most appropriate way of concluding the sentence. "Theater", however, is not the most probable word in all contexts; at the end of a sequence such as *It was agreed that he would meet me at the* ———, the word "station" has a very much higher probability of occurring than "theater" and a number of other words.

We can now test our hypothesis that prior knowledge results in the reduction in the number of visual features required to identify a word in a meaningful context. We shall flash the two words onto a screen, and ask two groups of people to try to identify them. For one group we shall flash the word "theater" after they have been told the other words of the first sentence, and the word "station" after they have been given the words of the second sentence. For the other group we shall reverse the order, flashing "station" after the first sentence and "theater" after the second. You will notice, of course, that both words are equally feasible in each context. There is nothing nonsensical about going to the station after dinner or arranging to meet at the theater. It is just that these combinations are less likely. Our experimental assumption is that if more people manage to identify a word from a brief exposure on one occasion than on another, then they must be identifying it on less visual information; they are making use of other sources of information.

The result of the experiment should come as no surprise at this point. A much greater proportion of viewers is able to recognize the word "theater" from a brief flash if it follows the first sentence than if it follows the second. And more people identify the word "station" after the second sentence than after the first. It must be noted that the viewers are not guessing; they are making use of visual information because they do not respond "theater" when *station* is presented. But the amount of information required to identify either word depends on the sequence of words that it follows, on the sense that the reader can predict.

To nail down the point, let us see once more if you can identify the elements printed in our pretest 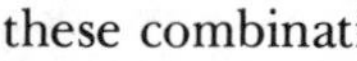. You probably can now. If you cannot, then you should have no difficulty in the context "There was a happy reunion at the ."

Compelling evidence that meaning can be used to avoid the identification of *any* words is the fact that fluent readers can extract words from text at a rate that would absolutely preclude individual word identification. Many people can follow the meaning of a novel or newspaper article at the rate of a thousand words a minute, which is four times faster than their probable speed if they were identifying every word, even with meaning to help them. There is a prevalent misconception that for this kind of fast reading the reader must be identifying only one word in every four and that this gives sufficient information at least for the gist of what is being read. But it is very easy to demonstrate that identifying one word in four will not contribute very much towards the intelligibility of a passage. Here is every fourth word from a film review: *Many* — — —*been* — — —*face* — — —*business* — — —*sour* — — —*If* — — —*to*. . . . The passage is even less easy to comprehend if the selected words are in groups, with correspondingly larger gaps between them. It is somewhat easier to comprehend what a passage is about if every fourth *letter* is provided rather than every fourth word, and, of course, my argument is that reading at a thousand words a minute is possible only if the omissions occur at the *featural* level. A skilled reader may need to discriminate only a fraction of the features available in every word, but not if these features are all concentrated in a single letter.

It should not be thought from the preceding discussion that there is a special kind of distinctive feature for meaning in print, different from the distinctive features of letters and words. There is no "semantic feature", for example, that *house* and *residence* physically have in common that we should expect to find in the inkmarks on the page. What makes visual features distinctive as far as meaning is concerned is precisely what makes them distinctive for individual letters and words as well — the particular alternatives that already exist in the reader's uncertainty. The same features that can be used to distinguish the letter *m* from the letter *h* will also distinguish the word *mouse* from the word *house* and the meaning of *we went to the mill* from the meaning of *we went to the hill*. It is not possible to say what the specific features are that readers employ to distinguish meanings; this would depend upon what the reader is looking for, and, in any case, it is not possible to describe the features of letters or words either. The situation is only additionally complicated by the fact that we cannot say what a meaning is.

As I pointed out in Chapter 6, in the discussion of the chasm between the surface structures and the deep structure of language, meaning lies beyond words. One cannot *say* what meaning is in general, any more than one can say what the meaning of a particular word or group of words is, except by saying other words which are themselves surface structure. The meaning itself can never be exposed. This inability to pin down meaning is not a theoretical defect or scientific oversight. We should not hope that a marvelous discovery will be made one day to enable us all to say what meanings are. Meaning, to repeat myself, cannot be trapped in a net of words.

A reader does not comprehend the written word *table* by saying the spoken word "table" either aloud or silently, any more than the spoken word "table" can itself be understood simply by repeating it to oneself. (Would you understand the Spanish word *"mesa"* by saying it to yourself if you did not understand the language?) And neither the written nor the spoken word *table* is understood by saying silently to oneself "a four-legged flat-topped piece of furniture", or whatever other definition might come to mind, because of course the understanding of the definition would itself still have to be accounted for. There can be no understanding and no explanation unless the web of language is escaped. The actual *words,* written or spoken, are always secondary to meaning, to understanding. We no more need to repeat the word *"table"* in any form to understand the word than we need to say "table" in order to recognize an object as a table before we can say the name by which it is known.

We are normally unaware of *not* identifying individual words when we read because we are not thinking about words in any case. Written language (like speech) is *transparent* — we look through the actual words for the meaning beyond, and unless there are noticeable anomalies of meaning, or unless we have trouble comprehending, we are not aware of the words themselves. (When we deliberately attend to specific words, for example in the subtle matter of reading poetry, this is a consequence of asking a different kind of question in the first place. The sounds that we can give to the words do not so much contribute to a literal interpretation as establish a different — a complementary or alternative — kind of mood or meaning.)

Of course, word identification is necessary for reading aloud, but as I have tried to show, the identification of words in this way depends upon the identification of meaning. The voice lags behind the understanding, and is always susceptible, to some extent, of diverging from the actual text. The substitution of words and even phrases with appropriate meanings is again not something that the reader will be aware of; the reader's main concern, even in reading aloud, must be with the sense of the passage. Misreadings would have to be pointed out by a listener following both the text and the reading. Misreadings of this kind are not normally made with words that are not part of meaningful text, for example words that have to be read in isolation or from lists, but then there is no way that meaning could be sought or utilized in the first place. Besides, in such circumstances readers usually have the leisure to scrutinize sufficient visual information to identify individual words precisely (giving the words a label rather than a meaning) because nothing is lost by reading slowly.

Subvocalization (or reading silently to oneself) cannot in itself contribute to meaning or understanding any more than reading aloud. Indeed, like reading aloud, subvocalization can only be accomplished with anything like normal speed and intonation if it is preceded by comprehension. We do not listen to ourselves mumbling parts of words or fragments of phrases and then comprehend. If anything, subvocalization slows readers down and interferes with comprehension. The habit of subvocalization can be broken without loss of comprehension (Hardyck and Petrinovich, 1970). Besides, most people do not subvocalize as much as they think. Whenever we "listen" to see if we are subvocalizing, subvocalization is bound to occur. We can never hear ourselves not subvocalizing, but that does not mean that we subvocalize all the time. Why do we subvocalize at all? The habit may simply be a holdover from our younger days, perhaps when we were expected to read aloud; a teacher knows that children are working if their fingers are moving steadily along the lines and their lips are moving in unison. Subvocalization may also have a useful function in providing "rehearsal" to help hold in short-term memory words that cannot be immediately understood or otherwise dealt with. But in such cases subvocalization indicates lack of comprehension rather than its occurrence. There is a general tendency to subvocalize when reading becomes difficult, when we can predict less.

Readers do not normally attend to print with their minds blank, with no prior purpose and with no expectation of what they might find in the text. Readers normally look for meaning rather than strive to identify letters or words. The way readers look for meaning is not to consider all possibilities, nor to make reckless guesses about just one, but rather they predict within the most likely range of alternatives. In this way readers can overcome the information-processing limitations of the brain and also the inherent ambiguity of language. Readers can derive meaning directly from text because they bring expectations about meaning to text. The process is normally as natural, as continual and effortless as the way we bring meaning to every other kind of experience in our lives. We do not go through the world saying "There's a chair; there's a table; a chair is something I can sit on," struggling to make sense of every bit of information our sensory systems direct towards the brain. Instead we look out for those aspects of our environment that will make the world meaningful to us, especially with respect to our particular purposes and interests. Com-

prehension is not a matter of putting names to nonsense and struggling to make sense of the result, but of operating in the realm of
meaningfulness all the time.

LEARNING TO IDENTIFY MEANING

The remarks that concluded the preceding discussion should have
made the present discussion largely unnecessary. There is no need for
a special explanation about how children learn to identify meaning
from print because no special process is involved. Children will naturally tend to put meaning into print. For them there is no point in
language that is not meaningful, whether spoken or written. They
perceive spoken language by looking for meaning, not by focussing
on the sounds of words.

There is a classic illustration of the priority that meaning takes as
children learn to talk. Even when children try to "imitate", it is meaning that they imitate, not meaningless sounds. McNeill (1967) has
reported an exchange between mother and child which went like this:

Child: Nobody don't like me.
Mother: No, say "nobody likes me."
Child: Nobody don't like me.
(eight repetitions of this dialogue)
Mother: No, now listen carefully; say *"nobody likes me."*
Child: Oh! Nobody don't likes me.

Even when children are asked to perform a language exercise,
they expect that it will make sense. Like the child in the above example, it takes them a long time to understand the task if they are
required to attend to surface structure, not to meaning. Children do
not need to be told the converse, to look for sense; that is their natural
(and only) way of learning about language in the first place. Indeed,
they will not willingly attend to any noise that does not make sense to
them.

Just as children do not need to be told to look for meaning in
either spoken or written language, so they also do not need to learn
special procedures for finding meaning. Prediction is the basis of
meaning identification, and all children who can understand the spoken language of their own environment must be experts at prediction.
Besides, the very constraints of reading — the constant possibility of
ambiguity, tunnel vision, and memory overload — can only serve as
reminders to learners that the basis of reading must be prediction.

Certainly there is no need for a special explanation of how comprehension should be *taught*. Comprehension is not a new kind of skill that has to be learned for reading but is the basis of all learning. Rather it may happen at school that children are taught the *reverse* of comprehension, being instructed instead to take care to "decode" correctly and not to make "guesses" if they are uncertain. They may even be expected to learn to read with materials and exercises specifically designed to discourage or prevent the use of nonvisual information. I shall return to these general issues more in the next chapter.

Of course, there is a difference between the comprehension of written language and the comprehension of speech or of other kinds of events in the world, but these are not differences of process. The differences are simply that the reader must use the distinctive features of print to test predictions and reduce uncertainty. Children need to become familiar with these distinctive features for print and with how they are related to meaning. This familiarity and understanding cannot be taught, any more than the rules of spoken language can be taught, but formal instruction is similarly unnecessary and in fact impossible. The experience that children require to find meaning in print can only be acquired through meaningful reading, just as children develop their speech competence through using and hearing meaningful speech. And until children are able to do meaningful reading on their own account, they are clearly dependent on being read to, or at least on being assisted to read.

A final point. It is not necessary for any readers, and especially not for beginners, to understand the meaning of *everything* that they attempt to read. Whether adults are reading novels and other lengthy texts or menus or advertisements, they always have the liberty to skip quite large passages and certainly to ignore many small details, either because they are not comprehensible, or simply because they are not relevant to their interest or needs. Children when they are learning spoken language seem able and willing to follow adult conversations and television programs without comprehending every word. A grasp of the theme, a general interest and the ability to make sense on the basis of a few comprehensible parts can be more than sufficient to hold a child's attention. Such partially understood material is indeed the basis for learning; no one will pay attention to any aspect of language, spoken or written, unless it contains some information that is new. For children, a good deal that is not comprehensible will be tolerated for the opportunity to discover something that is new. But children are rarely given credit for their ability to ignore what they cannot understand and to attend only to that from which they will learn.

Unfortunately, the right of children to ignore what they cannot understand may be the first of their freedoms to be taken away when they enter school. Instead, attention is likely to be focussed on what each child finds incomprehensible in order to "challenge" them to further learning. Anything a child knows already is likely to be set aside as "too easy". Paradoxically, many reading materials are made intentionally meaningless. Obviously, in such cases there is no way in which children will be able to develop their ability to seek and identify meaning in text.

MEDIATED MEANING IDENTIFICATION

Reading usually involves bringing meaning *immediately* or directly to the text without awareness of individual words or their possible alternative meanings. There are occasions, however, when the meaning of the text or of particular words cannot be immediately comprehended. On these occasions, mediated meaning identification may be attempted, involving the identification of individual words before comprehension of a meaningful sequence of words as a whole. I propose to divide the discussion into two parts, the first concerned with the mediated meaning identification of entire sequences of words, such as phrases and sentences, and the second concerned with the mediated identification of the meaning of occasional individual words.

I have already argued that the first is rarely possible. The meaning of a sentence as a whole is not understood by putting together the meanings of individual words (Chapter 6). Individual words have so much ambiguity — and usually alternative grammatical functions as well — that without some prior expectation about meaning there is little chance for comprehension even to begin. In addition limitations of visual information processing and memory are difficult to overcome if the reader attempts to identify and understand every word as if it had nothing to do with its neighbors and came from many thousands of alternatives. So although some theories of reading and many methods of reading instruction would appear to be based on the assumption that comprehension of written text is achieved one word at a time, the present analysis leaves little on this topic to be discussed. To attempt to build up comprehension in such a way must be regarded as highly inefficient and not likely to succeed. Certainly computers cannot be programmed to deal with language in this way. Computers need instead some prior knowledge of the world, that is to say, the ability to bring possible meaning to the text and thus to identify meaning immediately.

But the second sense of mediated meaning identification — where the passage in general is comprehensible and perhaps just one word is unfamiliar and not understood — is a more general and useful characteristic of reading. In this case the question is not one of trying to use the meanings of individual words to construct the meaning of the whole, but rather of using the meaning of the whole to provide a possible meaning for an individual word. And not only is this possible; I would regard it as the basis of much of the language learning that we do.

I have seen no figures, but it seems likely to me that the bulk of the vocabulary of most literate adults must come from reading. It is not necessary to understand thousands upon thousands of words to begin to learn to read — basically all that is required is a general familiarity with the words and constructions in the written material from which one is expected to learn, and then not all of those. And it seems highly unlikely that our understanding of many of the words that we have learned as a result of reading should be attributed to thousands of trips to the dictionary or to asking someone else what the word might be. We learn the meaning from the text itself.

Evidence that we quite coincidentally learn new words while reading comes from those words whose meaning or reference we know well but which we are not sure of pronouncing correctly, so there is no way we could have learned about them from speech. I am referring to words like *Penelope* (Penny-loap?), *misled* (mizzled? myzelled?) and *gist* (like guest or jest?), and perhaps *slough, orgy,* and *gaol.* There is what I like to call the *facky-tious* phenomenon (*tious* to rhyme with "pious") after the occasion when the mother of a friend commented that one did not often hear the word "facky-tious" these days. My friend confessed that he could not remember the last time he heard the word and asked what it meant. "A little sarcastic or supercilious," he was told. Something clicked. "You mean *facetious*", he said. "No", replied his mother thoughtfully, "though the two words do have a similar meaning. Come to think of it," she added, "I don't think I've ever seen the word *facetious* in print."

The question, of course, is where she got the correct meaning of facky-tious, which she had never heard in speech and had obviously never asked anyone about. And the answer must be that she learned it the way most of us learn the meaning of so many of the words that we know, by making sense of words from their context, using what is known to comprehend and learn the unfamiliar. Mediated meaning identification from context is something that fluent readers probably do all the time, without awareness, and is the basis not just of comprehension but of learning.

Learning new words without interference with the general comprehension of text is another example of the way in which children — and all readers — can continually learn to read by reading. The vocabulary that develops as a consequence of reading provides a permanent basis of knowledge for determining the probable meaning and pronunciation of new words. If you know both the meaning and the pronunciation of *auditor* and *visual,* you will have little difficulty in comprehending and saying a new word like *audiovisual.* The larger your capital, the faster you can add to it — whether with words or material wealth. The best way to acquire a large and useful vocabulary for reading is by meaningful reading. If the text makes sense, the mediation and the learning take care of themselves.

PREDICTIONS AND INTENTIONS — GLOBAL AND FOCAL

So far throughout this book I have talked as if predictions are made and dealt with one at a time. As we read, a particular prediction may range over a set of alternative meanings, words, or letters. As we drive we may predict the future position of our car with respect to an approaching truck, a pedestrian, or a landmark that we expect to see. But all of this has been oversimplified. Predictions are multiplex; usually we handle more than one at any one time. Some predictions are overriding; they carry us across large expanses of time and space. Other predictions occurring at the same time are far more transient, arising and being disposed of relatively rapidly. Predictions are layered and interleaved.

Consider again the analogy of driving a car downtown. We have a general intention and prediction that we shall reach a certain destination, leading to a number of relatively general predictions about landmarks that will be met along the route. Call these predictions *global,* since they tend to influence the entire journey. No matter how much our exact path might have to be varied because of exigencies that arise on the way, swerving to avoid a pedestrian or diverting down a side street because of a traffic holdup, these overriding global predictions tend to bring us always towards our intended goal.

But while global predictions influence every decision until our intended goal is reached, we simultaneously make more detailed predictions related to specific events during the course of the journey. Call predictions of this nature *focal,* since they concern us for short periods of time only and have no lasting consequence for the journey as a whole. Focal predictions must be made, usually quite suddenly, with respect to the oncoming truck or the pedestrian or as a consequence of a minor diversion. In contrast to global predictions, we cannot usually be specific about focal predictions before the journey begins. It would be futile to try to predict before starting the specific location of incidents that are likely to occur on the way. Yet while the occasion for a focal prediction is likely to arise out of particular sets of local circumstances, the prediction itself will still be influenced by our global predictions about the journey as a whole. For example, the modified focal predictions that will result if we have to make an unexpected detour will still be influenced by our overriding intention of eventually reaching a particular destination.

Now I want to suggest that we make similar global and focal predictions when we read. While reading a novel, for example, we may handle a number of quite different predictions simultaneously, some global that can persist up to the entire length of the book, others far more focal that can rise and be disposed of as often as every fixation. We begin a book with extremely global predictions about its content from its title and from what perhaps we have heard about it in advance. Sometimes even global predictions may fail — we discover that a book is not on the topic we anticipated. But usually global predictions about content, theme, and treatment can persist throughout the book.

At a slightly more detailed level, there are likely to be expectations still very global that arise and are elaborated within every chapter. At the beginning of the book we may have such predictions about the first chapter only, but in the course of reading the first chapter expectations about the second arise, and so on to the end. Within each chapter there will be rather more focal predictions about paragraphs, each paragraph being a major source of predictions about the next. At lower layers within each paragraph there will be predictions about sentences and within each sentence some predictions about words.

Lower level predictions arise more suddenly; we will rarely make focal predictions about words more than a sentence ahead of where we are reading, nor predictions about sentences more than a paragraph ahead, nor predictions about paragraphs more than a chapter ahead. The more focal the prediction, the sooner it arises (since it is based on more immediate antecedents) and the sooner it is disposed of (since it has fewer long-range consequences). In general, the more focal a prediction, the less it can be specifically formulated in advance. You would be unlikely to predict the content of the present sentence before you had read the previous sentence, although the content of the present chapter as a whole was probably predictable from the previous chapter. On the other hand, predictions at the various layers inform each other. While focal level predictions are largely determined by the particular situation in which they arise, they are also influenced by our more global expectations. Your focal predictions about my next sentence will depend to some extent on your comprehension of the present sentence but also on your expectations about this paragraph, this chapter, and the book as a whole. But similarly, the global predictions that we make at the book and chapter level must be constantly tested and if necessary modified by the results of our predictions at more focal levels. Your comprehension of one sentence could change your view of a whole book. The entire process is at once extremely complex and highly dynamic, but in Figure 11.3 I shall try to illustrate it with a considerably simplified and static diagram.

In general, the expectations of Figure 11.3 should be regarded as developing from left to right; the past influences our expectations for the future. But it can frequently help at all levels of prediction in reading to look ahead. Meaning can be sought in many ways. Similarly, there should be vertical lines all over the diagram, as the outcomes of focal predictions have their effect on global predictions and the global expectations exert their constant influence on specific focal predictions.

Do not take the diagram too literally. It is not necessary to predict at every level all of the time. We may become unsure of what a book as a whole is about and, for a while, hold our most global predictions to the chapter or even a lower level while we try to grasp where the book might be going. Sometimes we may have so much trouble with a

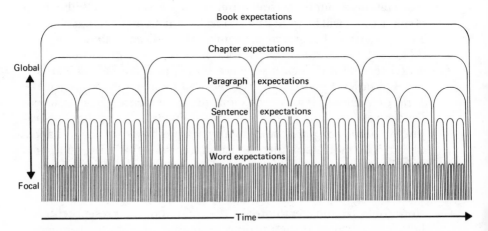

FIGURE 11.3   Layers of prediction in reading a book.

paragraph that we find it impossible to maintain predictions at the chapter level. At the other extreme we may find a chapter or paragraph so predictable, or so irrelevant, that we omit predictions and tests at lower levels altogether. In plain language, we skip. It is only when we can make no predictions at all that a book is completely incomprehensible. It should also not be thought that there are clearly defined boundaries between the different levels of prediction; the global-focal distinction does not describe alternatives but extreme ends of a continuous range of possibilities. A better analogy for reading a novel than my drive downtown might be the weaving of a richly structured tapestry of subtly shaded colors.

In the car-driving analogy I tended to use the words "prediction" and "intention" interchangeably. When we drive, our predictions to a large extent reflect our intentions about where we want to go, how soon we want to get there, and the route we prefer. It is instructive to consider the analysis of prediction in reading that I have just made from the point of view of the intentions of the writer. To some extent, the predictions and intentions can be seen as reflections of each other.

Writers usually begin with global intentions of what the book as a whole shall be about and about the way the subject shall be treated. These global intentions then determine lower-level intentions for every chapter. Within each chapter will be more focal intentions about every paragraph, and within each paragraph, quite detailed focal intentions regarding sentences and words. And just as the more focal predictions of the reader (or the driver) tend to arise at shorter notice and to be dispensed with more quickly, so the more focal intentions of the writer extend over a shorter range in both directions. What I want to say in the present sentence is most specifically determined by what I wrote in the previous one and will, in turn, place a considerable constraint upon how I compose the next sentence. But these focal constraints are at the detailed level. My intention in every sentence that I write is influenced by the more global intentions for the paragraph as a whole, and of course my intention in every paragraph reflects the topic I have selected for the chapter and more generally for the book.

It may be from the perspective of predictions and intentions that one can best perceive the intimate relationship between readers and writers. It might be said that a book is comprehended (from the writer's point of view at least) when the reader's predictions mirror the writer's intentions at all levels. Certainly one important aspect of writing is the intentional manipulation of the reader's predictions. A textbook writer must try to lead readers in a Socratic sense so that the answers to one set of predictive questions set up the succeeding predictions that the readers should make. In a more dramatic context an author may strive for tension by maintaining a particular degree of uncertainty in the reader's predictions at all levels throughout a book. And in a mystery story an author might quite deliberately lead readers into inappropriate predictions so that the inevitable consequence of predictions that fail — surprise — becomes a part of the reading experience.

But readers should also have intentions of their own. When we read a book purely for its literary or even entertainment merit we may willingly submit our expectations to the control of the author or poet. But certainly for textbooks — like the present one, for example — readers should not only be seeking certain information for their own particular ends, quite independently of the intentions of the author, but they should constantly be on guard to resist having their predictions entirely controlled by the author's arguments. The critical mind always reserves some questions of its own. And in all reading, as I have several times reiterated in my assertion that comprehension is relative, there is bound to be an idiosyncrasy in the predictions that readers make at all levels, reflecting their personal interests and purposes and expectations.

Some of the constraints upon authors at all levels are highly conventional. Writers of prose and poetry must temper many of their intentions to the particular stylistic demands of the medium in which they work. In the same way it might be expected that the kinds of predictions that readers make at various levels should also reflect these conventions. Such issues I think lie at the basis of the debates about the "right way" to read poetry or literature. These are difficult questions. On the one hand, I think there is a distinction to be made between what a child has to learn in order to read — a topic which has been a major concern of this book — and what a child is sometimes expected to be able to do as a result of reading. "Drawing inferences" and "evaluating arguments", for example, seem to me to fall into the latter category. Yet I would not want to suggest that there is a clearcut division between the processes and the consequences of reading. I certainly would not want to support a distinction between "reading" on the one hand and "thinking" on the other. Reading should not be regarded as different from thinking or devoid of thinking. Many of the so-called "higher-level skills" associated with the critical reading of literature and poetry seem to me best regarded as specialised questions or predictions that are asked from perspectives beyond the range of this book. Such perspectives do not alter the fundamental nature of reading, but they can add immeasurably to its richness.

SUMMARY

Comprehension, the basic objective of reading, also facilitates the process of reading in two ways. **Immediate meaning identification** makes unnecessary the prior identification of individual words, and comprehension of a passage as a whole facilitates the comprehension and, if necessary, identification of individual words. Immediate meaning identification reduces the probability of tunnel vision, memory overload and ambiguity caused by overreliance on visual information. The prediction that is the basis of comprehension may be carried on at a number of interleaved levels simultaneously.

Notes to Chapter 11 begin on page 231.

CHAPTER 12

**READING
and learning
to read**

The major themes of this book have tended to organize themselves into pairs, not of alternatives or opposites but of complementary considerations. There was the initial assertion, for example, that an understanding of how children learn to read would have to be approached from two points of view — the nature of fluent reading and the way in which all children learn. An understanding of fluent reading would itself require twin perspectives — the way in which language works and the capacities and limitations of the human brain. This final chapter will attempt to review briefly and consolidate these major themes, beginning with the analysis of reading and continuing with how children learn to read. A concluding section will offer some comments on the topic many readers will think primary — reading instruction and the role of teachers.

READING

The emphasis throughout has been on comprehension and meaning. There has been no formal definition of reading, because like other common words in our language the word "reading" can take a variety of meanings depending on the context in which it occurs. Sometimes, for example, the verb "to read" clearly implies comprehension; it would usually be redundant if not rude to say to a friend "Here's a book you might like to read and comprehend." But at other times the verb does not entail comprehension; our friend might reply "I've read that book already and didn't understand it." Obviously there is little to be gained by asking such abstract questions as "Does reading involve comprehension (or thinking, or inferential reasoning) or does it not?" Everything depends on the context in which the words are used. In its specific detail the act of reading itself depends on the situation in which it is accomplished and the intention of the reader. Consider for example the differences between reading a novel, a poem, a social studies text, a mathematical formula, a telephone directory, a recipe, an advertisement, a street sign. Always it is better to try to *describe* the situation than to *define* what words mean.

A general description of what is taking place in all of the preceding examples might be that the reader is seeking information to answer questions that will vary according to the particular situation. This leads to a definition that I did offer, that comprehension is getting one's questions answered. The twin foundations of reading are to be able to ask specific questions (make predictions) in the first place, and to know how and where to look at print so that there is at least a chance of getting these questions answered. What are these questions? Obviously they can range from the price of an article in a catalog to the style, symbolism, and world view of the author of a novel. I have avoided any attempt to catalog and characterize all these different questions because of their very specific — and sometimes specialized — nature. Instead, I have focussed on three kinds of questions that all fluent readers seem able to ask and answer in most reading situations, related to the identification of letters, words, and meaning. These three kinds of question are seen as alternatives, all three cannot be asked simultaneously, and it is unnecessary for the reader to attempt to ask them in sequence. Reading is not a matter of identifying letters in order to recognize words in order to get the meaning of sentences. Meaning identification, I have argued, does not require the identification of individual words, just as word identification does not require the identification of letters. Indeed, any effort on the part of a reader to identify words one at a time, without taking advantage of the sense of the whole, indicates a failure of comprehension and is unlikely to succeed. In the same way any endeavor to identify and perhaps "sound out" individual letters is unlikely to lead to efficient word identification.

From this perspective it would not make sense to try to say whether print basically consists of letters, words, or meanings. Print is discriminable visual contrasts, for example ink marks on paper, that have the potential of answering certain questions — usually implicit — that readers might ask. Print is *visual information,* in which readers can select *distinctive features* and make decisions among the alternatives in which they are interested. Readers find letters in print when they ask one kind of question and select relevant visual information; they find words in print when they ask another kind of question and use the same visual information in a different way; and they find meaning in print, in the same visual information, when they ask a different kind of question again. It should be rare for a reader to ask questions about specific letters (except when letters themselves have a particular relevance, for example as a person's initials or as a compass direction *N, S, E,* or *W*). It should also be rare for a reader to attend specifically to words, unless again there is a particular reason to identify a word, for example a name.

It is interesting to see how people use the visual information on clockfaces to answer questions rather than to identify particular numbers. The next time you notice someone glancing at a clock or watch, ask what time it is. Usually the person has to look again because at the first glance the question was not concerned with the precise time, but with whether the coffee break was over, or how long it was to lunch, or whether the person was on time for an appointment.

Comprehension, then, is relative; it depends on getting an answer to the question being asked. A particular meaning is the answer a reader gets to a particular question. Meaning therefore also depends on the questions that are asked. A reader "gets the meaning" of a book or poem from the writer's (or a teacher's) point of view only when the reader asks questions that the writer (or teacher) implicitly expected to be asked and brings an expected background of prior knowledge. Disputes over the meaning of text, or the "correct" way to comprehend text, are disputes over the questions that should be asked. A particular skill of writers (and of teachers), based usually on exceptional experience, understanding, and sensitivity, is to lead a reader to ask the questions that they consider appropriate. Thus, the basis of fluent reading is the ability to find answers in the visual information of print to the particular questions that are being asked. Print makes sense when readers can relate it to what they know already (including those occasions when learning takes place, that is to say when there is a comprehensible modification of what the reader knows already). And reading is interesting, and relevant, when it can be related to what the reader wants to know.

The Role of the Reader

It should therefore be evident that both comprehension and learning depend on prior knowledge, or what the reader knows already. I have called this relevant prior knowledge *nonvisual information*. Throughout this book I have tried to emphasize that reading is possible only when the reader can bring sufficient nonvisual information to bear to reduce the amount of visual information that must be attended to in the text, or at least to utilize the visual information as economically and efficiently as possible. The nonvisual information lessens the reader's uncertainty in advance and reduces the amount of visual information required to eliminate the remaining uncertainty. Here is a summary of reasons why the balance of nonvisual and visual information is critical:

1. The visual system can be overloaded if too much visual information is required to eliminate the reader's uncertainty, and tunnel vision will result. Nonvisual information reduces alternatives.
2. Short-term memory will also be overloaded by the need to pay attention to small fragments of the text, and the possibility of comprehension will be greatly diminished. Nonvisual information ensures that short-term memory is concerned with sense.
3. Long-term memory functions efficiently only when reading is meaningful, when new information can be integrated directly into what the reader knows already. Nonvisual information is the basis of effective learning and recall.

4. Reading must be fast and not overcautious. Slow reading (less than 200 words a minute unless the text is already understood) interferes with comprehension and learning because it overloads the visual system and memory. Nonvisual information permits fast reading (and is in fact the only way to make slow reading possible).
5. Language is intrinsically ambiguous. This is basically the distinction between the surface structure and deep structure of both spoken and written language. Nonvisual information, through the elimination of unlikely alternatives in advance, ensures that meaning is brought to text at the deep structure level and that the reader does not become enmeshed in the pointless detail of surface structure.

To crystalize all the preceding points, fluent reading entails maximizing what the brain can do best, namely the utilization of what it knows already, and minimizing what the brain is least efficient at, namely the processing of a lot of new information, especially when that new information makes little sense.

LEARNING TO READ

There is only one way to summarize everything that a child must learn in order to become a fluent reader, and that is to say that the child must learn to use nonvisual information efficiently when attending to print. Learning to read does not require the memorization of letter names, or phonic rules, or large lists of words, all of which are in fact taken care of in the course of learning to read, and little of which will make sense to a child without some experience of reading. Nor is learning to read a matter of application to all manner of exercises and drills, which can only distract and perhaps even discourage a child from the business of learning to read. And finally learning to read is not a matter of a child relying upon instruction, because the essential skills of reading — namely the efficient uses of nonvisual information — cannot be taught.

In a sense, learning to read is for children very much like the cat-and-dog problem. No one can teach them directly what the relevant categories, distinctive features, and interrelationships are, yet children are perfectly capable of solving the problem for themselves provided they have the opportunities to generate and test their own hypotheses and to get appropriate feedback. In quite a literal sense, learning to read is like learning spoken language. No one can even begin to explain to infants what are the essential features of speech that should be learned, let alone construct a course of study for them to follow; yet even this complex problem is solved by children, without any apparent strain or difficulty, provided again that they have the opportunity to exercise their innate learning ability. All that children require to master spoken language, both to produce it themselves and more fundamentally to comprehend its use by others, is to have experience of using language. Children easily learn about spoken language when they are involved in its use, when language has the possibility of making sense to them. And in the same way children will try to understand how to read by being involved in its use, in situations where it makes sense to them and they can generate and test hypotheses.

It should not be a cause for dismay that we cannot say with exactitude what a child has to learn in order to read, or that a foolproof method of instruction cannot be found to direct a child's progress in learning to read. It was not possible to specify the content or course of a child's learning spoken language either (or the difference between cats and dogs for that matter). But it is possible to specify the *conditions* under which a child will learn to read, and these are again the general conditions that are required for learning anything — the opportunity to generate and test hypotheses in a meaningful context. And to reiterate the constant theme, the only way a child can do all this for reading is to read. If the question arises how children can be expected to read by reading before they have learned to read, the answer is very simple. At the beginning — and at any other time when it is necessary — the reading has to be done for the children. Before children acquire any competence in reading, everything will have to be read to them, but as their ability expands they just need help.

One of the beautiful things about written language that makes sense (to the child) is that to a growing extent it will itself provide learning assistance to the child. Helpful adults are not always necessary. Meaningful written language, like meaningful speech, not only provides its own clues to meaning, so that children can generate appropriate learning hypotheses, but it also provides the opportunity for tests. If a child is not sure about the likely meaning of what is currently being attended to, the context (before *and* after) can provide clues. And the subsequent context will provide the feedback about whether the child's hypotheses were right or wrong. Reading text that makes sense is like riding a bicycle; children do not need to be told when they are falling off.

Let us list the advantages a child gains from reading meaningful written language — building vocabulary, making sense of letter-

sound relationships, developing mediated meaning and word identification ability, acquiring speed, avoiding tunnel vision, preventing
memory overload, relying on sense; in short, increasing relevant nonvisual information and using it more efficiently, the key aspects of
reading that cannot be taught. And always the child will be the best
guide to learning in the most efficient manner, because children will
not willingly limit their vision, overload memory, or tolerate nonsense.
Children also will not tolerate *not learning,* so just as there is no reason
to expect that they will be satisfied with what has become simple for
them, so also they should not be expected to remain in situations
where no learning or comprehension is possible at all.

It is easy also to list the conditions required for children to take
advantage of the learning opportunities that reading meaningful text
provides. There are only four: access to meaningful and interesting
reading material (ideally the child's own choice), assistance where
needed (and only to the extent that it is required), a willingness to take
the necessary risks (anxiety increases the proportion of visual information a reader needs), and freedom to make mistakes. On the last
point, there is nothing to learn if you know everything already, and in
any case, a hypothesis is a hypothesis only if there is a possibility of
being wrong. One only learns the right alternative by discovering
which alternatives are inadequate.

I have not said anything about motivation, not because it is not
important, but because it is not something that can be artificially
promoted or maintained, certainly not by means of extrinsic "reinforcers" such as irrelevant material rewards, improved grades, or
even extravagant praise. None of these is necessary for a child to learn
spoken language. All the satisfaction that a child requires is in the
learning itself. It is not learning, not comprehending, that destroys
motivation. And the impetus in the first place? Why do children set
themselves the enormously time-consuming task of learning spoken
language? Not, I think, in order to communicate. Children cannot
understand this use of language until they have got some. And certainly not to get their material needs fulfilled or to control the behavior of others. Children are never so well looked after as before they
can use language; afterwards they can be told to wait, to do without,
or to do it themselves. Even adults when language fails can feel the
urge to revert to earlier, nonlanguage and more assertive ways of
trying to get their way. I think there can be only one reason why
children apply themselves to learning spoken language — because it
is *there,* in the world around them. As they learn they see its sense, its
utility, its meaningfulness. And because language is meaningful, because it changes the world and is not arbitrary or capricious, not only

do children succeed in learning it, but they want to learn it. Children will not stop learning anything that is meaningful to them, unless the learning becomes too difficult or too costly for them, in which case the learning itself becomes meaningless.

Children need adults as models; they will endeavor to learn and understand anything that adults do — provided they see adults enjoying doing it. If meaningful written language exists in the child's world, and is visibly used with satisfaction, then the child will strive to master its mystery; that is in the nature of childhood. There is no need for special explanations about why children should want to learn to read, only for why they might come to the conclusion that it is pointless or too costly.

All this has been very general. I have argued that no special theories are required for how and why children learn to read. There is nothing unique about reading, whether from the point of view of the language skills involved (no different in principle from those of spoken language comprehension), the visual skills involved (no different from discriminating any aspects of the visual world) or of the learning procedures involved. There are however two special insights that children must have in order to learn to read. The insights are fundamental, in the sense that children who do not have them are bound to find reading instruction nonsensical, and will not therefore succeed in learning to read. Yet not only are these insights not taught in school, much of what constitutes formal reading instruction might be seen as contrary to these insights, and thus likely to inhibit them. The insights, which I shall discuss in turn, are first, that print is meaningful, and second, that written language is not the same as speech.

Insight 1: Print Is Meaningful

There is no need to belabor why the insight that print is meaningful is essential for learning to read. After all, reading *is* a matter of making sense of print, and meaningfulness is the basis of learning. The issue concerns how children might initially acquire the insight — or at least hypothesize — that print is meaningful, that differences in print make a difference in the world. And just as children must and do begin learning spoken language by finding that meaning can be brought to speech — before they have the language skills that would produce that speech — so it must be possible for children to test and prove the hypothesis that print is meaningful even before they are able to read a word. In other words, the roots of reading are prior to reading, and the topic now is the "prereading" child.

In Chapter 7 I examined the possibility that children are as much immersed in written language as they are in speech, and that all of the print in the world around them is potentially meaningful; every bit makes a difference. All the everyday print of signs and instructions and labels can have meaning brought to it; the context provides opportunity for hypotheses about its purpose to be generated and tested. Thus self-directed learning is possible with written language as with speech, provided the initial insight is achieved and maintained that print is meaningful.

Very little print is meaningful in school, in the sense that it would not be possible to substitute one word for another. A teacher writes the words *table* or *chair* on the board but could just as well write *horse* or *cow*. The words in word lists, or the sentences in many "stories", could be changed without any child noticing anything "wrong". Perhaps the most meaningful print in schools is the names of teachers, and the highly significant labels *boys, girls,* and *staff,* on different doors.

To make sense of any aspect of language children must bring meaning to it, which means they must perceive a purpose for it. In school, this need implies that children should be able to understand not only the content of the instruction — the materials they are expected to read — but also the purpose of the instruction itself. Teachers may understand the reason for a particular exercise or procedure (although this is not invariably the case), but if children cannot see the sense of the enterprise, then for our purposes it can reasonably be regarded as incomprehensible. A brief list of fundamentally incomprehensible aspects of reading instruction to which children may be exposed would include:

1. The decomposition of spoken words to "sounds". The spoken word "cat", in some contexts, can make sense, but the sounds "kuh", "a", "tuh" do not.
2. The decomposition of written words to letters. The printed word *cat,* in some contexts, can make sense — it refers to an object in the real world with which children can meaningfully interact. But the letters *c, a,* and *t* refer to specialized visual symbols that have nothing to do with anything else in the child's life.
3. The relating of letters to sounds. For a child who has no idea of reading to be told that some peculiar shapes called letters — which have no apparent function in the real world — are related to sounds that have no apparent independent existence in the real world must be the purest jabberwocky.
4. Meaningless drills and exercises. There are so many candidates for

this category, ranging from deciding which of three ducks is facing the wrong way to underlining silent letters in words, that I shall not attempt to make a list. Children may learn to score high on boring, repetitive, and nonsensical tasks (especially if they happen to be competent readers) but such a specialized ability will not make readers of them.

The preceding kinds of activity may through their very incomprehensibility make learning to read more complicated, arduous, and nonsensical than need be. It is not until children have begun reading that they have a chance of making sense of such activities at all. Children who do not have the insight that written language should make sense may never achieve it, while children who have it may be persuaded that they are wrong.

Insight 2: Written Language Is Different from Speech

The first insight was concerned primarily with written language in the form of single words (or small groups of words) like labels and signs. These kinds of print function very much like the everyday spoken language of the home in that contextual cues to meaning (and constraints on interpretation) are provided largely by the physical situation in which they occur. Now I want to consider written *text*, where constraints on substitutability and interpretation are placed not by the physical environment but by the syntax and semantics of the text itself. As I discussed in Chapter 6, written and spoken language are evidently not the same, and probably for very good reason, including the fact that written language has especially adapted itself for being read.

Children who expect written language to be exactly the same as speech are likely to have difficulty in predicting and comprehending text and thus in learning to read. They must be familiar with written language. It does not matter that we cannot say with any precision what exactly the differences between spoken and written language are. We cannot list the rules of spoken language; yet children learn to make sense of speech. Immersion in functional language, the possibility of making sense, a plentiful experience, and the opportunity to get feedback to test hypotheses would seem to be just as easily met with written language as with speech. In fact, written language might seem to have several advantages, since a number of tests can be conducted on the same piece of material, a second hypothesis tried if the first one fails. By virtue of its internal consistency the text itself can provide relevant feedback about the correctness of hypotheses.

How might children who cannot yet read acquire and develop the insight that speech and written language are not the same? Only by being read to, or at least by hearing written language read aloud. When a child's predictions of written language fail because they are based on knowledge of spoken language, then the occasion exists for the insight to arise that spoken and written language are not precisely the same. And a similar process of hypothesis-testing as written language is heard and comprehended will develop an understanding of the particular conventions of written language, considerably augmented of course as children become able to do more and more of their own reading.

The kind of reading that would most familiarize children with written language is coherent *stories*, ranging from items in newspapers and magazines to traditional fairy tales, ghost and adventure stories, history, and myth. All of these types of story are truly written *language* — produced for a purpose in a conventional medium and distinguishable from most school texts by their length, sense, and semantic and syntactic richness. There is no evidence that it is any harder for children to understand such complex texts (when they are read to them) than it is difficult for children to understand the complex adult speech that they hear around them and on television.

Children at school are usually not provided with complex written material as part of their reading instruction for the obvious reason that they could not be expected to read it by themselves. Since most of the material in which children are likely to be interested — and from which they would be likely to learn — tends to be too difficult for them to read by themselves, less complex material is found or produced in the expectation that children will find it "simpler". And when these specially-tailored-for-children texts also seem to confound beginners, the assumption may be made that the fault lies with the children, or with their "language development".

And indeed, it probably is the case that the language of such texts is unfamiliar to most children. But this inadequacy need not have its roots in the particular kind of spoken language with which the child is familiar nor even in the possibly limited experience of the child with print. The reason is more likely to be associated with the child's unfamiliarity with the artificial language of school books, whether of the truncated "Sam the cat sat on the mat" variety or the more florid "Down the hill, hand in hand, skipped Susie and her friend." This is all so different from any other form of language, spoken or written, that it is probably safest to put it into an exclusive category of "school language".

Of course, such material tends to be quite unpredictable for many children who consequently have enormous difficulty understanding it and learning to read from it. And ironically it may be concluded that written language is intrinsically difficult for children who would be better off learning from "spoken language written down". The text is then based on the intuition of a professional textbook writer or classroom teacher about what constitutes spoken language — or more complex still, a dialect of that language or even children's language. All of these are problems that would confound a professional linguist. The result is quite unlike written language yet has none of the advantages of speech, since it will have to be comprehended out of context. Children may learn to recite such print, but there is no evidence that it will make them readers. Any insight they might have in advance about the nature of written language is likely to be undermined, and worse, they might become persuaded that the print which they first experience in school is a model for all the written language that they will meet throughout their lives — a conviction that would be as discouraging as it is misleading.

THE ROLE OF THE TEACHER

Throughout this book I have taken strands of evidence about the nature of language and about the capacities and limitations of the human brain from the experiments, observations, and analyses of scientists in various fields of linguistics and psychology. I have tried to weave these strands into a coherent picture that might both reflect and respect the subtle complexities of reading. And I have come to the practical conclusions that reading cannot be formally taught, that children learn to read only by reading, but that provided children have adequate opportunity to explore and test their hypotheses in a world of meaningful print, they can and do succeed in learning to read. Now that we come to consider the educational implications of such a picture of reading, it might be asked whether there is any role for teachers at all. My final aim will be to argue that teachers have a critical function in helping children learn to read, and that they must be trusted more because formal instructional systems — prepackaged materials and programs — must be trusted less. The issues are complex and deserve far more space than I have available. My attempts to be both brief and comprehensive may sound more prescriptive than I would like to be. The following points are all considerations which may be debatable but which cannot, I think, be ignored.

The view of reading that I have presented sees the teacher not as a classroom manager or ringmaster nor as a dispenser of instructional routines, but as a facilitator and guide. Only teachers can develop the intuition, understanding, and insight required to help children learn to read. Not only must they understand the nature of fluent reading and of the general way in which children learn, they must have a sympathetic awareness of the particular children for whom they are responsible and a sensitivity for their individual feelings, interests, and abilities at any particular time. All of this, obviously, is harder for a teacher than programmed instruction. But no formal program of instruction can be relied upon to address itself to all these concerns.

Indeed, the more formal and structured the program, the more important becomes an understanding teacher to ensure that it stays relevant and adequate to a child's needs. Programmed instruction can often be viewed as the systematic deprivation of information.

The Practice of Reading

The primary function of reading teachers can be summed up in very few words — to ensure that children have adequate opportunity to read. Where children see little relevance in reading, then teachers must provide a model. Where children find little interest in reading, then teachers must change the situation. And where children have difficulty in reading, teachers must see that they are helped. In part, this assistance can be given by developing the confidence of children to read for themselves, in their own way, taking the risk of making mistakes and being willing to ignore the completely incomprehensible. Even bizarre personal interpretations are better than none at all; children find out soon enough the mistakes that make a difference. But children will also from time to time look for help from others, either in answering specific questions or in assisting with reading generally. Such reading on behalf of the child can be provided by the teacher, an aide, by other children, or by recordings.

Always teachers should strive to ensure that reading is easy, permitting children themselves to judge whether materials or activities are too difficult, too incomprehensible, or too dull. Anything children would not listen to, or understand, if it were read to them is unsuitable material for them to be expected to read. A child's preference is a far better yardstick than any readability formula, and grade levels have no reality in a child's mind. Teachers need not be afraid that children will engage in reading so easy that there is nothing to learn; that would be boring. Children learn about reading as long as they read, but they can never learn to read by not reading.

There is no simple formula to ensure that reading will be easy; no materials or procedures are guaranteed not to interfere with a child's progress. Instead teachers must understand the situations that make reading difficult, whether induced by the child, the teacher, or the task. For example: the concentration on visual detail that will cause tunnel vision; the overloading of short-term memory by attention to fragments of text that make little sense; log jams in long-term memory (so that the child can answer lots of questions afterwards, or write "reports"); attempts to sound out words at the expense of meaning; slow reading; anxiety not to make a mistake; lack of assistance when a child needs it for sense or even word identification; or too insistent "correction" that may be irrelevant to the child and that may in the long run inhibit the self-correction that is an essential part of learning. All of these ways in which reading can be made harder can be characterized as limitations on the extent to which children can use nonvisual information.

And conversely, what makes reading easy for children is the teacher's facilitation of the use of nonvisual information. Not only should a child come into every reading situation with relevant nonvisual information — equipped with, in plain English, an adequate prior understanding — but also the child must feel free to use it. A child's fund of knowledge and confidence should be constantly developed, but this will occur as a consequence of reading. Not only should the teacher try to avoid materials or activities that are nonsense to the child, there should be active encouragement for the child to predict, to understand, to enjoy. The worst habit for any learner to acquire is to treat text as if it were nonsense. Where there is a mismatch, where there is little likelihood that a child will comprehend the material, then the preference should be to change the material rather than to try to change the child. For older children there may be reluctance to change material because a certain content is expected to be learned, but teachers still have a choice. Students cannot learn two things at the same time; they cannot simultaneously learn to read and master an unfamiliar subject matter like history or math. If the teacher's intention is to improve reading, then students must have material they can easily understand. If the intention is to extend subject matter knowledge — which will in turn make reading easier — then until the student can read it with some fluency it must be taught in some other way, by lecture, film, board work, or individual tuition. The two can be taught *concurrently* — the math need not wait for the reading competence any more than the reading need wait for math skills — but they cannot be learned simultaneously.

Teachers sometimes try to resolve problems the hard way, for example in expecting poor readers to improve while in fact doing less reading than better readers. When children have trouble understanding text, they may be given isolated word drills, while problems with word identification may provoke attention to letter identification and sound blends. But letters (and their phonic interrelations) are recognized and learned best when they are parts of words, and words are recognized and learned more easily when they are in meaningful sequences. Good readers tend to be good at letter and word identification and at phonic drills, but these more specific skills are a consequence, not a cause, of good reading (Samuels, 1971). Good readers tend also to understand the technical jargon of reading such as *letter, word, verb, sentence, paragraph,* but this again is a result of being able to read. Practice with definitions does not make readers (Downing and Oliver, 1973–74).

Many poor readers make "reversal" errors, saying "p" for *q* and "b" for *d,* or perhaps "was" for *saw* or "on" for *no.* This is not a matter of "seeing backwards" (which is an impossibility) but of faulty knowledge of distinctive features in a difficult discrimination task. No other visual object has a different name depending on whether it is facing right or left, and reversals are a common mistake for even fluent readers to make in situations where they have limited visual information, for example, in the kinds of experiments described in Chapters 3 and 8. Good readers do not usually make reversal errors, partly because they have had a wealth of experience but also because there are many other clues that they can use. Text would still be understandable if every *d* and *b* were interchanged — text woulb still de unberstanbadle if every *b* and *d* were interchangeb — anx certainly if they were ignorex altogether or printex with an *x.* But if children have difficulty with reversals — which is only likely to happen when they are reading out of context (or reading as if context tells them nothing) — they may be taken away from reading text altogether and given exercises with individual words. They may be required to practice with words like *big* and *dig,* which would never be confused in a meaningful context but are relatively similar in isolation. If they continue to exhibit difficulty with words, the children may then be given the far more difficult task of distinguishing *b* and *d* in isolation (while deprived of some important relational cues) and even one letter alone (which removes even the possibility of comparison).

Children may also be confounded by instruction that is as unnecessary as it is futile, often as a consequence of a theoretical vogue among specialists. When, for example, Noam Chomsky popularized transformational linguistics as a technical method of analyzing language, many people thought children would not learn to read unless they became miniature linguists themselves, and made children spend a lot of time doing transformational exercises that made no apparent difference to their language ability. After psychologists became interested in the theoretical notion of distinctive features there were several efforts to teach children the distinctive features of letters, although no one could convincingly demonstrate what these features might be. Children who had difficulty with the alphabet or with these exercises were sometimes diagnosed as having poor feature discrimination, although they had no reported difficulty with knives and forks or Chevrolets and Volkswagens. Phonic-based reading programs and materials have flourished whenever linguists get particularly interested in the spelling-sound correspondences of language, and more recently there have been moves towards teaching "prediction" as if it were something foreign to most children's experience. In all these cases, concepts that scientists have found useful as hypothetical constructs in their attempts to understand their discipline have become, with little justification, something a child must learn as a prerequisite for learning to read. (How children learned to read before these concepts were devised is not explained.) There is a growing acknowledgement today of the importance of comprehension as the basis of learning, but at the same time there is a feeling that comprehension itself must be taught, that it can be broken down into a series of "comprehension skills" which presumably can be taught without comprehension.

I am not saying that nothing should be taught, that children should not learn the alphabet or build up sight vocabularies or even that the relationships between the spelling of words and their sounds should be concealed. But all of these are by-products of reading that make more sense as reading itself is mastered and understood. It is pointless for teacher and child to labor over abilities that will not facilitate learning to read and that will be easily achieved once reading competence develops. It is certainly not the case that teachers should never correct. But correction or even advice may be offered too soon. A child pauses while reading aloud and half the class shouts out the next word although the reader may be thinking about something else six words behind or ahead. But there is no harm in *any* correction provided the child can ignore it if it is incomprehensible or otherwise irrelevant. Problems arise when corrections and explanations sap children's confidence or stop them in their tracks for what might be quite extraneous purposes. The teacher's question always should be "Does the child understand?" or "What is causing the confusion here?"

The First Steps

So how does a teacher begin to teach reading? I do not think there is a first lesson; reading does not compartmentalize itself like that. Children begin to read with the first intuition that print is meaningful or the first time they listen to a story being read aloud. Reading has begun with the first word a child can recognize. Nonvisual information is so important that reading potential is enhanced with every expansion of a child's knowledge of the world or of spoken language. (But there is no particular need for extensive prior knowledge of the world or of spoken language for a child to begin to read — just enough to make sense of the first print that will be read. Much of the knowledge and language skills of fluent readers is again a consequence of literacy rather than its cause.)

Reading is not intrinsically different from all other activities. Unless the instruction is unusual in some way, reading should blend smoothly into all the other visual and linguistic and intellectual enterprises of a young child's life. There is no magical day when a "prereader" suddenly becomes a "learner", just as there is no landmark day when learning is completed and a reader graduates. No one is a perfect reader and we can all continue to learn. It is always possible to find something that a fluent reader will be unable to read, either because of the language or the topic (a matter of nonvisual information once again). The only difference with less fluent readers is that there is more they cannot read. But even with beginners it is possible to find something — a word even, perhaps in a familiar story — that they will be able to read fluently. Learning to read can be perceived as making sense of more and more kinds of language in more and more contexts, fundamentally a matter of experience.

Methods and Materials

There is no "method" of teaching reading that will take care of all the preceding considerations. Nor should the development of a foolproof method be expected, despite the millions of dollars spent in its pursuit. While some methods of teaching reading are obviously worse than others (because they are based on very weak theories of what reading is about, such as the decoding of letters to sound), the belief that one perfect method might exist to teach all children is contrary to all the evidence about the multiplicity of individual differences that every child brings to reading.

Research is of little help in the selection of appropriate methods. Research tells us that all methods of teaching reading appear to work for some children but that none works for all. Some teachers seem to succeed whatever the method they are formally believed to employ. We must conclude that the instructional method is not the critical issue. (Researchers recognize this point and have to control in their studies for the "variability" introduced first by the different abilities of children and second by the varying influences of teachers.) It might not be particularly unfair to say that many children learn to read — and many teachers succeed in helping them — despite the instructional method used.

One thing we do not need research to tell us is that millions of children learned to read before the sophisticated space-age reading programs that are being developed or promoted today, often on the basis of unsupported or unsophisticated theories of learning or reading. Many children of two and three years of age have learned to read, and so have many illiterate adults. Children from the poorest homes have learned to read and so have children from all cultures. Children who are not very smart have learned to read (while many otherwise bright children, even from "privileged" homes, have failed). A good deal more research is required before we can hope to understand what really helped those millions to read, sometimes despite substantial difficulties. It may have less to do with split-second programming and more with the labels on jars than we think.

Teachers should not rely on any method, but on their own experience and teaching skills. No one is in a better position than a teacher to identify a particular child's needs or interests or difficulties at a particular time. Teachers should not ask what they ought to do, but what they need to know in order to be able to make productive decisions. Even if teachers do get their "practical" questions answered — and there is no shortage of experts to give them advice or of materials producers to promote their wares — the final responsibility rests with the teacher. The teacher must still decide which expert to trust, which materials to try.

I am not saying that teachers should not be familiar with instructional materials, programs, and techniques. But teachers must still decide how and when to use particular materials and techniques with particular children at particular times, and such decisions require knowledge and understanding. Surgeons are not primarily characterized by the number or sophistication of the instruments that they have at their command; at a pinch the best surgeons could work with instruments found in a well-equipped kitchen. What makes a surgeon, of course, is ability to use instruments appropriately, an ability that does not come from asking experts which is the best.

I am also not recommending that teachers blindly trust everything they do, even if they are generally successful. It is too easy for teachers — and the public in general — to give credit where it is not deserved. We imagine that we are taught — or that we teach — by a particular method, all of the time, and that learning to read is entirely attributable to that method. As if teachers and children did nothing else that was relevant to reading than work through the particular course. But the method itself may have little to do with the success and may even be a handicap. The experience and intuition that I think teachers should trust is more connected with what individual children have found easy and what they have found hard, comprehensible or nonsense, interesting or dull, inspiring or bland. Once more I must assert that to understand what helps children to read, one must be sensitive to the complexities of both children and reading.

None of this is to say that all children will easily learn to read; there has always been evidence that such is unlikely to be the case. But I do not believe that failure should be attributed to *dyslexia,* a disease that only strikes children who cannot read and which is invariably cured when they can read. I have argued there is nothing unique about reading, either visually or as far as language is concerned. There are no evident visual defects that are specific to reading, but this does not mean that there are no general visual anomalies that will interfere with learning to read. Children who need glasses will not find reading easy until their sight is corrected. The few children who have difficulty learning to understand speech, or learning anything, may also find learning to read difficult.

But there is no convincing evidence that children who can see normally, with or without glasses, and who have acquired a working competence in the language spoken around them, might be physically or congenitally incapable of learning to read. It cannot be denied that some children who seem "normal" and even bright in all other respects may fail to learn to read. But there can be other reasons for this failure that do not presuppose any organic dysfunction on the part of the child. Children do not learn to read who do not want to, or who see no point in doing so, or who are hostile to the teacher, or to the school, or to the social or cultural group to which they perceive the teacher and the school as belonging. Children do not learn to read who expect to fail, or who believe learning to read will be too costly, or whose preferred image of themselves, for whatever reason, is of a nonreader. Children do not learn to read if they have the wrong idea of what reading is about, if they have learned — or been taught — that reading does not make sense.

On Changing the World

My closing point is perhaps an obvious one: that theories of reading cannot be expected to change the world. The kinds of situations that I have characterized as making reading more difficult, and thus likely to interfere with children's learning to read, are a fact of life in many classrooms, that many teachers feel they can do very little about. Tests must be administered; instruction must be directed towards the texts; children will be categorized and streamed; teachers must be accountable; certain curricula must be followed; parents and trustees must be assuaged; work must be graded; competition and anxiety is unavoidable. And it is true, all of these considerations interfere with teachers and children in the task of learning to read. But then we have to recognize that relatively little of what goes on in many schools is in fact directly concerned with the actual process of learning, about reading or about anything else. Much of a teacher's time is necessarily directed to classroom management, many activities are engaged in to satisfy guidelines or other demands laid down by external sources, and few teachers can find the time or the resources to provide an ideal learning environment for children all the time.

A theory of reading will not change all this (although it might hopefully provide ammunition for anyone who tries to make a dent). The kind of change that will make a difference in schools will not come with better theories or with better materials or even with better-informed teachers, but only with individuals taking action towards change. The problem of improving reading instruction, in the long run, is a political question. But whether teachers can change their world or not, they will still be better off, the more they understand about reading and how children learn to read. Teachers who cannot free children from the disruptions of irrelevant activities and demands may at least protect them. Teachers can make their own informed decisions about conditions likely to interfere with learning to read and conditions likely to promote it and see that the latter are not completely swamped. Fortunately, most children seem able to tolerate a good deal of tedium, anxiety, and even nonsense in the process of learning to read. Extraneous activities may not help them learn to read but children often do not take such activities too seriously. Perhaps teachers could capitalize more on this innate toughness of young learners. Recognizing the conditions that favor learning, and of course doing their best to provide them, teachers might also consider taking children into their confidence about the rest. They might make it clear for example that drills designed to improve performance on a certain test, and performance on the test itself, have in fact nothing to do with reading and should not be considered a part of reading or learning to read. Children understand ritual.

What matters for progress in reading is a child's own capacity to derive sense and pleasure from any form of print in the world. Teachers can see that there is always time for this. Teachers and children can truly be partners in the enterprise of understanding reading.

SUMMARY

Circumstances that facilitate comprehension in reading also facilitate learning to read. These circumstances can be summed up as the possibility of using relevant nonvisual information without hindrance or anxiety. Teachers have a crucial role in helping children learn to read by modifying circumstances, responding to children's needs, and making reading meaningful to a degree that formal instructional programs, with their necessarily limited objectives, cannot be expected to achieve.

Notes to Chapter 12 begin on page 235.

NOTES

Changes in the Second Edition

All of the chapters have been substantially rewritten, with major revisions or additions to the sections on mediated word identification (new Chapter 10) and on comprehension (new Chapters 5 and 11). The basic framework of the two editions is the same with the following exceptions: The earlier chapters on eye and brain (old Chapters 7 and 8) have been consolidated, condensed, and moved forward (new Chapter 3). The "behaviorism" chapter on habit learning (old Chapter 5) has been eliminated, with some material carried through to the Notes to new Chapter 7. New Chapter 7, on learning, also contains and elaborates upon material on language learning (old Chapter 4) which has also been eliminated. The small section on memory in old Chapter 6 has now been expanded into a chapter in its own right (new Chapter 4). The earlier chapter on features (old Chapter 11) has been dropped entirely, mainly because I felt that the discussion of semantic features did not contribute to the general argument.

I have tried to solve the perennial problem of a harmonious marriage between readability and documentation with a judicial separation. The main body of text in each chapter is as nontechnical as I can make it, while specific references to research and to detailed theoretical issues have been segregated into the following Notes. The elaboration of topics in the Notes has permitted me to expand considerably on the number of references cited. A full list of

197

references now appears in the conventional position at the end of the book, where a glossary has also been added.

Notes to Chapter 2, Communication and Information, pp. 11–24

Measuring Information and Uncertainty

Only a small proportion of the Notes throughout this book will have a mathematical flavor. But a brief introduction to some elementary concepts of Information Theory measurement will be useful for subsequent chapters when we try to estimate the rate at which the brain can process visual information and also the uncertainty of letters and words of English in differing circumstances.

It is necessary to be a little circumlocutionary in putting actual figures to information and uncertainty because although both are measured with respect to alternatives, the measure is not simply the number of alternatives. Instead, information is calculated in terms of a unit called a *bit,* which always reduces by half the uncertainty on any particular occasion. Thus the card player who discovers that an opponent's strongest suit is red (either diamonds or hearts) gets one bit of information, and so does a child trying to identify a letter who is told that it comes from the second half of the alphabet. In the first case two alternatives are eliminated (the two black suits) and in the second case thirteen alternatives are removed (and thirteen still remain). In both cases the proportion of uncertainty reduced is a half and therefore the amount of information received is regarded as one bit.

The uncertainty of a situation in bits is equal to the number of times a "yes or no" question would have to be asked and answered to eliminate all uncertainty if each answer reduced uncertainty by a half. Thus there are two bits of uncertainty in the card-playing example because two questions will remove all doubt, for example: *Q1. Is it a black suit? Q2. If yes, is it clubs? (If no, is it hearts?),* or *Q1. Is it spades or diamonds?   Q2. If yes, is it spades? (If no, is it hearts?).*

You can see it does not matter how the questions are posed, provided they permit a yes-no answer that will eliminate half the alternatives. The final qualification is important. Obviously, a single lucky question such as "Is it clubs?" will eliminate all alternatives if the answer is "yes", but will still leave at least one and possibly more questions to be asked if the answer is "no". The most efficient way of reducing uncertainty when the answer can only be "yes" or "no" is by a binary split, that is, by partitioning the alternatives into two equal sets. In fact the word *bit,* which may have sounded rather colloquial, is an abbreviation of the words *binary digit,* or a number representing a choice between two alternatives.

The uncertainty of the 26 letters of the alphabet lies somewhere between four and five bits. Four bits of information will allow selection among 16 alternatives, not quite enough, the first bit reducing this number to 8, the second to 4, the third to 2, and the fourth to 1. Five bits will select among 32 alternatives, slightly too many, the first eliminating 16 and the other four removing the rest of the uncertainty. In brief, X bits of information will select among 2^x alternatives. Two bits will select among $2^2 = 4$, 3 bits among $2^3 = 8$, four bits among $2^4 = 16$, and so on. One question settles only $2^1 = 2$ alternatives, and no questions at all requires that you have only one alternative to begin with ($2^0 = 1$). Twenty bits ("Twenty questions") are theoretically sufficient to distinguish among $2^{20} = 1,048,576$ alternatives. There is a mathematical formula that shows that the theoretical uncertainty of the 26 letters of the alphabet is almost precisely 4.7 bits, although, of course, it is not easy to see how one could ask just 4.7 questions. (The formula is that the uncertainty of X alternatives is $\log_2 X$, which can be looked up in a table of logarithms to the base 2. $\log_2 26 = 4.7$, since $26 = 2_{4.7}$.) Can you calculate the uncertainty in a deck of 52 playing cards? Since 52 is just twice 26, the uncertainty of the cards must be one bit more than that of the alphabet, or 5.7 bits.

Measuring Redundancy

It will be helpful to pursue the matter of redundancy a little more deeply, partly because of the importance of the concept of redundancy to reading, but also because the discussion of how *bits* of uncertainty or information are computed contained an oversimplification that can now be rectified. We shall consider two aspects of redundancy, termed *distributional* and *sequential*.

Distributional redundancy is associated with the relative probability that each of the alternatives in a particular situation can occur. Surprising as it may seem, there is less uncertainty when some alternatives are less probable than others. And because there is less uncertainty when alternatives are not equally probable, there is redundancy. The very fact that alternatives are not equally probable is an additional source of information that reduces the uncertainty of the set of alternatives as a whole. Redundancy that occurs because the probabilities of alternatives are not equally distributed is therefore called distributional redundancy.

Uncertainty is greatest when every alternative has an equal chance of occurring. Consider a coin-tossing game where there are only two alternatives, head or tail, and there are, in fact, equal chances of a head or tail turning up. The informativeness of knowing that a particular toss of the coin produced a head (or a tail) is one bit, because whatever the outcome uncertainty is reduced by a half. But now suppose that the game is not fair, and that the coin will come down head nine times out of ten. What is the uncertainty of the game now (to someone who knows the coin's bias)? The uncertainty is hardly as great as when the odds were 50–50, because then there was no reason to choose between head and tail while with the loaded coin it would be foolish knowingly to bet tail. By the same token, there is likely to be far less information in being told the outcome of a particular toss of the loaded coin. Not much uncertainty is removed if one is told that the coin has come down head because that is what was expected all the time. In fact the informativeness of a head can be computed to be about .015 bit compared with 1 bit if the game were fair. It is true that there is much more information in the relatively unlikely event of being told that a toss produced a tail — a total of 3.32 bits of information compared with the 1 bit for a tail when heads and tails are equally probable — but we can expect a tail to occur only once in every 10 tosses. The *average* amount of information available from the loaded coin will be nine-tenths of the .015 bit of information for head and one-tenth of the 3.32 bits of information for tail which when totaled is approximately .35 bit. The difference between the 1 bit of uncertainty (or information) for the 50–50 coin, and the .35 bit for the 90–10 loaded coin, is the distributional redundancy.

The earlier statements that every bit of information halves the number of alternatives, and that the number of bits of uncertainty is the number of yes-no questions that would have to be asked and answered to eliminate all the alternatives, hold only when all the alternatives are equally probable. If some alternatives are less probable than others, then an *average* amount of uncertainty or information has to be computed, taking into account both the number of alternatives and the probability of each. Because uncertainty and information are at their maximum when alternatives are equally probable, the average uncertainty of situations where this does not occur is necessarily less than the maximum, and redundancy is present.

The statement that the uncertainty of the letters of the English language is 4.7 bits is perfectly true for any situation involving 26 equally probable alternatives — for example drawing a letter from a hat containing one instance only of each of the 26 letters of the alphabet. But the letters of English do not occur in the language with equal frequency; some of them, such as *e, t, a, o, i, n, s,* occur far more often than others. In fact *e* occurs about 40 times more often than the least frequent letter, *z*. Because of the inequality, the average uncertainty of letters is somewhat less than the maximum of 4.7 bits that it would be if the letters all occurred equally often. The actual uncertainty of letters, considering their relative frequency, is 4.07 bits, the difference of about .63 bit being the distributional redundancy of English letters, a measure of the prospective informativeness that is lost because letters do not occur equally often. If letters were used equally often, we could achieve the 4.07 bits of uncertainty that the 26 letters currently have with a little over 16 letters. We could save ourselves about 9 letters if we could find a way (and agree) to use the remainder equally often.

Words also have a distributional redundancy in English. One of the oldest and still least understood findings in experimental psychology concerns the "word-frequency effect", that more common words of our language can be identified on less visual information than less frequent words (Broadbent, 1967; Howes and Solomon, 1951). Computations of the distributional redundancy of letters and words in English are contained in Shannon (1951) and are discussed in Cherry (1966) and Pierce (1961).

Sequential redundancy exists when the probability of a letter or word is constrained by the presence of surrounding letters or words in the same sequence. For example, the probability that the letter *H* will follow *T* in English words is not one in 26 (which would be the case if all letters had an equal chance of occurring in any position) nor about one in 17 (taking distributional redundancy into account), but about one in 8 (because only 8 alternatives are likely to occur following T in English; namely, R, H, or a vowel). Thus the uncertainty of any letter that follows T in an English word is just 3 bits ($2^3 = 8$). The average uncertainty of all letters in English words is about 2½ bits (Shannon, 1951). The difference between this average uncertainty of 2½ bits and a possible uncertainty of 4.07 bits (after allowing for distributional redundancy) is the *sequential redundancy* of letters in English words. An average of 2½ bits of uncertainty means that letters in words have a probability of about one-in-six instead of one-in-26. This figure, of course, is only an *average* computed over many readers, many words, and many letter positions. There is not a progressive decline in uncertainty from letter to letter, from left to right, in all words. An English word beginning with q, for example, has zero uncertainty about the next letter u, an uncertainty of about two bits for the four vowels that can follow the u, and then perhaps four bits of uncertainty for the next letter, which could be one of over a dozen alternatives. Other words have different uncertainty patterns, although in general the uncertainty of any letter goes down the more other letters in the word are known, irrespective of order. Because of constraints in the spelling patterns of English — due in part to the way words are pronounced — there is slightly more uncertainty at the beginning of a word than at the end, with slightly less in the middle (see Bruner and O'Dowd, 1958).

There will be many references to the sequential redundancy of English letters and words in subsequent chapters of this book (and a few more calculations in some of the Notes). The orthographic (spelling) redundancy of print to which I have referred comprises both distributional and sequential redundancy for letters *within* words, while syntactic (grammar) and semantic (meaning) redundancy are primarily sequential redundancy *between* words.

Signal Detection Theory

As I said, observers (whether radar operators or readers) always have the choice of reducing the number of their absolute errors while increasing "misses" or of achieving maximum hits while increasing the number of "false alarms". In effect, observers can place themselves at any point along a curve ranging from zero false alarms (but zero hits) to 100 percent hits (but a maximum of false alarms). This curve is called a *receiver operating characteristic*, or ROC curve, and varies with every individual and situation. At any one time an observer can choose where to be placed on the ROC curve — the criterion level selected depending upon the perceived relative costs of hits, misses, and false alarms. But to shift the ROC curve as a whole — to improve the ratio of hits, misses, and false alarms — requires an improvement in the clarity of the situation (e.g., better illumination) or in the ability of the observer (e.g., more skill). Encouragement or "reinforcement" has the effect of moving an observer up an ROC curve, just as anxiety will move the observer down, but only a change in ability — or for example an increase in the availability of non-visual information — will shift the ROC curve in its entirety.

There is an interesting example of the ability of human observers to penetrate noise and extract information-carrying signals in what Cherry (1966) calls the *cocktail party problem*. The example illustrates a point frequently made in this book that the prior knowledge of the perceiver contributes so much to comprehension. The problem is this: How can listeners in a crowd of people all talking loudly at the same time manage to follow what one person is saying, and tune out everything else? The communication channel to each listener's ear is full of noise (both literally and technically), yet the individual can select from within the noise the information coming from one source only. And this "selected" voice is the only one that is heard — unless someone else happens to say something particularly relevant personally, such as the listener's name, in which case it is demonstrated that the listener has really been monitoring all the conversations all the time, "listening without hearing". No one has yet been able to devise a machine that, using the same communication channel, could unscramble more than one voice at a time. Yet the human receiver can separate intermingled messages, and not because they come in different voices, or from different directions (it has been shown experimentally that we can follow one message even if successive words are produced by different voices), but by following the sense and syntax of the message being attended to. Such a feat can be accomplished only if listeners draw upon their own knowledge of language to extract a message from all the irrelevant noise in which it is embedded.

Further Reading

For communication theory and information theory generally, see Pierce (1961) and Cherry (1966). Attneave (1959) discusses specifically applications of information theory to psychology. Miller (1964) reprints useful brief articles on both information theory and signal detection theory. An introductory psychology text that employs concepts from both theoretical domains is Lindsay and Norman (1972). Garner (1962, 1974) also develops psychological descriptions from an information theory point of view. A classic article on signal detection theory is Swets, Tanner, and Birdsall (1961); at a more popular level see Swets (1973) and, more technically, Pastore and Scheirer (1974).

Notes to Chapter 3, Between Eye and Brain, pp. 25–42

Limits of Visual Information Processing

That there is a limit to how much print can be identified at any one time, varying according to the use a reader can make of redundancy, is not exactly a recent discovery. The illustration in this chapter of how much can be identified from a simple glance at a row of random letters, random words, and meaningful sequences of words, is derived directly from the researches of Cattell (1885, republished 1947) and of Erdmann and Dodge (1898). Descriptions of many similar experimental studies were included in a remarkably broad and insightful book by Huey (1908, republished in 1967) which remains relevant today and is the only classic in the psychology of reading. A good deal of recent research on perception in reading is basically replication of early studies with more sophisticated equipment; nothing has been demonstrated to controvert them. Yet the pioneer research was neglected by experimental psychologists for nearly half a century and is still widely unknown in education, partly because behaviorism inhibited psychologists from studying "mental phenomena" (see the Notes to Chapter 6) and partly because "systematic" or "operationalized" piecemeal approaches to reading instruction have concentrated on decoding and word attack — the "tunnel vision" extreme — at the expense of comprehension.

The mathematics of information theory, introduced in the Notes to Chapter 2, can be applied directly to the Cattell findings to show that readers identifying just four or five random letters, a couple of random words, or a meaningful sequence of four or five words, are each time processing the same amount of visual information. The differences among the three conditions can be attributed to the varying amounts of nonvisual information that readers are able to contribute, derived from distributional and sequential redundancy within the print.

The random letter condition suggests that the limit for a single glance (the equivalent of a second of processing time) is about 25 bits of information. The calculation is based on a maximum of five letter identifications of about five bits of uncertainty each (2^5 bits = 32 alternatives). In random sequences of letters, of course, there is no distributional or sequential redundancy that a reader can utilize. That 25 bits per second is indeed a general limit on the rate of human information processing has been argued by Quastler (1956) from studies not only of letter and word identification but of the performance of piano players and "lightning calculators" as well (see also Pierce and Karlin, 1957).

How is it possible then to identify two random words, consisting on the average of 4.5 letters each, with just 25 bits of visual information? Nine or ten letters at five bits each would seem to require closer to 50 bits. But as I pointed out in the Chapter 2 Notes, because of distributional and sequential redundancy the average uncertainty of letters in English *words* is about 2½ bits each (Shannon, 1951) making a total average uncertainty for letters in two random words of something under 25 bits. From a different perspective, random words taken from a pool of 50,000 alternatives would have an uncertainty of between 15 and 16 bits each (2^{15} = 32,768, 2^{16} = 65,536), but due to distributional redundancy among words — and probably also because unusual words are unlikely to be employed in reading studies — we can probably again accept the estimate of Shannon that the average uncertainty of English words without syntactic or semantic constraints (sequential redundancy) is about 12 bits per word. So whether we look at the random word condition from the point of view of letter uncertainty in words (about 2½ bits per letter) or of isolated word uncertainty (about 12 bits per word) the result is still that the reader is making the identification of about nine or ten letters or two words with roughly 25 bits of visual information. The fact that both the number of letters identified and the effective angle of vision double in the random word condition compared with the four or five letters that can be perceived in the random letter condition reflects the use that the reader can make of redundancy. In other words, the viewer in the isolated word condition contributes the equivalent of 25 bits of nonvisual information to enable twice as much to be seen in a single glance. Anyone who did not have the relevant nonvisual information would have had to rely on visual information alone and therefore have seen only half as much.

In meaningful and grammatical passages of English there is considerable sequential redundancy among the words themselves. Speakers and authors are not free to choose any word they like whenever they please, at least not if they expect to make any sense. From statistical analyses of long passages of text and also by a "guessing game" technique in which people were actually required to guess letters and words, Shannon calculated that the average uncertainty of *words* in meaningful sequences was about seven bits (a reduction over isolated words of about a half) and that the average uncertainty of *letters* in meaningful sequences was only slightly over one bit (again reducing by half the uncertainty of letters in isolated words). On this basis, one would expect viewers in the meaningful word sequences condition to see twice as much again compared with isolated words, which is of course the experimental result. A phrase or sentence of four or five words can be seen in one glance, a total of 20 letters or more. This is four times as much as can be seen in the random letter condition, but still on the basis of the same amount of visual information; four or five random letters at about five bits each, or 20 letters in a meaningful sequence at just over one bit each. Put in another way, when reading sequences of meaningful words in text the reader can contribute at least three parts nonvisual information (in the form of prior knowledge of redundancy) to one part visual information so that four times as much can be perceived.

For a more detailed discussion of the preceding argument, see Smith and Holmes (1971). Other examinations of uncertainty and redundancy in English are included in Garner (1962, 1974) and in Miller, Bruner, and Postman (1954), the latter using carefully constructed "approximations to English". McNeill and Lindig (1973) provide a recent demonstration that what listeners perceive in spoken language also depends on how much they are looking for — individual sounds, syllables, or entire words.

The Rate of Visual Decision-Making

Seventy years after the first demonstrations of a limit to how much can be seen in a single glance, other tachistoscopic studies showed that the limit cannot be attributed to any restriction on the amount of visual information that the eye can gather from the page, nor because viewers forget letters or words that have already been identified before they can report them. Rather the bottleneck occurs as the brain labors to process what is transiently a considerable amount of raw visual information, organizing "seeing" after the eyes have done their work. Perceptual decision-making takes time, and there is a limit to how long visual information sent back by the eyes remains available to the brain.

Subjects in the kind of tachistoscopic experiment that I have described often feel that they have potentially seen more than they are able to report. The brief presentation of visual information leaves a vaguely defined "image" that fades before subjects are fully able to attend to it. The validity of this observation has been established by an experimental technique called *partial recall* (Sperling, 1960) in which subjects are required to report only four letters out of a presentation of perhaps twelve, so that the required report is well within the limits of short-term memory (see Chapter 4). However, the subjects do not know *which* four letters they must report until after the visual presentation, so they must work from visual information that remains available to the brain after its source has been removed from before the eyes. At one stroke the experimental technique avoids any complication of memory by keeping the required report to a small number of items, while at the same time testing whether in fact viewers have information about all twelve items for a brief time after the eyes' work is complete.

The experimental technique involves presenting the twelve test letters in three rows of four letters each. Very soon after the 50 msec presentation is ended, a tone is sounded. The subject already knows that a high tone indicates that the letters in the top row are to be reported, a low tone calls for the report of the bottom row, while an intermediate tone indicates the middle line. When this method of partial recall is employed, subjects can normally report back the four required letters, indicating that for a short while at least they have access to raw visual information about all twelve letters. The fact that subjects can report any four letters, however, does not indicate that they have identified all twelve, but simply that they have time to identify four before the visual information fades. If the cue tone is delayed more than half a second after the end of the presentation the number of letters that can be reported falls off sharply. The "image" is unprocessed visual information that decays by the time about four letters have been identified.

Other evidence that visual information remains available in a "sensory store" for about a second, and that the entire second is required if a maximum report of four or five letters is to be identified, has come from the "masking" studies described in this chapter (e.g., Averbach and Coriell, 1961; Smith and Carey, 1966). If a second visual array is presented to the eye before the brain has finished identifying the maximum number of letters that it can from the first input of visual information, then the amount reported from the first presentation declines. The second input of visual information erases information from the first presentation.

However, it can be as disruptive for reading if visual information reaches the eye too slowly as if it is too fast. Kolers and Katzman (1966), Newman (1966), and Pierce and Karlin (1957) have shown an optimum rate of about six presentations a second for receiving visual information about individual letters or words; at faster rates the brain cannot keep up and at slower speeds there tends to be a greater loss of earlier items through forgetting. These studies and the earlier calculations of Quastler all tend to support the view that the "normal reading rate" of between 200 and 300 words a minute (Tinker, 1965; S. Taylor, 1971) is an optimum; slower reading is more than inefficient, it is almost certainly disruptive to comprehension.

There is another historic strand of evidence leading to the same conclusion that perception is a judgmental process that takes time, with the amount of time required depending on the number of alternatives among which the brain must choose. These are the studies of *reaction times*, or of the *latency* between the presentation of visual information to a subject and the identification response. Latency always increases with the number of alternatives within a category. For example, it took subjects an average of 410 msec to name a letter of the alphabet (out of 26 alternatives) but only 180 msec to say whether a light was flashed (a simple yes-no choice). Interestingly, short words could be identified faster (388 msec) than single letters — and no one has ever satisfactorily explained why this should be the case. I have taken these figures from a long and interesting section on vision and eye movements in Woodworth and Schlosberg's compendious *Experimental Psychology* (1954); even more basic detail about early studies of reading is included in the original Woodworth (1938) edition.

Eye Movements in Reading

Classic studies of the nature of eye movements and rate of fixation changes in reading are reported in Tinker (1951, 1958). S. Taylor, Frackenpohl, and Pettee (1960) report the stabilization of fixation rates by Grade 4. Llewellyn Thomas (1962) discusses the eye movements of speed readers, who sample visual information over such a broad area that they break free of the constraint of moving their fixations along lines of type and rather move down and even up the center of pages (without, however, increasing their rate of fixations). More recent studies of eye movements in reading, involving sophisticated equipment and theorizing, are provided by Hochberg (1970), Rayner (1975), and Spragins, Lefton, and Fisher (1976). Hochberg has been influential among a number of experimental psychologists with his development of the view that reading is a highly selective process as the brain determines in advance the best place for each fixation to fall. More generally, and very technically, Treisman (1969) has argued that perception is most efficient when the viewer is in control of what the eyes will look for. Garner (1966) has also summarized a number of experiments demonstrating the selective nature of perception.

It might be asked why the most general and most efficient fixation rate in reading seems to be about four a second when the information from a single glance persists for a second or more and indeed a second is required for processing all the information that can be read out of a single fixation. There has not been a good research answer to this question, but my hypothesis would be related to the view that the brain is less concerned with squeezing the last bit of information from each fixation than it is with receiving a smooth inflow of selected visual information as it builds up its own coherent picture of the text. Prolongation of a fixation in reading is similar to an unblinking stare at a picture or other scene, not a sign that more visual information is being processed but rather that the viewer can make little sense of what is being looked at.

Further Reading

For vision generally, Gregory (1966) is a brief, easily read and well illustrated introduction, while more technical detail (and an excellent paper by Hochberg) is included in a useful collection by Haber (1968). There are some good psychology texts with an information-processing basis to their discussions of visual perception, notably Neisser (1967), Lindsay and Norman (1972), Calfee (1975), and Massaro (1975).

Notes to Chapter 4, Bottlenecks of Memory, pp. 43–54

Theories of Memory

One of the earliest and most coherent attempts to distinguish short-term and long-term characteristics of memory was by Norman (1969), recently revised and expanded into a comprehensive analysis of the processes and contents of memory (Norman, 1976). The underlying perspective also pervades the Lindsay and Norman (1972) introductory psychology text. A more technical basic paper is Baddeley and Patterson (1971) and there are useful reviews by Shiffrin (1975) and Schneider and Shiffrin (1977), who particularly emphasize the relationship between short-term memory and attention. There are of course alternative points of view. Craik and Lockhart (1972) have proposed an influential *levels of processing* model, arguing that the different short-term and long-term "stages" of memory are in fact reflections of different "levels" or "depths" to which processing is done. The additional processing, from their point of view, required to identify words rather than letters, or meanings rather than words, accounts for evidence often used to account for stage theories. On the other hand, it is not clear that word identification is a deeper level of perception or memory, or that it involves more processing, than letter identification; short-term and long-term memory effects can be found with both letters and words. The argument is not really about the evidence, but about the way it is most usefully interpreted. The same comment applies to an interesting proposal by Tulving (Tulving and Thomson, 1973; Tulving and Watkins, 1975) that there are two different kinds of memory, but not the kinds proposed by the stage or depth theorists. Instead Tulving distinguishes an *episodic* memory, which is concerned with the order or sequence of events, and a *semantic* memory (similar to what I have been referring to as long-term memory) where "facts" are stored independently of the order in which they were acquired. Most people, for example, can reply immediately to questions of whether John F. Kennedy and Charles de Gaulle are dead, but not give an immediate reply to the question of who died first. Tulving stresses something that few cognitive psychologists these days would argue with, that the quality of a particular memory depends upon the processes involved in the original learning. For a recent review of episodic and semantic memory research, see Friendly (1977).

The notion that memory is constructive, or reconstructive, rather than a simple recall of original information also has a long history in psychology, with its own classic by Bartlett (1932). More recent arguments that present perspectives influence recall of past events are offered by Cofer (1973) and Mandler and Johnson (1977).

Chunking

The two apparent bottlenecks of memory — the limited capacity of short-term memory and the slow entry into long-term memory — can both be circumvented by the strategy known as *chunking,* or organization of information into the most compact (most meaningful) unit. For example, it is easier to retain and recall the sequence of digits 1491625364964 as the first eight square numbers, or the letters JFMAMJJASOND as the initials of the months of the year, than to try to remember either sequence as a dozen or so unrelated elements. But it is a mistake to think that we normally perceive first and chunk afterward; we no more read the letters *h, o, r, s,* and *e* which we then chunk into the word *horse* than we perceive a particular nose, ears, eyes, and mouth which we then chunk into a friend's face. Rather the size or quality of a chunk is determined by what we are looking for in the first place (the "levels of processing" issue again). The word "chunk" has become something of a minor fad term in education, with some teachers asking, "How can we teach children to chunk?" or even, "What do I do about a child who can't chunk?" But chunking is not something you learn to do, but rather a simple consequence of what you know; if you can recognize *horse* as a word there is no chunking problem in the first place. Chunking also has its own classic paper in the psychological literature, written with the flair suggested by its title, "The magical number seven, plus or minus two" (Miller, 1956). Another readable and informative paper on the same topic is by Simon (1974).

One important and common means of chunking is to employ imagery to remember; there is a substantial literature demonstrating the unsurprising fact that our recall of particularly graphic sentences that we have heard or read is more likely to be related to scenes that we imagine from the descriptions provided by the words than to the words themselves (Bransford and Franks, 1971; Bransford, Barclay, and Franks, 1972; Barclay, 1973; Sachs, 1974). These papers will be relevant to later arguments that meaning lies beyond words in any case; whenever possible everyone, including children, tends to remember the meaning of words rather than the words themselves. But while we remember some sequences of words in terms of the pictures they conjure up, we also often remember scenes or pictures in terms of their descriptions. We recall birds flying over a town but not whether they were seagulls or pigeons, nor how many there were. There is nothing remarkable about any of this: We naturally try to remember in the most efficient manner possible. If a scene is easiest to remember, or most efficiently remembered, in terms of a description, because perhaps we are interested in particular things rather than in the scene as a whole, then the memorization will proceed accordingly. Not only is our recall influenced by the way we learned or perceived in the first place, but the manner of memorization will tend to reflect the most probable way in which we shall want to recall or use the information in the future. For important discussions of the role of imagery in memory, see Paivio (1971) and Brooks (1968), and for a technical analysis of the relationship of words to images see Reid (1974).

Children's Memory

There is no evidence that children have poorer or less well developed memories than adults. Simon (1974) argues that children have the same memory capacity as adults but do not chunk as efficiently; however there is probably an adult bias behind the notion of chunking "efficiently" in the first place. We tend to chunk — or to perceive and remember in rich meaningful units — that which is most rich and meaningful to us. Recall of strings of unrelated letters and digits, which is the test by which children are usually judged to have inferior memories to those of adults, is not the most meaningful of tasks, for children especially. The number of digits a child can repeat after a single hearing increases from an average of two at the age of 2½ to six at the age of ten (and eight for college students). But rather than suppose that children's memory capacity grows with their height and weight, one can argue that the younger children have had little experience, and see little sense, in repeating sequences of numbers, especially before they have become accustomed to using the telephone. The memory span of adults can be magically increased by teaching them little tricks or strategies, for example to remember strings of numbers not as single digits (two, nine, four, three, seven, eight. . . .) but as two-digit pairs (twenty-nine, forty-three, seventy-eight . . .). Adults are so familiar with two-figure numbers through their use of dollars and cents that separate digits, like 2 and 9, can become chunked into a single unit 29. Practice improves performance on any memory task, but does not seem to improve memory beyond the particular skill into unrelated areas or activities. The best aid to memory for anyone of any age is a general understanding of the structure and purpose behind the required memorization. Skilled chess players can recall the layout of most or all of the pieces on a board after just a couple of glances while beginners can remember the positions of only a few pieces — but only if the pieces are arranged as part of an actual game. If the pieces are organized randomly then the skilled player can remember no more than the beginner, because then the skilled player's experience of hundreds of games and positions is of no relevance or utility.

Baer and Wright (1975) argue that children's memory is not inferior to adults' but that they *encode* (or organize memory) differently. Huttenlocher and Burke (1976) refer to the additional difficulty (lesser experience) of children in identifying items and especially information about order in memory tasks in the first place. Paris and Carter (1973) report that children use imagery in remembering sentences just like adults (see also G. Olson, 1973).

Further Reading

Klatzky (1975) provides a relatively nontechnical introduction to the highly technical area of memory, and Norman (1972) is highly recommended though rather more advanced. There is a good summary in Calfee (1974), embedded in discussion of reading somewhat different from the approach taken in this book. For the structure or contents of memory — which gets close to the topic of concern of the next chapter — there are useful reviews as well as some idiosyncratic points of view in Tulving and Donaldson (1972), Anderson and Bower (1973), and Crowder (1976). By contrast there is a very easy to comprehend paper by Jenkins (1974) relating his conversion from a traditional *associationistic* view of memory to a more meaningful cognitive approach, entitled "Remember that old theory of memory? Well, forget it!"

Notes to Chapter 5, Knowledge and Comprehension, pp. 55–68

Theories of Comprehension

Comprehension is not a topic that has attracted a great deal of attention among psychologists until quite recently, with the notable exception of Piaget. The notion that everyone's brain contains a structure of knowledge concerning the world, into which all incoming information is assimilated, is a central aspect of Piaget's theorizing. Piaget's writings are voluminous and not always transparent; one might begin with his book entitled *The Construction of Reality in the Child* (Piaget, 1954) or one of his collaborative efforts, such as Piaget and Inhelder (1969). Alternatively there are some useful general introductions to Piaget's thought, for example, Flavell (1963), Firth (1969), and Ginsburg and Opper (1969).

Paradoxically, the computer has provided a great impetus to many psychologists interested in comprehension, not necessarily because the brain is conceptualized as a kind of computer (although such a notion does seem to underlie some theorizing) but because the computer has proved a useful tool for simulating knowledge structures and memory processes. Some experimentalists believe that theories about mental processes "lack rigor" unless they can be simulated on a computer to prove that they are at least "workable", while others find such a requirement constricting if not misleading. There can be no doubt that some very ingenious though limited models of cognitive processes have been explored through computer simulations; for examples, see Norman and Rumelhart (1975), Meyer and Schvaneveldt (1976), Kintsch (1974), and E. Smith, Shoben, and Rips (1974), as well as some of the memory theorists listed in the Notes to the preceding chapter. As I have already pointed out, there is a large degree of overlap between recent studies of memory and those of the structure of human knowledge. All agree that the basis of comprehension, whether of language or of the world in general, must be some internal organization of knowledge (or beliefs) about the world. An earlier, classic book on the interaction between world and brain, presaging computer analogs but remaining readably untechnical, is Miller, Galanter, and Pribram (1960). For a brief but thought-provoking paper about the knowledge background of comprehension, see Attneave (1974).

Karl Popper is a philosopher who argues for an active process of comprehension and learning similar to the discussions of the present volume; he suggests that the knowledge that each of us (and of our cultures) has accumulated is a record of the problems we have had to solve. Popper tends to be repetitive and fairly heavy going in his technical writing (e.g., Popper, 1973), but his views are expressed more concisely in an engaging autobiography (Popper, 1976) and even more clearly in a biography (Magee, 1973).

Prediction as I have discussed it in this chapter is not a topic that has been widely explored, although there is an extensive psychological literature on the consequences of expectancy, for example in word recognition (Broadbent, 1967) and in pattern recognition (Garner, 1970). Bruner (1957) wrote an influential paper on "perceptual readiness", and Neisser (1977) has more recently published a book exploring the notion that perception is based on anticipated information from the environment.

The standard work on the fact that we do not have direct access to the knowledge stored in our heads is Polanyi (1966), and there is a relevant, more recent paper by Nisbett and Wilson (1977).

Further Reading

The basic ideas in this and the following two chapters are presented at greater length in (F. Smith, 1975a). Miller and Bruner are perhaps the two psychologists who have written most on a wide variety of topics relevant to comprehension and learning from a cognitive, information-processing point of view (and have certainly stimulated my own thought). For examples of their investigations of the organization and processes of human knowledge see Bruner (1973) and Miller and Johnson-Laird (1975).

Notes to Chapter 6, Language — Spoken and Written, pp. 69–84

Linguistic Theories

Noam Chomsky's influential theory of *generative transformational grammar* is in fact a theory of the way language functions in the human mind, an attempt to describe the kind of knowledge that underlies language skills. The theory has been through a number of modifications, by Chomsky and others, since its first publication (N. Chomsky 1957), and has continually provoked dissent as well as enthusiasm. Later I shall discuss an alternative theoretical approach, called *generative semantics*, which I believe offers more towards an understanding of comprehension. But first I shall give a flavor of Chomskian grammar, partly because of its historical and theoretical significance, and partly because it is still the basis of what is considered "new grammar" in many schools. Sometimes parts of this grammar are taught to children in the apparent belief that their language development will be facilitated if they become precocious linguists. But Chomsky himself has never argued that children should be instructed in what is, after all, a partial attempt to describe what all language users, from schoolchildren to Chomsky himself, know implicitly, namely the mechanisms of the language they speak.

Chomsky's basic notion is that grammar is the bridge between surface structure and deep structure. These latter terms are employed in a variety of ways by different theorists. In this book I am using them in their most contrastive sense — regarding surface structure as the observable sounds of speech or inkmarks of print and deep structure as meaning, beyond the realm of language itself. Chomsky keeps deep structure as part of language, lodged securely within his system of grammar, the input to an underlying semantic (meaning) system which "interprets" the abstractions of deep structure. Similarly, surface structure for Chomsky is another intangible abstraction at the opposite pole of his grammatical system, the input to a phonological (sound) system, which "interprets" surface structures into actual speech. Other linguists, like the generative semanticists whom I shall discuss, propose that there must be several layers of depth in language, with abstract forms of sentences going through a number of hypothetical changes as they rise from the abysses of meaning to the surface of realized sound.

Chomsky's view, then, is that the link between deep and surface structures, and ultimately between meaning and sound (or print), is *grammar*, which consists of two components: (1) a *lexicon*, or "dictionary" of *lexical entries* (roughly speaking words); and (2) a *syntax*, or set of *rules*, for the selection and ordering of lexical entries. These syntactic rules are not to be confused with the traditional "rules of grammar" which are classroom precepts for "correct" language use; they constitute a dynamic language system that Chomsky sees in everyone's head, producing and comprehending sentences. The particular lexicon and syntax possessed by different individuals depend upon the language that they use. In this sense, there is just as much grammar in the mind of a person who always produces double negatives as there is in another who would never say "I ain't got no . . . ."

Chomsky's grammar is a device that *generates* sentences. With only a few rules and a small number of words it can produce an infinite number of utterances, all "grammatical" (according to the built-in syntactic rules), and all potentially new to the language user. Thus the theory offers a description of how individuals might be able to produce and comprehend sentences they have never heard before. I shall give a very simple illustration to show the potential productivity and creativity of even the smallest generative grammar. This grammar will consist of just three syntactic rules and a lexicon of eight words. The syntactic component is always in the form of "rewrite rules", indicated by the single arrow → which means that a symbol on the left side of the arrow must be replaced or "rewritten" by the symbols on the right. Here are three rewrite rules:

(1) $S \to NP + VP$
(2) $VP \to V + NP$
(3) $NP \to D + N$

The actual choice of letters as symbols is purely for convenience; they could be called X, Y, and Z but instead S is used (for "sentence") NP for "noun phrase", VP for "verb phrase", N for "noun", V for "verb", and D for "determiner".

The eight lexical entries might be chosen as follows:

$N \to dog, cat, man$
$V \to chases, frightens, ignores$
$D \to the, a$

To produce a grammatical sentence, we simply put the grammar to work, starting at the beginning with S (because we want a sentence) and following the instructions of the rewrite rules. Rule 1 says that we erase S and replace it with $NP + VP$; rule 2 changes VP to $V + NP$, giving us $NP + V + NP$, and rule 3 (applied twice) rewrites each NP as $D + N$, giving us a "terminal string" of the symbols $D + N + V + D + N$. Then we enter the lexicon, where we can exercise choice. For the first D we might perhaps select *the*, and for the first N *dog*. V can be rewritten as *chases*, the second D as *a* and the second N as *cat*, giving us the sentence *the dog chases a cat*. Eminently grammatical, you will agree. With different lexical selections we could have produced *a man frightens the cat* or *the cat ignores the dog* or indeed a total of no fewer than 108 sentences ($2 \times 3 \times 3 \times 2 \times 3$ alternatives), all of them grammatical. Add a few more rules (Chomsky estimated about a hundred) for alternative sentence structures, and a larger lexicon, and you would have — theoretically — a grammar with the productive power of the human mind.

Some of the additional rules would be *transformational* rather than *generative*, which is the reason Chomsky's grammar is sometimes called by one or other of the two labels alone and sometimes by the two together. A transformational rule operates on entire sequences of symbols on the left of the arrow instead of taking them one at a time like a generative rule. The transformational arrow has a double shaft, ⇒. Thus a transformational rule might take a sequence like the $D_1 + N_1 + V + D_2 + N_2$ that we just produced (the subscripted numbers are required to keep track of the different Ds and Ns) and reorganize it as follows:

$D_1 + N_1 + V + D_2 + N_2 \Rightarrow D_2 + N_2 + is + V + by + D_1 + N_1$.

Thus *the dog chases a cat* would be "transformed" (with an additional slight modification of the verb which I have ignored for the sake of simplicity) into *a cat is chased by the dog* — a perfectly grammatical passive sentence. Similarly *a man frightens the cat* would by the same rule be transformed into *the cat is frightened by a man.* In fact every active sentence that our original generative grammar produced could be transformed into a passive by this simple transformational rule, at one stroke doubling the number of sentences that the grammar could produce. A second transformational rule, say for negatives, would quadruple the total number of possible sentences (active positives, active negatives, passive positives, passive negatives) while a third transformational rule, say for interrogatives, would give eight times the power, permitting sentences as complex as *Isn't a cat chased by the dog?* Three generative rules, eight lexical entries, and three transformational rules, producing a total of $108 \times 8 = 864$ possible sentences. Other transformational rules permit combinations of sentences (*the dog chases a cat, the cat is limping* $\Rightarrow$ *the dog chases a limping cat*) making the grammar's potential output infinite, because there is no theoretical limit to the length of sentences.

All this is simplified in the extreme. To experience the complexity of unadulterated Chomsky you should sample his work directly (e.g., N. Chomsky 1957, 1965, 1972, 1975), and also N. Chomsky and Halle (1968) which makes some comments on spelling relevant to reading. A brief and clear explanation of Chomsky's theoretical positions, and their radical changes, in 1957 and 1965, together with a discussion of related psycholinguistic research, can be found in an excellent paperback by Greene (1972). A more technical description of transformational grammar is in Jacobs and Rosenbaum (1968).

A frequent criticism of Chomsky's theory concerns his treatment of meaning. In fact Chomsky ignores meaning, at least as far as his grammar is concerned. He claims that grammar works without reference to meaning. But there are in fact many sentences whose grammar cannot be decided if the meaning is unknown. Even the noun "dog" in our eight-word illustrative lexicon could have been a verb. A sentence like *the child opens the door* cannot involve the same generative rules as *the key opens the door,* since you could not say *the child and the key open the door* (and *the door opens* is another case again). But you can only explain the difference between what the child does to open the door and what the key does by reference to meaning, not to grammar. Similarly the sentence *Sarah was soaked by the fountain* is passive (a transformation of *the fountain soaked Sarah*) but *Sarah was seated by the fountain* is not passive (it is not a transformation of *the fountain seated Sarah*), although the same syntactic markers might appear to be present. In these and many other quite familiar kinds of sentence, meaning must be comprehended before the grammar can be determined; grammar is not the bridge to meaning.

Moreover, Chomsky's grammar might be considered too productive. Any rules that will generate a sentence like *the runaway car frightens the angry invalid* will also generate nonsense like *the runaway invalid frightens the angry car.* But Chomsky's theory is not concerned with sense. It does not explain how we usually finish up with a sentence that more or less expresses the meaning we want to convey, nor how meaning is brought to words that are not labelled "noun" or "verb" in advance. It is not easy to see how the system works in reverse for comprehension. While Chomsky's grammar may *describe* the grammatical competence of language users, it does not convincingly explain how particular sentences are produced or comprehended on particular occasions, nor indeed does it claim to.

Generative semantic theories, by contrast, are solely concerned with how language develops out of meaning. These theories consider syntax to be subordinate to meaning or taken care of by meaning altogether. Sentences are seen not as arrangements of syntactic structures but as expressions or *propositions,* related of course to the intentions of whoever produces them. Propositions may be analyzed in terms of *case relations* between the various nouns in a sentence, whether expressed or understood, and the verb. For example, the deep structure (meaning) of a particular sentence might be centered on the verb *open,* which has different "case" relations to such nouns as *child* (the agent of the opening), *key* (the instrument of the opening), *door* (the object of the opening), and so forth. These and other relations are represented in the following diagram:

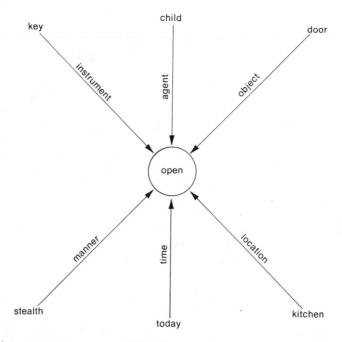

The diagram represents meaning, not surface structure. Each relationship (indicated by arrows) is a case relationship, of which there are perhaps a dozen altogether, their names and number depending on the particular theorist. The actual surface structure of an utterance will result from various transformations applied to the base structures (or case relations). In English, for example, the agent and object of a proposition are usually indicated by word order while the instrumental case may be represented by a preposition such as *with* or *by,* the locative case by *at* or *on* or *in,* manner by *with* (*with stealth*) or by an adverb (*stealthily*). You will notice that there are often alternatives —

the choice will depend on the precise information the language producer wishes to convey — and that some forms are ambiguous; they can represent more than one case relation. It is not necessary for all underlying case relationships actually to be expressed. When we read, *the window broke* we usually assume that there was an agent (someone) who broke the window and perhaps an instrument too (a stone). In *John was anxious to leave,* John is the deep structure subject, while in *John was asked to leave,* despite the similarity of surface structure, John is the deep structure object and a subject is implied (someone asked John to leave).

Generative semantic theories have little trouble with explaining how we usually manage to produce sentences that seem (to the producer at least) to express the intended meaning, because of course they arise out of meaning. And it is not necessary for such theories to run in reverse for comprehension provided the listener or reader is able to make predictions; the listener or reader will start from roughly the same meaning base as the producer of a sentence and be as unlikely as the producer to be aware of potential ambiguity.

A classic article on generative semantics is called "The case for case" (Fillmore, 1968), and there is a more elaborate exposition in Fillmore and Langendoen (1971). Case grammar has been extended across sequences of sentences in paragraphs by Grimes (1975). Other rather technical discussions are provided by Perfetti (1972) and Chafe (1970). Excellent reviews of case grammars and their concepts generally are provided coincidentally by Brown (1973), in his excellent volume on child language learning, and by Anderson and Bower (1973), in a book about memory. Many introductory books on semantics have relatively nontechnical discussions of generative theories (e.g., Palmer, 1976; see also Carroll and Freedle, 1972). A rather longer discussion of the topics of these Notes so far, and their relation to the theory of comprehension that I have presented, will be found in F. Smith (1975a).

There are of course other kinds of theory about language, notably that of B. F. Skinner (1957), who sees language production and comprehension in terms of stimulus-response connections. A violent critique of Skinner's views is in a classic review by N. Chomsky (1959), and there is a little more about Skinner in the Notes to Chapter 7.

Some Technical Terms

One might think that there could not be too much complication about the fact that the basic elements of language are sounds. The word "bed", for example, is made up of three distinctive sounds /b/, /e/, and /d/ (it is a useful convention that the sounds of language are printed between oblique // strokes). With a few perverse exceptions, each sound of the language is represented by a particular letter of the alphabet, so the number of alternative sounds in English must be about 26. Unfortunately, none of the preceding statements is correct.

English has rather more functionally different sounds than it has letters in the alphabet, about 40. These sounds have the special name *phonemes*. As we shall see later, a variety of letters can represent a single phoneme and a variety of phonemes can be represented by a single letter or letter combination. It is necessary to be tentative in making statements about the total number of phonemes because it depends on who is talking and when. All dialects have roughly the same number of phonemes, but not always the same ones, so that words that are individually distinguishable in some dialects, such as "guard" and "god" may not be distinguishable in others unless in a meaningful context. We often think we make distinctions between words when in fact we do not — redundancy in context is usually sufficient to indicate which alternative we intend. Many literate speakers do not have phonemes to distinguish among "Mary", "marry", and "merry", or "cot", "caught", and "court". Say these words one at a time and ask a listener to spell what you have just said. You may find that the listener cannot observe all the differences you think you are making. Phonemes often drop out of casual or colloquial speech.

A phoneme is not so much a single sound as a collection of sounds, all of which sound the same. If that description seems complicated, a more formal definition will not appear much better — a phoneme is a class of closely related sounds constituting the smallest unit of speech that will distinguish one utterance from another. For example, the /b/ at the beginning of the word "bed" distinguishes "bed" from words like "fed" and "led" and "red", the /e/ in the middle distinguishes "bed" from "bad" and "bide" and "bowed", and the /d/ distinguishes the word from such alternatives as "bet" and "beg". So each of the three elements in "bed" will serve to distinguish the word from others, and each also is the smallest unit that can do this. Each is a *significant difference*. It does not matter if the /b/ pronounced at the beginning of "bed" is a little different from /b/ at the beginning of "bad", or if the /b/ in "bed" is pronounced in different ways on different occasions. All the different sounds that I might make that are acceptable as the sound at the beginning of "bed" and "bad", and that serve to distinguish them from "fed" and "fad", and so forth, qualify as being the same phoneme. A phoneme is not one sound, but a variety of sounds any of which is acceptable by listeners as making the same contrast. The actual sounds that are produced are called *phones,* and the sets of "closely related" phones that all serve as the same phoneme are called *allophones* of each other (or of the particular phoneme). Allophones are sounds that the listener learns to treat as equivalent and to hear as the same.

When electronic equipment is used to analyze sounds heard as the same, quite marked differences can be found, depending on the sound that follows them. For example, the /d/ in "dim" is basically a high-pitched rising sound, while its allophone at the beginning of "doom" is much lower pitched and falling (Liberman, *et al.;* 1957). A tape recorder will confirm that the two words have no /d/ sound in common. If they are recorded, it is impossible to cut the tape in order to separate the /im/ or /oom/ from the /d/. Either one is left with a distinct /di/ or /doo/ sound, or else the /d/ sound disappears altogether, leaving two quite different kinds of whistle. Other phonemes behave in equally bizarre ways. If the first part of the tape-recorded word "pit" is cut and spliced at the front of the final /at/ of a word such as "sat" or "fat", the word that is heard is not "pat", as we might expect, but "cat". The /k/ from the beginning of "keep" makes "top" when joined to the /op/ from "cop" and makes "poop" when combined with the /oop/ from "coop".

There is a simple way to demonstrate that sounds that we normally hear to be the same can be quite different. Say the word "pin" into the palm of your hand and you will feel a distinct puff of air on the /p/; however, the puff is absent when you say the word "spin". In other words, the /p/ in "pin" is not the same as the /p/ in "spin" — and both are different from the /p/ in "limp". If you now pay careful attention to the way you say the words, you can probably detect the difference. Usually the difference is ignored, because it is not significant. Other word pairs provide a similar demonstration — for example, "kin" and "skin", or "team" and "steam". You may also be able to detect a difference between /k/ in "cool" and /k/ in "keen", a difference that is allophonic in English and phonemic in Arabic, or in the /l/ at the beginning and end of "level". Japanese often have difficulty in distinguishing between English words such as "link" and "rink" because there is no contrast at all between /l/ and /r/ in their language. In short, a phoneme is not something present in the surface level of spoken language — it is something that the listener constructs. We do not hear different sounds when we are listening to speech, but instead we hear significant differences, phonemes instead of phones. The preceding distinctions may be further illustrated by reference to writing, where a comparable situation holds. Just as the word "sound" is ambiguous in speech, since it can refer to a phone or a phoneme, so the word "letter" is ambiguous in writing. We call "a" one letter of the alphabet, as distinguished from "b", "c", "d", etc., but we also talk about *a, A, а*, etc. as being letters, although they all in a way represent the same "letter". In the first case, the letter of the alphabet "a" is really a category name for a variety of written symbols such as a, A, а. The 26 category names for the letters in the English alphabet may be called *graphemes,* the written symbols (which are innumerable in their various forms) may be called *graphs,* and the graphs that constitute alternatives for a single grapheme are known as *allographs.*

The same defining framework can now be used for the basic elements of speech and writing. A *phoneme* (*grapheme*) is a class of closely related *phones* (*graphs*) constituting the smallest significant differences in speech (writing) that will distinguish one meaningful unit from another. The set of functionally equivalent *phones* (*graphs*) constituting a single *phoneme* (*grapheme*) are termed *allophones* (*allographs*). Allographs may not seem to have as much in common as allophones; in fact, some allographs, such as *a* and *A,* or *g* or *G,* would appear to have nothing in common at all. But they do have a *functional equivalence* in that their differences are not significant for reading, any more than the differences between allophones are significant for comprehending speech.

Linguists make several other distinctions along the same lines. A *morpheme* is the smallest meaningful part of a word. A word may consist of one or more morphemes, some "free" like *farm* or *like* because they can occur independently, and some "bound", like *-er* (meaning someone who does something) and *-s* (meaning plural) or *un-* (meaning negative), which have to be joined to a free morpheme. Thus *farmers* is three morphemes, one free and two bound, and so is *unlikely*. Different *morphs* may represent the same morpheme — thus for plurality we can have not only *-s* but *-es, -en,* and a lot of quite odd forms like the vowel change in *man-men* or even nothing at all, as in the singular and plural *sheep*. Morphs that constitute the same morpheme are called *allomorphs*. Meaning itself may be considered in the form of elements sometimes called *sememes*. "Bachelor", for example, comprises sememes related to maleness, age, marriage, and negation. Words in a dictionary — earlier referred to as "lexical entries" — may similarly be termed *lexemes*.

More about Words

A number of my observations about the ambiguity of words are derived from the work of the linguist Fries (1945), who calculated that each of the 500 most common words of our language has an average of 28 distinct dictionary meanings. The most detailed analyses about the relation between word frequencies and their different meanings are by Zipf (1960), and there are interesting and more readable summaries in Miller (1952). Miller points out that the 50 most common words of our language do the bulk of our communicative work, constituting 60 percent of talk and 40 percent of writing. A mere seven words constitute 20 percent of our language — *the, of, and, a, to, in,* and *is*. The ten most common French words — *à, de, dans, sur, et, ou, que, ne, pas,* and *y* — constitute 25 percent of that language.

The eye-voice span phenomenon shows that when reading aloud we do not say the words we are looking at; the eye roves ahead over meaningful stretches of words and the brain deals in units that make sense. There is a flurry of small studies of the eye-voice span every decade or so; a recent review is included in Gibson and Levin (1975), and earlier in Geyer (1968).

Further Reading

For interesting discussions of why we select the particular words that we do, see R. Brown (1958, reprinted in R. Brown, 1973) and D. Olson (1970). Many of the topics in this chapter are elaborated, from various points of view, in introductory textbooks on psycholinguistics, such as Glucksberg and Danks (1975) and I. Taylor (1976). Miller (1965) sums up readably a number of important points. Excellent volumes that represent personal points of view rather than reviews of the field are R. Brown (1970, 1973) and Slobin (1971). More technical but of broad general interest is Bever, Fodor, and Garrett (1974). For psycholinguistics generally, see also Watt (1970) and G. Olson and Clark (in press).

Notes to Chapter 7, Learning about the World and about Language, pp. 85–98

An Alternative Perspective

There are basically two alternative psychological theories about learning, the extremes of which are diametrically opposed. The *behaviorist* view is that all learning is *habit formation,* and that the only data of importance are the observable cirumstances in which habits are established. The *cognitive* view is that learning involves the *acquisition of knowledge,* and that what is interesting is the unobservable manner in which information is acquired and organized by the brain. The present book, obviously, has a cognitive bias.

The most famous contemporary exponent of behaviorism is B. F. Skinner, whose very name has become a conditioned response to the box (actually a cage) that he invented and in which many of the principles of behaviorist theory have been analyzed and elaborated. In the Skinner box the behavior of rats, pigeons, fish, worms, and other living organisms has been studied and extrapolated, with considerable facility, to describe and even explain the behavior of human beings. Behaviorists assert that all behavior can be understood — in Skinnerian terminology "predicted and controlled" — in terms of *habits* established by the *reinforcement* of a *response* in the presence of a particular *stimulus.*

A response, quite simply, is a piece of observable behavior; not an idea, or a prediction, or an emotion, or a memory — all of these are unobservable, and therefore in the behaviorist view "fictions" — but an explicit movement or physical change. A stimulus, also quite simply, is an occasion for a response. A red light is the stimulus for stopping a car; the words, "pass the salt, please" are the stimulus for passing the salt; a baby is a stimulus for protective and nurturant behavior, and the printed word *cat* is a stimulus for the spoken word "cat". Learning is the establishing, or conditioning, of a bond between a particular stimulus and response, the establishing of a habit. The actual nature of the habit is determined by S-R (stimulus-response) contingencies. If a pigeon is conditioned to peck at a disk when a red light shines, then the S-R bond will be formed between the red light and a peck at the disk.

Reinforcement determines whether conditioning actually takes place. A particular S-R bond will be established only if the behaving organism is reinforced in a particular way while responding in the presence of a stimulus. Technically, reinforcement is defined operationally: Positive reinforcement is anything that increases the probability that a response will recur in the presence of a particular stimulus; negative reinforcement reduces that probability. In everyday life positive reinforcement is associated with reward, negative reinforcement with punishment. (However, there are differences between punishment and negative reinforcement. Negative reinforcement, such as the withholding of a reward, reduces the probability that a type of behavior will recur in the future. Punished behavior is likely to recur as soon as the punishment is stopped; the removal of punishment is positively reinforcing.)

After that slab of definition, examples are in order. I shall offer two: one animal and one human. Imagine a rat in a box equipped with stimulus, response, and reinforcement apparatus — a Skinner box, in other words. In this particular box there are two stimuli: a red light and green light, and two available responses in the form of levers that the rat can press, one on the left and one on the right. The reinforcement apparatus is a chute down which a pellet of food may be dropped. Ignoring for a moment the question of how the rat first learns to make the right kinds of responses, we shall watch the acquisition of an S-R habit. The rat is at 85 percent of its normal body weight, so it is no surprise that a pellet of food is positive reinforcement. The rat pushes one of the levers when no light is on, and nothing happens. A red light comes on, but it pushes the "wrong" lever, and still nothings happens. Eventually, the rat pushes the "correct" lever when the red light comes on, and it receives positive reinforcement, the reward of a pellet of food. But if it pushes the same lever when the green light comes on, there is, of course, no pellet. Very soon the rat is pushing one lever every time the red light comes on, and the other lever for the green. Quite a complex piece of discriminative behavior has been conditioned. Similar behavior can be conditioned in quite a different way, by negatively reinforcing the animal if the correct response is not made — for example, with a mild electric shock.

The second example reveals a child in a classroom also equipped with stimulus, response, and reinforcement apparatus, but not called a Skinner box. The stimulus apparatus is called a teacher, who asks questions, and the response apparatus is the child's voice. The child is not at 85 percent of normal body weight, but then the child will not be reinforced with pellets of food. The stimulus apparatus holds up a card bearing the word *cat,* and the child responds by gazing mutely out of the window. There is no reinforcement. The child responds by uttering the word "dog". There is no reinforcement. Eventually the child utters the word "cat", and is reinforced: The teacher smiles, or says "Correct" or "Very good" or "Go out and play now," or stops referring to the child sarcastically as a genius, or does something else that is a reinforcer by our operational definition. This increases the probability of the child's saying "cat" when confronted with the printed word *cat.*

The process of setting up the exact kind of behaviour that it is desired to reinforce is known as *shaping.* The term is appropriate; the behaviour is literally molded by a series of *successive approximations.* Consider again the lever-pressing rat, from the moment an untrained animal — "naive" is the felicitous term employed — is first put into the box. The experimenter, to show the rat how it is to be reinforced, drops a pellet of food down the chute into a food tray, and the rat eats and looks for more. The next problem is to get the rat to focus attention on the lever. If the experimenter waited until the rat actually pushed the lever, it might take all day. Instead, the experimenter reinforces the rat for a very rough approximation, namely entering the end of the box at which the levers are situated. Very quickly the rat "learns"[1] that it is reinforced only at that end of the cage, but by then the experimenter reinforces only if the rat comes to the corner where the levers are. The rat concentrates its attention on that particular corner and inevitably bumps against one of the

---

[1] Even with behaviorist theory there is a temptation to put the descriptions into everyday cognitive words like "learns", "thinks", and "decides", although a behaviorist would simply say that the probability of a particular response is increased.

levers, for which again it is reinforced. As soon as the experimenter has got the rate to push the lever, the serious business begins of reinforcing only when the rat pushes the right lever at the right time. The whole process takes an experienced trainer less time to accomplish than to describe. Training a naive rat to lever-press to a particular light or a sound is a five-minute laboratory demonstration. And once the shaping has been accomplished the rest of the training and data collection can be controlled quite automatically, programmed circuits organizing S-R contingencies so that every move by the conditioned animal is inexorably followed by a predetermined consequence.

By an associated process called *chaining*, quite elaborate sequences of behavior can be built up out of small elements. As a rather trivial example, pigeons can be trained to play table tennis. In both shaping and chaining the underlying principle is the same, made quite explicit in the terminology of the behaviorist experimenter: first get one piece of behavior *under control*. Once a system is established by which an organism will respond in order to receive reinforcement, the schedule of reinforcement can be adapted to develop the particular pattern of behavior required. What happens when the rat gets too fat on all those constant pellets of food, or a teacher runs out of rewards for the child? The remarkable fact is that the actual reinforcer comes to play only a minor part in the conditioning process once behavior has been brought under control. In fact the conditioning of really complex behavior is accomplished in the absence of reinforcement. Once reinforcement is expected, the experimenter works on the expectation. Pie in the sky is the most effective reinforcer of all.

In contrast to the behaviorist point of view, cognitive psychologists see human learners as discriminating information-seekers and creative decision-makers rather than as creatures of habit. In the cognitive view reinforcement affects behavior because it is informative; it provides feedback about the consequences of behavior. People scale mountains to see what is on the other side, not from force of habit, and they read for pleasure or to find the answers to questions. People do not permit their experiences or their knowledge to be determined for them by chance or inertia. Even children, as the discussion of language learning has tried to show, are selective and self-directed in their interactions with the world.

There can be no answer to the question of which view is "right", behaviorist or cognitive, because the question is inappropriate. Neither side can produce data that will contradict the other; there is no critical experiment that will decide between the two (Dulany, 1974), since basically they are both trying to make the same evidence explicable though in quite different ways. Rather the question should be which theory is the most useful, which sheds the most light in our efforts to understand various aspects of human behavior. No theory can claim to offer a complete account. I have already contrasted behaviorist and cognitive views of language in Chapter 6. My personal view is that little is added to our understanding of language learning by saying that it is the acquisition of conditioned responses. To suggest that reading is learned by reinforcing the conditioned response "cat" in the presence of the visual stimulus *cat* seems to me to leave out all the interesting as well as many of the difficult issues (F. Smith, in press). A behaviorist approach might be considered more productive as an analysis of *situations* in which learning takes place, or even simply of situations when attention is paid, rather than as an explanation of learning. As a theory of motivation, or at least a description of situations in which pigeons and even people are more or less likely to learn, the relevance of behaviorism may be more easily seen. But then it has to be recognized that reinforcement for humans is far more subtle than it might appear to be for animals. As I have argued in this chapter, human learning provides its own motivation and reward. The problem with extrinsic (or ir-relevant) reinforcers, such as "token" rewards of money, candy, or grades, is that while they may temporarily make learning more probable, their with-drawal is negatively reinforcing and even punishing. When irrelevant rein-forcement is taken away, the desired learning or behavior becomes less probable because it was not acquired for its own sake in the first place (Notz, 1975; Levine and Fasnacht, 1974). For Skinner's own views of learning and teaching, see Skinner (1953, 1968), and for further critiques, McKeachie (1974) and Dember (1974).

Language Development and Other Studies

It may be difficult to see how the behaviorist perspective relates to the self-direction and complexity of a child's early language learning, and indeed there is very little on the topic outside of the wealth of books and articles written from a cognitive (or psycholinguistic) point of view. In addition to references already cited in the main sections of this chapter, important dis-cussions of the way in which meaning is the basis of language learning include Bloom (1973) and Nelson (1973, 1974). Bloom, Rocissano, and Hood (1976) elaborate on the contribution of adult-child dialogs to language learning, and Harper (1975) considers the manner in which children actually control adult behavior to make learning possible. Bruner (1975) argues that the origin of language in children lies in their joint activities with adults, and Tough (1974) is another researcher who stresses that children learn language through use, not through prescription or instruction.

Children do not learn language by imitation, unless imitation is defined very specifically as the deliberate use of adult utterances on particular occa-sions as *models*, when the utterances are in fact already understood. For further discussion of the active and meaningful nature of imitation by chil-dren, and of its utility as a research tool, see Bloom, Hood, and Lightbown (1974) and Slobin and Welsh (1973). Certainly adults do not usually babble (in the infantile sense) yet the roots of meaningful language can be detected in infant babbling (Weir, 1962).

Piaget has not had a great deal to say about children's language learning, but an excellent introduction to Piagetian thought on the topic, emphasizing that it can only be understood by taking into account what a child knows already, is available in Sinclair (1970) and Sinclair-de-Zwart (1972). Additional general references on language learning are given below in the Further Reading.

Important studies of infant learning abilities generally, before they even turn their attention to language, are described by T. Bower (1971, 1974), Fantz (1964, 1966), and by Kagan (1970) and Kagan, Henker, Hen-Tov, Levine, and Lewis (1966). At the other extreme, the importance of meaningfulness in second language learning is discussed by McLaughlin (1977) and by Fillion, Smith, and Swain (1976).

More generally, the notion that the same principles underlie both comprehension and learning has been argued by Greeno (1974) while Haviland and Clark (1974) have demonstrated that the acquisition of new information is an intrinsic part of the comprehension of language.

Further Reading

The classic work on the biological basis of language and language learning is Lenneberg (1967). R. Brown (1973) and McNeill (1970) have already been cited as basic texts on the processes of children's language development; to these should be added Bloom (1970), Chukovsky (1968), Menyuk (1971), and two books with an educational emphasis, Cazden (1972) and Dale (1976). There are also a number of edited volumes containing important original chapters, including Hayes (1970), Moore (1973), Ferguson and Slobin (1973), and F. Smith and Miller (1967). For infant learning see T. Bower (1974), and also the general discussion by Gibson (1969). The more general argument that comprehension and learning are inseparable is in F. Smith (1975).

Notes to Chapter 8, Letter Identification, pp. 99–114

Theories of Pattern Recognition

Problems and theories of pattern recognition are discussed in the texts by Neisser (1967) and Lindsay and Norman (1972); there are more technical expositions in Kolers and Eden (1968) and Selfridge and Neisser (1960). Selfridge has proposed an intriguing "pandemonium" metaphor in which each analyzer is regarded as a "demon" looking out for its own particular feature, with the brain making letter-identification decisions based on the loudness of the combined shouts of recognition of the collective demons for particular letters.

It is not suggested that we have visual analyzers that function solely to collect information about letters of the alphabet. Information used in letter identification is received from analyzers involved in many visual activities, of which those concerned with reading are only a small part. The same analyzers might contribute information in other circumstances to the identification of words, digits, geometric forms, faces, automobiles, or any other set of visual categories, as well as to the apprehension of meaning. The brain makes a variety of specialized uses of very general receptor systems; thus statements can be made about analyzers "looking for" alphabetic features without the implication that a benign destiny has "prewired" mankind to read the alphabet. We all have a "biological inheritance" that enables us to talk and read, to ride bicycles and play the piano, not because of some specific genetic design, but because spoken and written languages, bicycles and pianos, were progressively developed by and for human beings with precisely the biological equipment that humans are born with.

Readers should resist any temptation to figure out what might be the particular features or tests specified in my illustrative feature list. They should not try to deduce what feature should be marked – on Test 1 for "A" and + on Test 1 for "B". The examples are quite arbitrary and imaginary. For an attempt to specify possible features of English letters, see Gibson (1965).

Incidentally, it is just as appropriate to talk about distinctive features of speech as it is to refer to distinctive features of written language. In fact, the feature model for letter identification that was developed in the 1960s was inspired by a feature theory of speech perception published in the 1950s (Jakobson and Halle, 1956). In both theories a physical representation, acoustic or visual, is scanned for distinctive features which are analyzed in terms of feature lists that determine a particular categorization and perceptual experience. The number of physical features requiring to be discriminated will depend upon the perceiver's uncertainty and other sources of information about the language (redundancy) that can be utilized.

Just as the basic elements of the written or printed marks on a page are regarded as distinctive features smaller than letters, so elements smaller than a single sound are conceptualized as distinctive features of speech. Distinctive features of sounds are usually regarded as components of the process by which a phoneme is articulated, such as whether or not a sound is *voiced* (whether the vocal chords vibrate as for /b/, /d/, /g/ compared with /p/, /t/, /k/), whether the sound is *nasal* (like /m/ and /n/), the sound's duration, and the position of the tongue. Each distinctive feature is a significant difference, and the discrimination of any one feature may eliminate many alternatives in the total number of possible sounds (the set of phonemes). Every feature cuts the set of alternatives in a different way, so that theoretically a total of only six distinctive features could be more than enough to distinguish among 40 alternative phonemes ($2^6 = 64$). There are many analogies between the distinctive features of print and those of speech. The total number of different features is presumed to be much smaller than the set of units that they differentiate (26 for letters, about 40 for sounds). The number of features suggested for phonemes is usually 12 or 13 (note again the redundancy). Phonemes can be confused in the same manner as letters, and the more likely two sounds are to be confused with each other, the more distinctive features they are assumed to share. Some sounds, such as /b/ and /d/, which probably differ in only one feature, are more likely to be confused than /b/ and /t/, which differ in perhaps two, and /t/ and /v/ which may differ in three features. Obviously, spoken words may differ by only a single feature just as written words may — "ban and "Dan", which have only a single feature's difference, should be rather more likely to be confused than "ban" and "tan", and much more likely than "tan" and "van"; experimental evidence suggests that assumptions of this kind are correct (Miller and Nicely, 1955).

Many people involved in the complexities of reading tend to think that the identification of spoken words is somehow more spontaneous and instantaneous and wholistic — almost as if the ears detect whole words rather than the patterned soundwaves that the brain has to analyze and interpret. Yet the perception of speech is no less complex and time consuming than that of reading; the sound that we hear is the end product of an information-processing procedure that leads to the identification (the categorization) of a sound or word or meaning prior to the perceptual experience. We rarely "hear" words and then identify them; the identification must precede the hearing, otherwise we would just hear noise. And we do not hear distinctive features of sound any more than we see distinctive features of writing; the unit that we are aware of discriminating is determined by the sense that the brain is able to make, the kind of question that it is asking. Usually we are aware only of meaning for both spoken and written language. Occasionally we may attend to particular words, but only rarely and in special circumstances will we be aware of the surface structure phonemes or letters. The features themselves evade our attention completely.

Making Letter Identification Easier

Letter identification as I have described it in this chapter is not the easiest task for any reader. Asking someone to identify a random letter flashed on a screen or even written on a chalkboard or piece of paper is in fact the most difficult task possible, given a constant size of type, duration of exposure, clarity of view, and so forth. The task is the most difficult in the given physical circumstances because there is no redundancy; the particular letter to be identified could be any one of the 26 alternatives in the alphabet, so the viewer requires a maximum of visual information and has no check if in fact an identification is incorrectly made. Letters are much easier to identify, and to learn, when they come from a smaller set of alternatives, or when they are not equally probable; in other words, when the viewer can make use of redundancy. As I pointed out in the Notes to Chapter 2, there is a marked reduction in the overall uncertainty of letters if they are selected at random from English text rather than drawn from a set of 26 equiprobable alternatives. The viewer can make use of the *distributional* redundancy of English letters if the particular letter to be identified is taken from a preselected point in a book, say the third letter of the fourth word of the seventeenth line of the eightieth page, in which case the nonvisual information that the letter is forty times more likely to be *e* than *z* can be used, with all the other letters ranked between. Distributional redundancy reduces uncertainty from the 4.7 bits for 26 equiprobable letters to about 4.07 bits, the equivalent of about 17 equiprobable alternatives, a considerable saving even without the sequential redundancy that becomes available from other letters or words in a sequence. The sequential redundancy of letters within English words is enormous. If all 26 letters of the alphabet could occur independently in each position of a five-letter word, the number of five-letter words there could be would be $26^5 = 11,881,376$, compared with perhaps 10,000 that actually exist. Even if permissible letter combinations are restricted to alternate consonants and vowels (CVCVC or VCVCV) there would still be a quarter of a million alternatives. And not only is it harder for viewers to identify letters without redundancy cues, it is far less familiar as an activity since the redundancy with which language is permeated is something which every language user capitalizes upon.

The identification of random letters is so uncharacteristic of reading and of so little relevance outside the specialized literature of experimental psychology that I can find no additional references on the topic sufficiently interesting to include under Further Reading, a section that must remain in abeyance for the next chapter or two while the discussion is at such a detailed level.

Notes to Chapter 9, Word Identification, pp. 115–132

Anderson and Dearborn (1952) include a basic discussion of the alternative assumptions underlying most theories of word identification (or more often theories of teaching the identification of words) prior to the development of the feature analytic view. I shall list some theorists whose approach to reading or instruction seems to rest on the belief that letter identification is a necessary step to word identification when "other points of view" are discussed in the Notes to the final chapter.

Letter Identification in Words

There is one type of experiment which might at first sight appear to indicate that words are *not* identified more easily than letters, but which actually provides an additional demonstration that words are indeed processed on a featural basis with the reader making use of sequential redundancy. The experimental method (F. Smith, 1967) involves projecting letters or words at such a low intensity that there is barely any contrast with the screen upon which they are shown, and then to increase the contrast slowly, gradually making more and more visual information available until observers are able to identify the word. Under this procedure the observers are not constrained by time or memory limitations and may choose to make either word or letter identifications with the information available at any moment. They typically identify letters within words before they say what an entire word is, although the entire word may still be identified before any of its letters could be identified in isolation. While this finding is not inconsistent with the classical evidence that words can be identified before any of their component letters in isolation it does make clear that words are, in fact, not recognized all-or-none "as wholes" but by analysis of their parts. The sequential redundancy among features that exists within the word configuration permits identification of the letters on fewer features than would be required if they were presented in isolation. Put in another way, criterial sets of features for words need not include sufficient information in any one position for the unique identification of an individual letter if all sequential redundancy were removed, but when sequential redundancy is present it may facilitate the identification of one or more letters even before the word as a whole can be identified. The letter *h* requires fewer features to identify if presented in the sequence *hat* than if presented alone, even if the reader identifies the *h* before the *at*. The additional information that enables the earlier letter identification to be made in words is based on orthographic redundancy in the spelling of words, reducing the uncertainty of letters from over four bits to less than three (about seven alternatives), as discussed in the Notes to Chapter 3. Even if a reader has not discriminated sufficient features in the second and third positions of the configuration *hat* to identify the letters *at* there is still some featural information available from those positions which, when combined with non-visual information about featural redundancy within words, permits identification of the letter in the first position on minimal visual information.

There is other evidence that although words are identified "as wholes", in the sense that featural information from all parts may be taken into account in their identification, they are by no means identified on the basis of the familiarity of their shape or contour. Examples were given earlier in this chapter of the ease with which quite unfamiliar configurations like rEaDiNg and HoRsE would be read. Entire passages printed in these peculiar configurations can be read about as fast as normal text (F. Smith, Lott, and Cronnell, 1969). In fact if the size of the capital letters is reduced slightly so that they do not interfere with the discriminability of the lower case letters, for example rEaDiNg, then there is no difference at all between the rates at which such words and normal text are read. The result is perhaps not surprising when we reflect upon the ease with which practiced readers can adapt to quite distorted forms of typography or handwriting. Indeed, the facility with which we can read passages of handwriting when individual letters and even words would be indecipherable is further evidence that reading does not depend upon letter identification.

It is obviously a gross oversimplification to talk about the relative "discriminability" of different letters of the alphabet or to assume that letters that are difficult to identify when standing alone must be difficult to perceive when in words.[1] The criterial features of letters are not a fixed and immutable set. The amount of visual information required to identify a letter has relatively little to do with the physical characteristics of the actual stimulus but depends much more on the reader's experience and the context in which the letter occurs. And precisely the same kind of argument applies to words. Children learning to read can often identify words in context that they cannot identify in isolation (Pearson and Studt, 1975). It is misleading to talk of children's word identification ability in terms of their "sight vocabulary" or word attack skills.

There is an extensive technical literature on the identification of letters in words, including Reicher (1969), Wheeler (1970), Meyer and Schvaneveldt (1971), Rumelhart and Siple (1974), Johnson (1975), and Cosky (1976). Brand (1971) shows that distinctions can be made between letters and digits without the identification of specific letters or digits (underlining the featural aspect of identification), and an article subtitled "Seek not and ye shall find" (Johnston and McClelland, 1974) describes how letters can sometimes be more easily identified in words if they are not specifically looked for. Further arguments for the priority of words over letters (and of meaning over individual words) are in Kolers (1970) and F. Smith and Holmes (1971).

Use of Redundancy by Children

There is no evidence that children need to be trained to seek or use redundancy in any way; indeed, part of the argument of this book is that all of perception depends upon the use of prior knowledge and that the youngest of children demonstrate ability to limit uncertainty by eliminating unlikely alternatives in advance. Studies with young readers have found ability to use sequential redundancy very early (Lott and Smith, 1970). First-grade children who had had a limited amount of reading instruction in kindergarten were shown letters in isolation and in simple three-letter words that they could normally identify easily. The children showed themselves able to identify letters in words on less visual information than when they were presented alone. For children in fourth grade the difference between the information on which letters were identified in words and that on which the same letters were identified in isolation was equal to that of skilled adult readers, indicating that for familiar three-letter words at least, fourth-graders could make as much use of sequential featural redundancy as adults. Krueger, Keen, and Rublevich (1974) subsequently confirmed that fourth-grade children may be as good as adults in making use of redundancy among letter sequences in words and nonwords.

---

[1]This argument applies especially to the question of "reversals" of letter pairs like *b* and *d*, which are particularly bothersome to some children (and teachers). Reversals are specifically considered in Chapter 12.

Distributional Redundancy among Words

The sequential redundancy that exists among words in text — which has a critical role in making reading possible — will be discussed in later chapters. But there is also a distributional redundancy among words, reflecting the obvious fact that some words are used far more often than others. The distributional redundancy of English words has not been formally calculated, but is probably related to the maximum theoretical uncertainty of between fifteen and sixteen bits for a set of about fifty thousand alternatives and the actual twelve bit uncertainty of isolated words computed by Shannon (1951) and discussed in the Notes to Chapter 3. Distributional redundancy among words complicates experimental studies of word identification because more frequent words are usually identified faster, more accurately, and on less visual information than less frequent words. The precise reason for this "word frequency effect" is itself the subject of a long and inconclusive debate in the technical literature (Howes and Solomon, 1951; Broadbent, 1967). The standard reference for relative word frequencies has long been the list of Thorndike and Lorge (1944) with a more recent compilation by Carroll, Davies, and Richman (1971).

Notes to Chapter 10, Phonics — and Mediated Word Identification, pp. 133–150

The Relevance of Phonics

The analysis I have given of the relationship between the spelling of written words and the sounds of speech is mainly derived from the work of a group of researchers (Berdiansky, Cronnell, and Koehler, 1969) associated with the Southwest Regional Laboratory (SWRL), an influential federally sponsored research and development center in California. SWRL researchers have not only endeavored to analyse the maze of spelling-to-sound correspondences in English, based largely on the work of Venezky (1967, 1970), but also begun to devise instructional programs to teach these correspondences to children, both native speakers and others, in the expectation that it will make them better readers and spellers. The ten-year history of this enterprise is recorded in a number of technical reports published by SWRL.

   The relevance of phonics instruction is the topic of a frequently cited volume by Chall (1967) entitled *Learning To Read: The Great Debate*, although her discussion is more about how reading is taught than how it is learned, and the conclusions may not be thought to follow inevitably from the evidence presented. On the other hand, Carol Chomsky (1970), drawing extensively from her own experience and from the theorizing of Noam Chomsky (N. Chomsky and Halle, 1968), argues that spelling does not so much represent sound as the underlying meaning structure of language. C. Chomsky (1971) recommends an early introduction to writing, not because it has anything directly to do with reading, but because it may help beginning readers make sense of phonics instruction. This view should not be confused with the occasional argument that children must be taught phonics to learn how to spell. In the first place, spelling has very little to do with reading, many good readers are poor spellers. And in the second place, children who spell words the way they are pronounced, as most children do at the beginning (Read, 1971), spell poorly. Spelling by rule is not an efficient strategy for spelling most common words (H. Brown, 1970). Although clues may be obtained from known words with similar meanings, the main requirement for good spelling is to *remember* individual spellings, a requirement that is not relevant to reading and which may, if allowed to, complicate learning to read. Gillooly (1973) argues that there is no justification for attempts to change the current spelling of English, which he says increases reading speed and is nearly optimum for learning to read. Further discussion about the relation of spelling to reading and writing is included in Chapters 6 and 10 of F. Smith (1973). Baron (1973) has demonstrated experimentally that decoding to sound is not necessary for comprehension, and conversely Calfee, Arnold, and Drum (1976) have disputed the frequent but undocumented assertion that it is possible for children to "decode" in the absence of comprehension.

A small but noteworthy controversy has developed out of a demonstration by Rozin, Poritsky, and Sotsky (1971) that poor readers who failed to learn through conventional phonics instruction could succeed when the Chinese characters for English meanings were substituted for the English spelling. After showing clearly that readers could extract meaning directly from written text, without the mediation of phonics, the authors rather remarkably concluded that reading would therefore best be taught by a syllabic method. Gleitman and Rozin (1973a) elaborated upon this notion of teaching reading through a syllabary, and responded vehemently (Gleitman and Rozin, 1973b) when Goodman (1973) commented that their proposal seemed to him to be another easy way to make learning to read difficult. The latter three articles are all contained in one lively issue of *Reading Research Quarterly*. On the relative ease with which children can learn to read in nonalphabetic written language, see also Makita (1968, 1976) for research with Japanese children.

Further Reading

The classic book on writing systems is Gelb (1963), although it reflects an occidental bias for crediting the Greeks with the sole discovery of an alphabet. A good case can also be made for the independent and alphabetic Sanskrit writing system devised about 3000 B.C. It all depends on whether you want to say that an alphabet must have vowel symbols that are separate from but equal to those for consonants. More recently, see Vachek (1973) for a discussion of writing systems.

Notes to Chapter 11, The Identification of Meaning, pp. 151–174

Effect of Meaningful Context

Meaningfulness clearly has a substantial role in facilitating the identification of words in reading, reducing their uncertainty from at least twelve bits (the equivalent of 4096 equiprobable alternatives) for words in isolation to fewer than eight bits (256 alternatives) for words in context (Chapter 3 Notes). It is really irrelevant to talk of letters at this stage — letters are not usually a concern when meaningful text is read. But as a yardstick, it is interesting to recall from the Chapter 3 discussion of the Cattell (1885) experiment that the uncertainty of letters falls from 4.7 bits to scarcely one bit when context is meaningful, enabling the brain to perceive four times as much of a line of print. Not only can twice as many words be identified in a single glance when they are in a meaningful context, thus overcoming bottlenecks of information-processing and memory, but problems of ambiguity and the gulf between surface structure and meaning are removed by the prior elimination from consideration of unlikely alternatives. Context has its effect not because it exists but because it can be *meaningful* and contribute information that reduces the uncertainty of individual words through sequential redundancy. It is important to be clear about the effect of context. Context places constraints on what each individual word might be.[1] These constraints constitute sequential redundancy, usable only if it is reflected in prior knowledge, or nonvisual information, that the reader can bring to bear. That is why I stress that context must be *meaningful,* with all the relative connotations of that word. If a particular context is not comprehensible to a reader, or if for one reason or another the reader is reluctant to take advantage of the redundancy and reduce the amount of visual information required for any aspect of reading, then the context might just as well be nonsense, a random arrangement of marks on the page.

Meaningful context as I have been using the term exercises its constraints on word occurrence in two ways, syntactic and semantic. These are two types of restriction upon the particular words an author can select — or a reader predict — at any time. (There are other constraints upon authors, such as the limited set of words a reader might be expected to understand.) Choice of words is always limited by what we want to say (semantics) and how we want to say it (syntax). I have not tried to separate the effects of syntax and semantics in this discussion for the simple reason that I have not found a good way to do so. The theoretical analysis of Chapter 6 argued that the two are inseparable; that without meaning it is pointless to talk about grammar. Triesman (1965) attempted to unravel the two experimentally and concluded that in normal language the syntactic component is subordinate to the semantic.

There is no shortage of research demonstrating the powerful facilitatory effect of meaningful context on word identification. Indeed, there is no evidence to the contrary. But before I begin to cite this research, a fundamental

---

[1]The present concern is with *language* context, the body of words in a text. But as I outlined in Chapter 7, words can also be constrained by more general *situational* contexts; for example there is a very small and highly predictable set of alternative words likely to occur on a toothpaste tube. There is also an important context in the receiver's expectations. As Olson (1970) has pointed out, words are selected and get meaning from what the listener or reader needs to know.

point must be reiterated: *Reading does not usually involve or rely upon word identification.* Banal though it may sound, the basic point about meaningful context is that it makes reading for meaning possible and word identification unnecessary. The fact that meaningful context makes individual words easier to identify is basically as irrelevant as the fact that individual letters are easier to identify in words; the research evidence is merely a demonstration of the effect of meaningful context. Even when reading aloud is involved, so that the accurate identification of words is required, the prior apprehension of meaning is an important prerequisite. Reading aloud is difficult if prior comprehension is limited, and if word identification is given priority there will be interference with comprehension (Howe and Singer, 1975).

In addition to the Tulving and Gold (1963) study used in this chapter as an example of how context facilitates word identification, see Morton (1964), Klein and Klein (1973), E. Smith and Spoehr (1974), and, for a summary of all the arguments of the preceding four chapters, Smith and Holmes (1971). In related studies demonstrating the effect of meaningfulness, Rothkopf and Coatney (1974) show that reading rate is determined by the reader's expectations of information in the text, and Rothkopf and Billington (1974) that comprehension is improved when answers to specific questions are sought and found. Carpenter and Just (1975, 1977) examine how reading normally involves the integration of new contextual information with what is already known (again showing that learning and comprehension are inseparable). Cohen (1970) provides a rare experimental demonstration that meaning can be sought without the identification of individual words. In a task involving a search through word lists, it took no longer to find an example of a category (such as "any flower") than to find a specific word in that category (such as *daisy*). Search tasks of this kind basically require rejecting irrelevant items on the list (much as we quickly dispose of names we are *not* looking for in a telephone directory) and show that it is not necessary to identify a word specifically to decide that it does not fall into a particular category (set of alternatives) in which we are interested. Lefton and Fisher (1976) have demonstrated that meaning is so prepotent that it will interfere with a search in which meaning is actually irrelevant. Neisser (1967) has an extensive discussion of such search tasks and the light they throw on visual decision-making. In a study entitled "Meaning in Visual Search" that is *not* about reading, Potter (1975) reports that viewers recognize pictures as accurately and almost as fast when all they know in advance is the "meaning" (given by a name or title, such as "a boat") as when they have already seen the picture itself. McNeill and Lindig (1973) show that context effects exist with spoken language just as with written (see also Miller, Heise, and Lichten, 1951). For a discussion of the relation between eye movements and comprehension, see Kolers (1976). It should not be surprising that the particular order and location of fixations is not a particularly good guide to how the reader comprehends text, especially as reading rate increases and a broader expanse of visual information is dealt with at one time. (Similarly the intermittent manner in which we flick our gaze around a room is not particularly suggestive of the stable perception of the room that the brain constructs.)

Use of contextual information to identify words deleted completely from text is the basis of the *Cloze test* (W. Taylor, 1957; Neville and Pugh, 1976–77), frequently employed to estimate the comprehensibility of a passage or the comprehension of a reader (although it is theoretically indefensible to expect any book to be equally readable to more than a few readers or to summarize the ability of any reader in a single score). The text in a Cloze test has words deleted at certain regular or systematic intervals, for example:

> A moth's ears are located _____ the sides of the rear _____ part of its thorax and _____ directed outward and backward into _____ constriction that separates the thorax _____ the abdomen. Each ear is _____ externally visible as a small _____, and within the cavity is _____ transparent eardrum.

Suppose six passages of this kind are presented to ten readers who are asked to fill in as many spaces as they can, scoring as a correct response every guess that coincides with the word that was actually deleted from a space. One way of interpreting a high score for a particular space would be that there are very few alternative words that could be put in that position — the uncertainty is low. And the only reason that uncertainty is low in that position is that most of the alternative words have been eliminated by information acquired from other parts of the passage, from the words that have not been removed. Passages that get a relatively large number of missing words correctly replaced may therefore be regarded as more easily comprehensible than those whose spaces are more dubious; thus this type of score is sometimes interpreted as a measure of the "intelligibility" or "readability" of a passage. On the other hand, a reader who succeeds in completing correctly a relatively large number of missing words might be regarded as one who is able to make greater use of the redundancy in the passage and who therefore comprehends it more. The Cloze test demonstrates that meaning is not something that suddenly appears when we have read to the end of a sequence of words, nor does it accumulate word by word from left to right across the page. Some clues to every deleted word in the example would be lost if all the words coming after the gap were removed. Indeed, a good strategy on any occasion when difficulty is encountered in comprehending print is to read further ahead instead of immediately going back to reread whatever preceded the troublesome passage.

Learners and Context

A variety of studies have demonstrated the readiness of children to make use of context in early reading (if they are so permitted), for example Klein, Klein, and Bertino (1974), Golinkoff (1975–76), and Doehring (1976). Rosinski, Golinkoff, and Kukish (1975) conclude that meaning is irresistible to children; it can interfere with performance on a task because they cannot ignore it. Such studies also tend to show that use of context and reading ability increase together. This correlation is often attributed to the fact that better readers can make more use of context; less often the possibility is considered that use of context makes better readers. For the relation between ability and use of context see also Clay and Imlach (1971) and Samuels, Begy, and Chen

(1975–1976). For analyses of children's errors, what Goodman calls "windows on the reading process", see Goodman (1965, 1969), Weber (1968), and Clay (1969). Studies of children's misreadings tend to highlight the important fact that many of the errors, especially those made by better readers, preserve the meaning of the context, and also that errors which make a difference to meaning are often subsequently corrected by children who are reading for meaning (and therefore are not errors that need be a great cause for concern). Children who read more literally, perhaps because of an emphasis on "accuracy" during instruction, may however make nonsensical errors without being aware of them.

The paradigm example of a child learning to read by meaning alone, without any possibility of decoding to sound, must be that of Helen Keller. Henderson (1976) reports the case of a deaf child who learned to recognize 4400 printed words in nine months at the age of six by relating them to manual signs in a meaningful context, basically in response to the child's own spontaneous questions.

Global and Focal Predictions

Several linguists have proposed that every sentence in a meaningful context contains some information that is old and some new. Chafe (1970) refers to information carried from one sentence to another as "foregrounding"; see also Halliday (1970), Bates (1976), and the Carpenter and Just (1977) chapter already cited. G. Bower (1976) observes that stories have a predictable structure at both general thematic and more specific episodic levels, and that children learn and use this structure in reading stories.

Further Reading

The discussion of reading has now become very general and suggestions for further sources are more appropriately consolidated with those of the final summary chapter which comes next.

Notes to Chapter 12, Reading — and Learning To Read, pp. 175–195

Learning To Read

Two important books on how young children learn to read, each with its own instructional predeliction, are Durkin (1966) and Clark (1976). Research on how children learn to read rarely remains uncontaminated by the influence that prior instruction has already had on them. Barr (1972, 1974) has written basic papers on the effect of instruction of children's reading strategies. Downing and Oliver (1974), Meltzer and Herse (1969), and Jenkins, Bausel, and Jenkins (1972) all report on the relevance of certain aspects of early reading instruction to children, while Pearson (1974) notes that comprehensibility is not improved in early reading books by fragmenting sentences and reducing grammatical complexity. Holdaway (1976) comments on the importance of self-correction for children learning to read and on the risk that some instructional techniques will take this responsibility away from the child. F. Smith (1977a) elaborates on some of the points made in this chapter about the relevance of reading instruction, and F. Smith and Goodman (1971) argue that psycholinguistic analysis of reading should never become the basis of a "psycholinguistic method" of teaching reading.

Of the allocation of blame for children's failure to learn to read there is no end. Guthrie (1973) offers one of many surveys of various systems for characterizing the disabilities of children who seem unable to capitalize on the resources available to modern reading pedagogy. Such children are frequently labeled "learning disabled", a diagnosis that is vigorously criticized by Glenn (1975) and Hart (1976). Serafica and Sigel (1970) note that some "reading disabled" children have superior visual discrimination to normal readers.

Carroll and Chall (1975) edited a report of the Committee on Reading of the U.S. National Institute of Education, discussing the research that was available or required to take advantage of modern technology and produce universal literacy. In a review of the Carroll and Chall book, D. Olson (1975) notes that not one of the contributing researchers queried the underlying assumption that technology could eradicate illiteracy.

Uses of Language

For general discussions about the context of language and its uses, see Wilkinson (1971), Halliday (1973), D.Olson (1972), and F. Smith (1977b). For discussions of the consequences of writing systems and literacy, see Havelock (1976), Goody and Watts (1972), and D. Olson (1977).

Further Reading

Authors never have the last word. The further reading which I suggest, and other sources which readers will doubtless find for themselves, will frequently represent divergent points of view, even those which I have cited for evidence or arguments supporting particular points that I have tried to make. I cannot of course counter every alternative argument in advance, but I can perhaps mute a little of their thunder by underlining where I think significant differences often lie. They are simply stated. From an *educational* point of view the argument will be met that my analysis must be wrong because phonics works. Reading must be a matter of decoding to sound because children who receive phonics instruction learn to read. The problem here seems to me to be one of different domains of discourse; we are not talking about the same thing. When I reject the decoding view of reading it is because I am talking about what I consider to be indisputable *facts* of reading, that spelling-to-sound correspondences cannot possibly be the basis of reading or learning to read because they do not translate print into comprehensible speech. The opposing point of view is concerned with a *strategy* of teaching, and just as a theoretical analysis cannot prove that an instructional method does not work, so the perceived success of an instructional method cannot disprove a theoretical analysis. Instructional methods may succeed for a variety of reasons, and children and teachers may succeed despite the method. Since no instructional method occupies all a child's waking hours — and "eclecticism" is a contemporary virtue — there is always the possibility of something else going on from which a child can in fact learn something useful about reading. Occasionally it is argued that phonics may not be necessary for fluent readers, but that it is still required when children learn to read, especially by those having difficulties. My position is exactly the reverse; that only good readers can make sense of spelling-to-sound correspondences, and that the more difficulty a child experiences in learning to read, the more the child needs meaningful reading experience. From the *psychological* point of view a common objection is that meaning is far too vague or impractical a concept on which to construct a theory of reading, which must begin with letter identification and be totally explicable in a purely reflex or programmatic fashion. I have characterized this approach to reading as "outside-in" as opposed to meaning-based views like my own which are "inside-out" (F. Smith, in press), and suggested that the preponderance of the outside-in perspective in both research and instruction is because it leads to more easily controlled and replicable experiments and to more structured and accountable instructional programs — the kinds of consideration that keep scientists and educators professionally respectable. But if science restricts consideration to questions that are amenable to experimental procedures, and educators and the world in general are persuaded that these questions are the only ones that have any significance, then a large number of important issues will be overlooked. The fact that there are theoretical problems of meaningfulness which do not lend themselves to anything but the most trivial kind of experimental study does not mean that meaning can be ignored or have its relevance minimized.

A typical alternative approach to both theory and instruction is that of Venezky (1976), who states explicitly at the outset of his book that "reading is the translation from writing to a form of language from which the reader is already able to derive meaning", an assertion for which I think there is no evidence and which is probably untestable. Kavanagh and Mattingly (1972) present a collection of papers on various aspects of reading and language generally, most of them from an outside-in point of view. Outstanding among such papers is one by Gough (1972), entitled "One Second of Reading" (which is as much of the process that is considered). Gough asserts that reading must progress from letters through sounds to words and finally meaning, and presents an elaborate diagram of these stages. But the arrows on the flowchart come to a theoretical full stop at comprehension, which is relegated to a mystical area of the brain called TPWSGWTAU (the place where sentences go when they are understood) presided over by a magician named Merlin. Gibson and Levin (1975) have put together a substantial compilation of research data and theorizations about reading and reading instruction; their book has received a critical review from Calfee, Arnold, and Drum (1976).

Chall (1967) has already been cited for her review of instructional methods leading to a decoding conclusion, and Samuels (1976, also LaBerge and Samuels, 1974) has consistently argued for a "subskills" approach to instruction, based on the notion that decoding is a central part of reading, although it becomes so rapid and automatic that it is not in fact detectable in any way. Atkinson (1974) exemplifies the not uncommon view that computers can teach children to read, even though the objectives are currently rather limited and the theory of reading underlying such programs is rarely evident or adequate.

On the other hand, Huey (1908) speaks such common and scientific sense about reading (despite some rather dated anxieties about the "hygiene" of certain reading habits) that many theorists, including the present author, have been tempted to claim him as an intellectual predecessor. For histories of research on reading and reading instruction see Venezky (1977), Mathews (1966), and Davies (1973). For comparative surveys of approaches to reading in different countries see Downing (1973) and Gray (1956). The Russian view, very much outside-in, is provided by Elkonin in Downing (1973), while Sakamoto (1976) discusses reading in Japan. Edited volumes covering various points of view include Singer and Ruddell (1976), Merritt (1976), Resnick and Weaver (in press), and F. Smith (1973). There are several chapters on reading in a two-volume international compendium on language generally, edited by Lenneberg and Lenneberg (1975).

Reading is widely a matter of national concern. In the United States a number of panel reports to a National Institute of Education conference on studies in reading have been published since 1974, outlining programs of research on such topics as semantics and learning and motivation; see especially Miller (1974). In the United Kingdom current opinions on reading and reading instruction are presented and argued in the "Bullock Report" (Bullock, 1975).

GLOSSARY

This list does not attempt to define words as a dictionary does, but rather indicates the general way that certain terms are employed in this book. Figures in parentheses indicate the chapter in which a term was first used or primarily discussed. Terms in *italics* themselves appear elsewhere in the Glossary.

Cat and dog problem: The fact that *distinctive features* cannot be explicitly taught but must be learned by the testing of *hypotheses* (7).

Category interrelationships: The various ways in which *cognitive categories* can be combined as a basis for *prediction* or action (5).

Channel capacity: Limit to the *information* that can pass through any part of an information-processing system (2).

Cognition: A particular organization of knowledge in the brain, or the process of organizing such knowledge (5). See *cognitive structure*.

Cognitive categories: Prior decisions to treat some aspects of experience as the same, yet as different from other aspects of experience; the constantly developing framework of *cognitive structure* (5).

Cognitive questions: The specific information sought by the brain to make a decision among alternatives; the range of a *prediction* (5).

Cognitive structure: The totality of the brain's organization of knowledge; everything an individual knows (or believes) about the world. Comprises *cognitive categories, feature lists,* and *category interrelationships.* Also referred to as *long-term memory* and the *theory of the world in the head* (5).

Comprehension: The interpretation of experience; relating new information to what is already known; finding answers to *cognitive questions* (5).

Constraint: A limitation that excludes or makes less probable certain alternatives; the mechanism of *redundancy* (11).

Context: The setting, physical or linguistic, in which words occur and which places constraints on the range of alternatives that these words might be (11).

Criterial set: A set of *distinctive features* within a *feature list* that permits an *identification* to be made on minimal information from a given set of alternatives (9).

Criterion level: The amount of information an individual requires to make a particular decision, varying with the perceived uncertainty of the situation and the perceived risk and cost of making a mistake (2).

Decoding to sound: The view that reading is accomplished by transforming print into actual or subvocalized (implicit) speech through the exercise of *spelling-to-sound correspondences* (10).

Deep structure: The meaningful aspect of language; the interpretation of *surface structure* (6).

Distinctive features: *Significant differences* among visual (or acoustic) patterns, i.e., differences that make a difference. For reading, any aspect of *visual information* that permits distinctions to be made among alternative letters, words, or meanings (2, 5, 8). See also *feature lists*.

Distributional redundancy: Reduction of *uncertainty* because alternatives are not equally probable (8, 9). May exist in letters or words (and, if an individual's mannerisms are sufficiently well-known, expressions). See also *featural redundancy*.

Featural redundancy: In reading, *redundancy* among the *distinctive features* of print as a consequence of constraints upon letter or word occurrence (8, 9).

Feature analysis: A theory of pattern recognition proposing that visual configurations such as digits, letters, or words are identified by the analysis of *distinctive features* and their allocation to *feature lists;* in contrast to *template theory* (8).

Feature list: A cognitive specification or "set of rules" for particular combinations of *distinctive features* that will permit *identification* in reading (8).

Feedback: Information that permits a decision whether an *hypothesis* is right or wrong (appropriate or inappropriate) in *learning* (7).

Fixation: The pause for the selection of *visual information* as the gaze rests at one place in the text between *saccades* (3).

Functional equivalence: Specification of the same *cognitive category* by two or more *feature lists* (9).

Grammar: See *syntax.*

Grapheme: A letter of the alphabet, one of 26 alternatives (10).

Hypothesis: A tentative modification of cognitive structure (*cognitive categories, feature lists,* or *category interrelationships*) that is tested as a basis for *learning* (7).

Identification: In reading, a cognitive decision among letter, word, or meaning alternatives based on the analysis of selected *visual information* in print (8–11).

Immediate meaning identification: The *comprehension* of language without the prior identification of words (11).

Immediate word identification: The *identification* of a word on sight, without *information* from another person and without the prior *identification* of letters or letter combinations within the word (9).

Information: Any property of the physical environment that reduces *uncertainty,* eliminating or reducing the probability of alternatives among which a perceiver must decide (2).

Learning: The modification or elaboration of *cognitive structure,* specifically the establishment of new or revised *cognitive categories, category interrelationships,* or *feature lists* (7).

Letter-sound correspondence: See *spelling-to-sound correspondence.*

Long-term memory: The totality of an individual's knowledge and beliefs about the world, including summaries of past experience in the world and ways of interacting with it (4).

Meaning: A relative term; the interpretation that a reader places upon text (the answer to a *cognitive question*). Alternatively, the interpretation an author or third party expects a reader to place upon text. The consequence of *comprehension* (5).

Mediated meaning identification: An inferior alternative to *immediate meaning identification,* attempting to derive meaning by the prior identification of words (11).

Mediated word identification: A less efficient alternative to *immediate word identification,* requiring information from letters or letter combinations within the word (10).

Memory: See *sensory store, short-term memory,* and *long-term memory.*

Noise: A signal that conveys no information (2).

Nonvisual information: Prior knowledge "behind the eyes" that reduces *uncertainty* in advance and permits *identification* decisions with less *visual information* (1).

Orthography: Spelling; the arrangement of letters in words (10).

Perception: *Identification* decisions made by the brain; subjective awareness of these decisions (3).

Phoneme: One of about 40 discriminable classes of *significantly different* speech sounds in English (10).

Phonetics: The scientific study of the sound structure of speech; has nothing to do with reading (10). See *phonics*.

Phonics: Reading instruction based on the assumption that reading is decoding to sound and requires learning *spelling-to-sound correspondences* (10). Sometimes mistakenly referred to as *phonetics*.

Prediction: The prior elimination of unlikely alternatives; the remaining set of alternatives among which an *identification* decision will be made from (in reading) selected *visual information* from print (5).

Psycholinguistics: An area of common concern in psychology and linguistics studying how individuals learn and use language.

Redundancy: *Information* that is available from more than one source. In reading, may be present in the *visual information* of print, in the *orthography*, the *syntax*, the *meaning*, or in combinations of these sources. Redundancy may be *distributional* or *sequential*. Redundancy must always reflect *nonvisual information;* prior knowledge on the part of the reader permits redundancy to be used (2).

Regression: An eye movement (*saccade*) from right to left along a line or from bottom to top of a page (3).

Saccade: Movement of the eyes as the gaze moves from one *fixation* to another in reading (3).

Semantics: The meaningful aspect of language; the study of this aspect (6).

Sensory store: In vision, the very brief retention of *visual information* while *identification* decisions are made; also called the *visual image* (4).

Sequential redundancy: Reduction of *uncertainty* attributable to *constraints* on the number or relative probability of likely alternatives in *context* (9, 11); may exist among letters or words and as a consequence of a reader's or listener's expectations. See also *featural redundancy*.

Short-term memory: The limited and constantly changing content of what is attended to at any particular moment (4).

Significant difference: A difference in the physical properties of an event that forms the basis of an *identification* decision (7).

Spelling-to-sound correspondence: The co-occurrence of a particular letter or group of letters in a written word and the assumed sound of the same part of the word in speech (10).

Surface structure: The physical properties of language; for reading — *visual information* (6).

Syntax: The manner in which words are organized in meaningful language; also referred to as "grammar" (6).

Tachistoscope: A projector or other viewing device with a shutter or timer controlling the presentation of *visual information* for brief periods of time (3).

Template theory: A theory of pattern recognition that visual configurations such as digits, letters, or words can be identified by comparison with prestored representations or templates in the brain of the range of alternative configurations; in contrast to *featural analysis* (8).

Text: A meaningful (or potentially meaningful) instance of written language; can range from a phrase to an entire book.

Theory: In science, a summary of a scientist's past experience, the basis for interpreting new experience and for predicting future events (5).

Theory of the world in the head: The brain's *theory;* also known as *cognitive structure* and *long-term memory* (5).

Uncertainty: The amount of *information* required to make an *identification* decision, determined by the number of alternative decisions that could be made, the perceived probability of each alternative, and the individual's *criterion level* for making the decision (2).

Visual image: See *sensory store.*

Visual information: In reading, *information* that is available to the brain through the eyes from the *surface structure* of print, e.g., from the inkmarks on a page (1).

REFERENCES

Anderson, John R. and Gordon H. Bower, *Human Associative Memory* (Washington, D.C.: Winston, 1973).

Anderson, I. H. and W. F. Dearborn, *The Psychology of Teaching Reading* (New York: Ronald, 1952).

Atkinson, Richard C., Teaching children to read using a computer, *American Psychologist*, 1974, *29*, 169–178.

Attneave, Fred, *Applications of Information Theory to Psychology* (New York: Holt, Rinehart and Winston, 1959).

Attneave, Fred, How do you know? *American Psychologist*, 1974, *29*, 493–499.

Averbach, E. and A. S. Coriell, Short-term memory in vision, *Bell Systems Technical Journal*, 1961, *40*, 309–328.

Bach, Emmon and R. T. Harms (eds.), *Universals of Linguistic Theory* (New York: Holt, Rinehart and Winston, 1968).

Baddeley, A. D. and Karalyn Patterson, The relation between long-term and short-term memory, *British Medical Bulletin*, 1971, *27*, 3, 237–242.

Baer, Donald M. and John C. Wright, Developmental psychology, in Mark A. Rosenzweig and Lyman W. Porter (eds.), *Annual Review of Psychology*, 1975, *25*, 1–82.

Barclay, J. R., The role of comprehension in remembering sentences, *Cognitive Psychology*, 1973, *4*, 229–252.

Baron, Jonathon, Phonemic stage not necessary for reading, *Quarterly Journal of Experimental Psychology*, 1973, *15*, 241–246.

Barr, Rebecca C., The influence of instructional conditions on word recognition errors, *Reading Research Quarterly,* 1972, *7,* 509–529.

Barr, Rebecca C., The effect of instruction on pupil reading strategies, *Reading Research Quarterly,* 1974, *10,* 555–582.

Bartlett, Frederick C., *Remembering: A Study in Experimental and Social Psychology* (London: Cambridge University Press, 1932).

Bates, Elizabeth, *Language and Context* (New York: Academic Press, 1976).

Berdiansky, Betty, Bruce Cronnell, and John A. Koehler, *Spelling-Sound Relations and Primary Form-Class Descriptions for Speech-Comprehension Vocabularies of 6–9 Year-Olds,* Southwest Regional Laboratory for Educational Research and Development, Technical Report No. 15, 1969.

Bloom, Lois, *Language Development: Form and Function in Emerging Grammars* (Cambridge, Mass.: M.I.T. Press, 1970).

Bloom, Lois, *One Word at a Time: The Use of Single Word Utterances Before Syntax* (The Hague: Mouton, 1973).

Bloom, Lois, Lois Hood, and Patsy Lightbown, Imitation in language development: If, when, and why, *Cognitive Psychology,* 1974, *6,* 380–420.

Bloom, Lois, Lorraine Rocissano, and Lois Hood, Adult-child discourse: Developmental interaction between information processing and linguistic knowledge, *Cognitive Psychology,* 1976, *8,* 521–552.

Bower, Gordon H., Experiments on story understanding and recall, *Quarterly Journal of Experimental Psychology,* 1976, *28,* 511–534.

Bower, Thomas G. R., The object in the world of the infant, *Scientific American,* 1971, *225,* 30–47.

Bower, Thomas G. R., *Development in Infancy* (San Francisco: Freeman, 1974).

Brand, H., Classification without identification in visual search, *Quarterly Journal of Experimental Psychology,* 1971, *23,* 178–86.

Bransford, John D., J. R. Barclay, and Jeffrey J. Franks, Sentence meaning: A constructivist vs. interpretive approach, *Cognitive Psychology,* 1972, *3,* 193–209.

Bransford, John D. and Jeffrey J. Franks, The abstraction of linguistic ideas, *Cognitive Psychology,* 1971, *2,* 331, 350.

Brooks, Lee, Spatial and verbal components of the act of recall, *Canadian Journal of Psychology,* 1968, *22,* 349–368.

Broadbent, Donald E., The word-frequency effect and response bias, *Psychological Review,* 1967, *74,* 1–15.

Brown, H. D., Categories of spelling difficulty in speakers of English as a first and second language, *Journal of Verbal Learning and Verbal Behavior,* 1970, *9,* 232–236.

Brown, Roger, How shall a thing be called? *Psychological Review,* 1958, *65,* 1, 14–21.

Brown, Roger, *Psycholinguistics* (New York: Free Press, 1970).

Brown, Roger, *A First Language: The Early Stages* (Cambridge, Mass.: Harvard University Press, 1973).

Brown, Roger and David McNeill, The "tip of the tongue" phenomenon, *Journal of Verbal Learning and Verbal Behavior,* 1966, *5,* 4, 325–337.

Bruner, Jerome S., On perceptual readiness, *Psychological Review,* 1957, *64,* 123–152.

Bruner, Jerome S., *Beyond the Information Given* (collected papers) (New York: Norton, 1973).

Bruner, Jerome S., The ontogenesis of speech acts, *Journal of Child Language,* 1975, *2,* 1–19.

Bruner, Jerome S. and D. O'Dowd, A note of the informativeness of parts of words, *Language and Speech,* 1958, *1,* 98–101.

Bullock, Alan (chairman, U.K. Department of Science and Education Committee of Enquiry), *A Language for Life* ("The Bullock Report") (London: Her Majesty's Stationery Office, 1975).

Calfee, Robert C., Memory and cognitive skills in reading acquisition, in Drake D. Duane and Margaret B. Rawson (eds.), *Reading, Perception and Language* (Baltimore: York Press, 1974).

Calfee, Robert C., *Human Experimental Psychology* (New York: Holt, Rinehart and Winston, 1975).

Calfee, Robert C., Richard Arnold, and Priscilla Drum, Review of *The Psychology of Reading* (by Eleanor Gibson and Harry Levin), in *Proceedings of the National Academy of Education,* 1976, *3,* 1–80.

Carpenter, Patricia A. and Marcel A. Just, Sentence comprehension: A psycholinguistic processing model of verification, *Psychological Review,* 1975, *82,* 45–73.

Carpenter, Patricia A. and Marcel A. Just, Integrative processes in comprehension, in David LaBerge and S. Jay Samuels (eds.), *Perception and Comprehension* (Hillsdale, N.J.: Erlbaum Associates, 1977).

Carroll, John B. and Jeanne S. Chall (eds.), *Toward a Literate Society* (New York: McGraw-Hill, 1975).

Carroll, John B., Peter Davies, and Barry Richman, *The American Heritage Word Frequency Book* (Boston: Houghton Mifflin, 1971).

Carroll, John B. and R. O. Freedle (eds.), *Language Comprehension and the Acquisition of Knowledge* (Washington, D.C.: Winston, 1972).

Cattell, James McKeen, Ueber die Zeit der Erkennung und Benennung von Schriftzeichen, Bildern und Farben, *Philosophische Studien,* 1885, *2,* 635–650; translated and reprinted in A. T. Poffenberger (ed.), *James McKeen Cattell, Man of Science, 1860–1944* (Vol. 1) (Lancaster, Pa.: Science Press, 1947).

Cazden, Courtney B., *Child Language and Education* (New York: Holt, Rinehart and Winston, 1972).

Chafe, Wallace L., *Meaning and the Structure of Language* (Chicago: University of Chicago Press, 1970).

Chall, Jeanne S., *Learning To Read: The Great Debate* (New York: McGraw-Hill, 1967).

Cherry, Colin, *On Human Communication* (Cambridge, Mass.: M.I.T. Press, 1966).

Chomsky, Carol, Reading, writing and phonology, *Harvard Educational Review*, 1970, *40*, 2, 287–309.

Chomsky, Carol, Write first, read later, *Childhood Education*, 1971, *47*, 6, 296–299.

Chomsky, Noam, *Syntactic Structures* (The Hague: Mouton, 1957).

Chomsky, Noam, Review of *Verbal Learning* (by B. F. Skinner), *Language*, 1959, *35*, 26–58.

Chomsky, Noam, *Aspects of the Theory of Syntax* (Cambridge, Mass.: M.I.T. Press, 1965).

Chomsky, Noam, *Language and Mind* (New York: Harcourt, 1972).

Chomsky, Noam, *Reflections on Language* (New York: Pantheon, 1975).

Chomsky, Noam and Morris Halle, *Sound Pattern of English* (New York: Harper & Row, 1968).

Chukovsky, Kornei (tr. Miriam Morton), *From Two to Five* (Berkeley: University of California Press, 1968).

Clark, Margaret M., *Young Fluent Readers* (London: Heinemann Educational Books, 1976).

Clay, Marie M., Reading errors and self-correction behavior, *British Journal of Educational Psychology*, 1969, *39*, 1, 49–56.

Clay, Marie M. and Robert H. Imlach, Juncture, pitch and stress and reading behavior variables, *Journal of Verbal Learning and Verbal Behavior*, 1971, *10*, 133–139.

Cofer, Charles N., Constructive processes in memory, *American Scientist*, 1973, *61*, 5, 537–543.

Cohen, Gillian, Search times for combinations of visual, phonemic and semantic targets in reading prose, *Perception and Psychophysics*, 1970, *8*, 5B, 370–372.

Cosky, Michael J., The role of letter recognition in word recognition, *Memory and Cognition*, 1976, *4*, 2, 207–214.

Craik, Fergus I. M. and Robert S. Lockhart, Levels of processing: A framework for memory research, *Journal of Verbal Learning and Verbal Behavior*, 1972, *11*, 671–684.

Crowder, Robert G., *Principles of Learning and Memory* (Hillsdale, N.J.: Erlbaum, 1976).

Dale, Philip S., *Language Development: Structure and Function* (New York: Holt, Rinehart and Winston, 1976).

Davies, W. J. Frank, *Teaching Reading in Early England* (London: Pitman, 1973).

Dember, William N., Motivation and the cognitive revolution, *American Psychologist*, 1974, *29*, 3, 161–168.

Doehring, Donald G., Acquisition of rapid reading responses, *Monographs of the Society for Research in Child Development*, 1976, *41*, 2, no. 165.

Downing, John (ed.), *Comparative Reading* (New York: Macmillan, 1973).

Downing, John and Peter Oliver, The child's conception of "a word," *Reading Research Quarterly*, 1973–74, *4*, 9/4, 568–582.

Dulany, Don E., On the support of cognitive theory in opposition to behavior theory: A methodological problem, in Walter B. Weiner and David S. Palermo (eds.), *Cognition and the Symbolic Process* (Hillsdale, N.J.: Erlbaum, 1974).

Dunn-Rankin, Philip, The similarity of lower case letters of the English alphabet, *Journal of Verbal Learning and Verbal Behavior*, 1968, *7*, 990–995.

Durkin, Dolores, *Children Who Read Early* (New York: Teachers College Press, 1966).

Erdmann, B. and R. Dodge, *Psychologische Untersuchungen ueber das Lesen auf Experimenteller Grundlage* (Halle: Niemeyer, 1898).

Fantz, Robert L., Visual experience in infants: Decreased attention to familiar patterns relative to novel ones, *Science*, 1964, *146*, 668–670.

Fantz, Robert L., Pattern discrimination and selective attention, in Aline H. Kidd and Jeanne L. Rivoire (eds.), *Perceptual Development in Children* (New York: International Universities Press, 1966).

Ferguson, Charles A. and Dan I. Slobin (eds.), *Studies of Child Language Development* (New York: Holt, Rinehart and Winston, 1973).

Fillion, Bryant, Frank Smith, and Merrill Swain, Language "basics" for language teachers: Towards a set of universal considerations, *Language Arts*, 1976, *53*, 7, 740–745.

Fillmore, Charles J., The case for case, in Emmon Bach and Robert J. Harms (eds.), *Universals in Linguistic Theory* (New York: Holt, Rinehart and Winston, 1968).

Fillmore, Charles J. and D. Terrance Langedoen (eds.), *Studies in Linguistic Semantics* (New York: Holt, Rinehart and Winston, 1971).

Firth, Hans G., *Piaget and Knowledge* (Englewood Cliffs, N.J.: Prentice-Hall, 1969).

Flavell, John H., *The Developmental Psychology of Jean Piaget* (New York: Van Nostrand, 1963).

Fodor, Jerry A., Thomas G. Bever, and M. F. Garrett, *The Psychology of Language* (New York: McGraw-Hill, 1974).

Friendly, Michael L., In search of the M-gram: The structure of organization in free recall, *Cognitive Psychology*, 1977, *9*, 188–249.

Fries, Charles C., *Teaching and Learning English as a Foreign Language* (Ann Arbor: University of Michigan Press, 1945).

Fries, Charles C., *Linguistics and Reading* (New York: Holt, Rinehart and Winston, 1963).

Garner, Wendell R., *Uncertainty and Structure as Psychological Concepts* (New York: Wiley, 1962).

Garner, Wendell R., To perceive is to know, *American Pscyhologist,* 1966, *21,* 1, 11–19.

Garner, Wendell R., Good patterns have few alternatives, *American Scientist,* 1970, *58,* 34–42.

Garner, Wendell R., *The Processing of Information and Structure* (Hillsdale, N.J.: Erlbaum, 1974).

Gelb, J., *A Study of Writing* (Chicago: University of Chicago Press, 1963).

Geyer, John J., Perceptual systems in reading: The prediction of a temporal eye-voice span constant, in H. K. Smith (ed.), *Perception and Reading* (Newark, Del.: International Reading Association, 1968).

Gibson, Eleanor J., *Principles of Perceptual Learning and Development* (New York: Appleton, 1969).

Gibson, Eleanor J., Learning to read, *Science,* 1965, *148,* 3673, 1066–1072.

Gibson, Eleanor J., The ontogeny of reading, *American Psychologist,* 1970, *25,* 2, 136–143.

Gibson, Eleanor J. and Harry Levin, *The Psychology of Reading* (Cambridge, Mass.: M.I.T. Press, 1975).

Gillooly, W. B., The influence of writing system characteristics on learning to read, *Reading Research Quarterly,* 1973, *8,* 2, 167–199.

Ginsburg, Herbert and Sylvia Opper, *Piaget's Theory of Intellectual Development: An Introduction* (Englewood Cliffs, N.J.: Prentice-Hall, 1969).

Gleitman, Lila R. and Paul Rozin, Teaching reading by use of a syllabary, *Reading Research Quarterly,* 1973, (a), *8,* 4, 447–483.

Gleitman, Lila R. and Paul Rozin, Phoenician go home? (A response to Goodman), *Reading Research Quarterly,* 1973, (b), *8,* 4, 494–501.

Glenn, Hugh W., The myth of the label "learning disabled child," *Elementary School Journal,* 1975, *75,* 6, 357–361.

Glucksberg, S. and J. H. Danks, *Experimental Psycholinguistics: An Introduction* (Hillsdale, N.J.: Erlbaum, 1975).

Golinkoff, Roberta Michnick, A comparison of reading comprehension processes in good and poor readers, *Reading Research Quarterly,* 1975–76, *11,* 4, 623–659.

Goodman, Kenneth S., A linguistic study of cues and miscues in reading, *Elementary English,* 1965, *42,* 639–643.

Goodman, Kenneth S., Reading: A psycholinguistic guessing game, *Journal of the Reading Specialist,* 1967, *6,* 126–135.

Goodman, Kenneth S., Analysis of oral reading miscues: Applied psycholinguistics, *Reading Research Quarterly,* 1969, *5,* 1, 9–30.

Goodman, Kenneth S., The 13th easy way to make learning to read difficult, *Reading Research Quarterly,* 1973, *8,* 4, 484–493.

Goody, Jack and Ian Watt, The consequences of literacy, in P. P. Gigliolo (ed.), *Language and Social Context* (London: Penquin, 1972).

Gough, Philip B., One second of reading, in James F. Kavanagh and Ignatius G. Mattingly (eds.), *Language by Ear and by Eye* (Cambridge, Mass.: M.I.T. Press, 1972).

Gray, William S. *The Teaching of Reading and Writing: An International Survey* (Paris: UNESCO, 1956).

Greene, Judith, *Psycholinguistics: Chomsky and Psychology* (London: Penguin, 1972).

Greeno, James G., Learning and comprehension, in Lee W. Gregg (ed.), *Knowledge and Cognition* (Hillsdale, N.J.: Erlbaum, 1974).

Gregory, R. L., *Eye and Brain: The Psychology of Seeing* (New York: McGraw-Hill, 1966).

Grimes, Joseph E., *The Thread of Discourse* (The Hague: Mouton, 1975).

Guthrie, John T., Models of reading and reading disability, *Journal of Educational Psychology*, 1973, *65*, 9–18.

Haber, Ralph N. (ed.), *Contemporary Theory and Research in Visual Perception* (New York: Holt, Rinehart and Winston, 1968).

Halliday, Michael A. K., Language function and language structure, in John Lyons (ed.), *New Horizons in Linguistics* (London: Penguin, 1970).

Halliday, Michael A. K., *Explorations in the Functions of Language* (London: Arnold, 1973).

Hardyck, C. D. and L. F. Petrinovich, Subvocal speech and comprehension level as a function of the difficulty level of reading material, *Journal of Verbal Learning and Verbal Behavior*, 1970, *9*, 647–652.

Harper, Lawrence V., The scope of offspring effects: From caregiver to culture, *Psychological Bulletin*, 1975, *82*, 5, 784–801.

Hart, Leslie A., Misconceptions about learning disabilities, *National Elementary Principal*, 1976, *56*, 1, 54–57.

Havelock, Eric A., *Origins of Western Literacy* (Toronto: Ontario Institute for Studies in Education, 1976).

Haviland, Susan E. and Herbert H. Clark, What's new? Acquiring new information as a process in comprehension, *Journal of Verbal Learning and Verbal Behavior*, 1974, *13*, 512–521.

Hayes, John R. (ed.), *Cognition and the Development of Language* (New York: Wiley, 1970).

Heckenmueller, E. G., Stabilization of the retinal image: A review of method, effects and theory, *Psychological Review*, 1965, *63*, 157–169.

Henderson, John M., Learning to read: A case study of a deaf child, *American Annals of the Deaf*, 1976, *121*, 502–506.

Hochberg, Julian, In the mind's eye, in Ralph N. Haber (ed.), *Contemporary Theory and Research in Visual Perception* (New York: Holt, Rinehart and Winston, 1968).

Hochberg, Julian, Components of literacy: Speculations and exploratory research, in Harry Levin and Joanna P. Williams (eds.), *Basic Studies on Reading* (New York: Basic Books, 1970).

Holdaway, Don, Self-evaluation and reading development, in John E. Merritt (ed.), *New Horizons in Reading* (Newark, Del.: International Reading Association, 1976).

Howe, M. J. A. and Linda Singer, Presentation variables and students' activities in meaningful learning, *British Journal of Educational Psychology*, 1975, *45*, 52–61.

Howes, D. H. and R. L. Solomon, Visual duration threshold as a function of word-probability, *Journal of Experimental Psychology*, 1951, *41*, 401–410.

Huey, Edmund Burke, *The Psychology and Pedagogy of Reading* (New York: Macmillan, 1908; reprinted Cambridge, Mass.: M.I.T. Press, 1968).

Huttenlocher, Janellen and Deborah Burke, Why does memory span increase with age? *Cognitive Psychology*, 1976, *8*, 1, 1–31.

Jacobs, Roderick A. and Peter S. Rosenbaum, *English Transformational Grammar* (Waltham, Mass.: Blaisdell Publishing Company, 1968).

Jakobson, Roman and Morris Halle, *Fundamentals of Language* (The Hague: Mouton, 1956).

Jenkins, James J., Remember that old theory of memory? Well, forget it! *American Psychologist*, 1974, *29*, 11, 785–795.

Jenkins, J. R., R. B. Bausel, and L. M. Jenkins, Comparison of letter name and letter sound training as transfer variables, *American Educational Research Journal*, 1972, *9*, 75–86.

Johnson, Neal F., On the function of letters in word identification: Some data and a preliminary model, *Journal of Verbal Learning and Verbal Behavior*, 1975, *14*, 1, 17–29.

Johnston, J. C. and J. L. McClelland, Perception of letters in words: Seek not and ye shall find, *Science*, 1974, *184*, 1192–1193.

Kagan, Jerome, The determinants of attention in the infant, *American Scientist*, 1970, *58*, 298–306.

Kagan, Jerome, Barbara A. Henker, Amy Hen-Tov, Janet Levine, and Michael Lewis, Infants' differential reactions to familiar and distorted faces, *Child Development*, 1966, *37*, 3, 519–532.

Kavanagh, James F. and Ignatius G. Mattingly (eds.), *Language by Ear and by Eye* (Cambridge, Mass.: M.I.T. Press, 1972).

Kintsch, Walter, *The Representation of Meaning in Memory* (Hillsdale, N.J.: Erlbaum, 1974).

Klatzky, Roberta L., *Human Memory: Structures and Processes* (San Francisco: Freeman, 1975).

Klein, Gary A. and Helen Altman Klein, Word identification as a function of contextual information, *American Journal of Psychology*, 1973, *86*, 2, 399–406.

Klein, Helen Altman, Gary A. Klein, and Mary Bertino, Utilization of context for word identification in children, *Journal of Experimental Psychology*, 1974, *17*, 79–86.

Kolers, Paul A., Reading and talking bilingually, *American Journal of Psychology*, 1966, *79*, 357–376.

Kolers, Paul A., Reading is only incidentally visual, in Kenneth S. Goodman and James T. Fleming (eds.), *Psycholinguistics and the Teaching of Reading* (Newark, Del.: International Reading Association, 1969).

Kolers, Paul A., Three stages of reading, in Harry Levin and Joanna P. Williams (eds.), *Basic Studies on Reading* (New York: Basic Books, 1970).

Kolers, Paul A., Buswell's discoveries, in R. A. Monty and J. W. Senders (eds.), *Eye Movements and Psychological Processes* (Hillsdale, N.J.: Erlbaum, 1976).

Kolers, Paul A. and M. Eden (eds.), *Recognizing Patterns: Studies in Living and Automatic Systems* (Cambridge, Mass.: M.I.T. Press, 1968).

Kolers, Paul A. and M. T. Katzman, Naming sequentially presented letters and words, *Language and Speech*, 1966, *9*, 2, 84–95.

Krueger, Lester E., Robert H. Keen, and Bella Rublevich, Letter search through words and nonwords by adults and fourth-grade children, *Journal of Experimental Psychology*, 1974, *102*, 5, 845–849.

LaBerge, David and S. Jay Samuels, Towards a theory of automatic information processing in reading, *Cognitive Psychology*, 1974, *6*, 293–323.

Lefton, Lester A. and Dennis F. Fisher, Information extraction during visual search: A developmental progression, *Journal of Experimental Child Psychology*, 1976, *22*, 346–361.

Lenneberg, Eric H., *Biological Foundations of Language* (New York: Wiley, 1967).

Lenneberg, Eric H. and Elizabeth Lenneberg, *Foundations of Language Development: A Multidisciplinary Approach*, 2 vols. (New York: Academic Press, 1975).

Levine, Frederic M. and Geraldine Fasnacht, Token rewards may lead to token learning, *American Psychologist*, 1974, *29*, 816–820.

Liberman, Alvin M., The grammars of speech and language, *Cognitive Psychology*, 1970, *1*, 301–323.

Liberman, Alvin M., F. S. Cooper, D. F. Shankweiler, and M. Studdert-Kennedy, Perception of the speech code, *Psychological Review*, 1957, *54*, 358–368.

Lindsay, Peter H. and Donald R. Norman, *Human Information Processing* (New York: Academic Press, 1972).

Llewellyn-Thomas, E., Eye movements in speed reading, in *Speed Reading: Practices and Procedures, No. 10* (Newark, Del.: University of Delaware Reading Study Center, 1962).

Lott, Deborah and Frank Smith, Knowledge of intra-word redundancy by beginning readers, *Psychonomic Science*, 1970, *19*, 6, 343–344.

Mackworth, Norman H., Visual noise causes tunnel vision, *Psychonomic Science*, 1965, *3*, 67–68.

Macnamara, John, Cognitive basis of language learning in infants, *Psychological Review*, 1972, *79*, 1, 1–13.

Magee, Bryan, *Popper* (London: Fontana, 1973).

Makita, Kiyoshi, The rarity of reading disability in Japanese children, *American Journal of Orthopsychiatry*, 1968, *38*, 4, 599–614.

Makita, Kiyoshi, Reading disability and the writing system, in John E. Merritt (ed.), *New Horizons in Reading* (Newark, Del.: International Reading Association, 1976).

Marshall, John C. and F. Newcombe, Syntactic and semantic errors in paralexia, *Neuropsychologia*, 1966, *4*, 169–176.

Mandler, Jean M. and N. S. Johnson, Remembrance of things parsed: Story structure and recall, *Cognitive Psychology*, 1977, *9*, 111–151.

Massaro, Dominic W., *Experimental Psychology and Information Processing* (Skokie, Ill.: Rand McNally, 1975).

Mathews, M. M., *Teaching To Read: Historically Considered* (Chicago: University of Chicago Press, 1966).

McKeachie, W. J., The decline and fall of the laws of learning, *Educational Researcher*, 1974, *3*, 3, 7–11.

McLaughlin, Barry, Second-language learning in children, *Psychological Review*, 1977, *84*, 3, 438–459.

McNeill, David, Developmental psycholinguistics, in Frank Smith and George A. Miller (eds.), *The Genesis of Language* (Cambridge, Mass.: M.I.T. Press, 1967).

McNeill, David, *The Acquisition of Language: The Study of Developmental Psycholinguistics* (New York: Harper & Row, 1970).

McNeill, David and Karen Lindig, The perceptual reality of phonemes, syllables, words, and sentences, *Journal of Verbal Learning and Verbal Behavior*, 1973, *12*, 4, 419–430.

Meltzer, Nancy S. and Robert Herse, The boundaries of written words as seen by first graders, *Journal of Reading Behavior*, 1969, *1*, 3–14.

Menyuk, Paula, *The Acquisition and Development of Language* (Englewood Cliffs, N.J.: Prentice-Hall, 1971).

Merritt, John E. (ed.), *New Horizons in Reading* (Newark, Del.: International Reading Association, 1976).

Meyer, David E. and Roger W. Schvaneveldt, Facilitation in recognizing pairs of words: Evidence of a dependence between retrieval operations, *Journal of Experimental Psychology*, 1971, *90*, 227–234.

Meyer, David E. and Roger W. Schvaneveldt, Meaning, memory structure and mental processes, *Science*, 1976, *192*, 27–33.

Miller, George A., *Language and Communication* (New York: McGraw-Hill, 1951).

Miller, George A., The magical number seven, plus or minus two: Some limits on our capacity for processing information, *Psychological Review*, 1956, *63*, 81–92.

Miller, George A., Some psychological studies of grammar, *American Psychologist*, 1962, *17*, 748–762.

Miller, George A. (ed.), *Mathematics and Psychology* (New York: Wiley, 1964).

Miller, George A., Some preliminaries to psycholinguistics, *American Psychologist*, 1965, *20*, 15–20.

Miller, George A., The organization of lexical memory, in G. A. Talland and Nancy C. Waugh (eds.), *The Pathology of Memory* (New York: Academic Press, 1969).

Miller, George A. (chairman), *Report of the Study Group on Linguistic Communication* (Washington, D.C.: National Institute of Education, 1974).

Miller, George A., Jerome S. Bruner, and Leo Postman, Familiarity of letter sequences and tachistoscopic identification, *Journal of Genetic Psychology*, 1954, *50*, 129–139.

Miller, George A., Eugene Galanter, and Karl H. Pribram, *Plans and the Structure of Behavior* (New York: Holt, Rinehart and Winston, 1960).

Miller, George A., G. A. Heise, and W. Lichten, The intelligibility of speech as a function of the context of the text materials, *Journal of Experimental Psychology*, 1951, *41*, 329–335.

Miller, George A. and Philip N. Johnson-Laird, *Language and Perception* (Cambridge, Mass.: The Belknap Press of Harvard University Press, 1975).

Miller, George A. and Patricia E. Nicely, An analysis of perceptual confusions among some English consonants, *Journal of the Acoustical Society of America*, 1955, *27*, 338–353.

Moore, Timothy E. (ed.), *Cognitive Development and the Acquisition of Language* (New York: Academic Press, 1973).

Morton, John, The effects of context on the visual duration threshold for words, *British Journal of Psychology*, 1964, *55*, 2, 165–180.

Neisser, Ulric, *Cognitive Psychology* (New York: Appleton, 1967).

Neisser, Ulric, *Cognition and Reality* (San Francisco: Freeman, 1977).

Nelson, Katherine, Structure and strategy in learning to talk, *Monographs of the Society for Research in Child Development*, 1973, *38*, 149.

Nelson, Katherine, Concept, word and sentence: Interrelations in acquisition and development, *Psychological Review*, 1974, *81*, 4, 267–285.

Neville, Mary H. and A. K. Pugh, Context in reading and listening: Variations in approach to Cloze tasks, *Reading Research Quarterly*, 1976–77, *12*, 1, 13–31.

Newman, Edwin B., Speed of reading when the span of letters is restricted, *American Journal of Psychology*, 1966, *79*, 272–278.

Newson, John and Elizabeth Newson, Intersubjectivity and the transmission of culture: On the social origins of symbolic functioning, *Bulletin of the British Psychological Society,* 1975, *28,* 437–446.

Nisbett, Richard E. and Timothy DeCamp Wilson, Telling more than we can know: Verbal reports on mental processes, *Psychological Review,* 1977, *84,* 3, 231–259.

Norman, Donald A., *Memory and Attention: An Introduction to Human Information Processing* (New York: Wiley, 1969; 2d. 1976).

Norman, Donald A. and David E. Rumelhart, *Explorations in Cognition* (San Francisco: Freeman, 1975).

Notz, William W., Work motivation and the negative effects of extrinsic rewards, *American Psychologist,* 1975, *30,* 9, 884–891.

Oettinger, Anthony G., *Run, Computer Run: The Mythology of Educational Innovation* (Cambridge, Mass.: Harvard Educational Press, 1969).

Olson, David R., Language and thought: Aspects of a cognitive theory of semantics, *Psychological Review,* 1970, 77, 257–273.

Olson, David R., Language use for communicating, instructing and thinking, in John B. Carroll and R. Freedle (eds.), *Language Comprehension and the Acquisition of Knowledge* (Washington, D.C.: Winston, 1972).

Olson, David R., Review of *Towards a Literate Society* (edited by John B. Carroll and Jeanne Chall), in *Proceedings of the National Academy of Education,* 1975, *2,* 109–178.

Olson, David R., From utterance to text: The bias of language in speech and writing, *Harvard Educational Review,* 1977, *47,* 3, 257–281.

Olson, Gary M., Memory development and language acquisition, in Timothy E. Moore (ed.), *Cognitive Development and the Acquisition of Language* (New York: Academic Press, 1973).

Olson, Gary M. and Herbert H. Clark, Research methods in psycholinguistics, in E. C. Carterette and M. P. Friedman (eds.), *Handbook of Perception, Vol. 7; Speech and Language* (New York: Academic Press, in press).

Paivio, Allan, *Imagery and Verbal Processes* (New York: Holt, Rinehart and Winston, 1971).

Palmer, F. R., *Semantics: A New Outline* (Cambridge: Cambridge University Press, 1976).

Paris, S. G. and A. Y. Carter, Semantic and constructive aspects of sentence memory in children, *Developmental Psychology,* 1973, *9,* 109–113.

Pastore, R. E. and C. J. Scheirer, Signal detection theory: Considerations for general application, *Psychological Bulletin,* 1974, *81,* 12, 945–958.

Pearson, P. David, The effects of grammatical complexity on children's comprehension, recall and conception of certain semantic relations, *Reading Research Quarterly,* 1974–75, *10,* 2, 155–192.

Pearson, P. David, and Alice Studt, Effects of word frequency and contextual richness on children's word identification abilities, *Journal of Educational Psychology,* 1975, *67,* 1, 89–95.

Perfetti, Charles A., Psychosemantics: Some cognitive aspects of structural meaning, *Psychological Bulletin,* 1972, *78,* 4, 241–259.

Piaget, Jean, *The Construction of Reality in the Child* (New York: Basic Books, 1954).

Piaget, Jean and Barbel Inhelder, *The Psychology of the Child* (New York: Basic Books, 1969).

Pierce, J. R., *Symbols, Signals and Noise: The Nature and Process of Communication* (New York: Harper & Row, 1961).

Pierce, J. R. and J. E. Karlin, Reading rates and the information rate of a human channel, *Bell Systems Technical Journal,* 1957, *36,* 497–516.

Pillsbury, W. B., A study in apperception, *American Journal of Psychology,* 1897, *8,* 315–393.

Polanyi, Michael, *The Tacit Dimension* (Garden City, N.Y.: Doubleday, 1966).

Popper, Karl R., *Objective Knowledge: An Evolutionary Approach* (Oxford: Clarendon Press, 1973).

Popper, Karl R., *Unended Quest: An Intellectual Autobiography* (London: Fontana/Collins, 1976).

Potter, Mary C., Meaning in visual search, *Science,* 1975, *187,* 965–966.

Pritchard, R. M., Stabilized images on the retina, *Scientific American,* 1961, *204,* 6, 72–78.

Quastler, Henry, Studies of human channel capacity, in Colin Cherry (ed.), *Information Theory* (London: Butterworths, 1956).

Rayner, Kenneth, The perceptual span and peripheral cues in reading, *Cognitive Psychology,* 1975, *7,* 68–81.

Read, Charles, Pre-school children's knowledge of English phonology, *Harvard Educational Review,* 1971, *41,* 1, 1–34.

Reicher, G. M., Perceptual recognition as a function of meaningfulness of stimulus material, *Journal of Experimental Psychology,* 1969, *81,* 275–280.

Reid, L. Starling, Towards a grammar of the image, *Psychological Bulletin,* 1974, *81,* 6, 319–334.

Resnick, Lauren and Phyllis Weaver (eds.), *Theory and Practice of Early Reading* (Hillsdale, N.J.: Erlbaum, in press).

Rosinski, Richard R., Roberta Michnick Golinkoff, and Karen S. Kukish, Automatic semantic processing in a picture-word interference task, *Child Development,* 1975, *46,* 1, 247–253.

Rothkopf, Ernst Z. and Richard P. Coatney, Effects of readability of context passages on subsequent inspection rates, *Journal of Applied Psychology,* 1974, *59,* 6, 679–682.

Rothkopf, Ernst Z. and M. J. Billington, Indirect review and priming through questions, *Journal of Educational Psychology,* 1974, *66,* 5, 669–679.

Rozin, Paul, Susan Poritsky, and Raina Sotksy, American children with reading problems can easily learn to read English represented by Chinese characters, *Science*, 1971, *171*, 1264–1267.

Rumelhart, David E. and Patricia Siple, Process of recognizing tachistoscopically presented words, *Psychological Review*, 1974, *81*, 99–118.

Sachs, Jacqueline S., Memory in reading and listening to discourse, *Memory and Cognition*, 1974, *2*, 1A, 95–100.

Sakamoto, Takahiko, Writing systems in Japan, in John E. Merritt (ed.), *New Horizons in Reading* (Newark, Del.: International Reading Association, 1976).

Samuels, S. Jay, Letter-name versus letter-sound knowledge in learning to read, *Reading Teacher*, 1971, *24*, 604–608.

Samuels, S. Jay, Automatic decoding and reading comprehension, *Language Arts*, 1976, *53*, 323–325.

Samuels, S. Jay, Gerald Begy, and Chau Ching Chen, Comparison of word recognition speed and strategies of less skilled and more highly skilled readers, *Reading Research Quarterly*, 1975–76, *1*, 11(1), 72–86.

Schneider, Walter and Richard M. Shiffrin, Controlled and automatic human information processing: I. Detection, search, and attention, *Psychological Review*, 1977, *84*, 1, 1–66.

Selfridge, Oliver and Ulric Neisser, Pattern recognition by machine, *Scientific American*, 1960, *203*, 2, 60–68.

Serafica, F. C. and I. E. Sigel, Styles of categorization and reading disability, *Journal of Reading Behavior*, 1970, *2*, 105–115.

Shallice, Tim and Elizabeth K. Warrington, Word recognition in a phonemic dyslexic patient, *Quarterly Journal of Experimental Psychology*, 1975, *27*, 187–199.

Shannon, Claude E., Prediction and entropy of printed English, *Bell Systems Technical Journal*, 1951, *30*, 50–64.

Shiffrin, Richard M., Locus and role of attention in memory systems, in P. M. A. Rabbitt and S. Dornic (eds.), *Attention and Performance V* (New York: Academic Press, 1975).

Simon, Herbert A., How big is a chunk? *Science*, 1974, *183*, 482–488.

Sinclair, Hermina, The transition from sensory-motor behavior to symbolic activity, *Interchange*, 1970, *1*, 3, 119–126.

Sinclair-de-Zwart, Hermina, Language acquisition and cognitive development, in John B. Carroll and R. O. Freedle (eds.), *Cognitive Development and the Acquisition of Language* (Washington, D.C.: Winston, 1972).

Singer, Harry and Robert B. Ruddell (eds.), *Theoretical Models and Processes of Reading*, 2d ed. (Newark, Del.: International Reading Association, 1976).

Skinner, B. F., *Science and Human Behavior* (New York: Macmillan, 1953).

Skinner, B. F., *Verbal Behavior* (New York: Appleton, 1957).

Skinner, B. F., *The Technology of Teaching* (New York: Appleton, 1968).

Slobin, Dan I., *Psycholinguistics* (Glenview, Ill.: Scott, Foresman, 1971).

Slobin, Dan I. and C. A. Welsh, Elicited imitation as a research tool in developmental psycholinguistics, in Charles A. Ferguson and Dan I. Slobin (eds.), *Readings in Child Language Acquisition* (New York: Holt, Rinehart and Winston, 1973).

Smith, Edward E., Edward J. Shoben, and Lance J. Rips, Structure and process in semantic memory: A featural model for semantic decisions, *Psychological Review*, 1974, *81*, 3, 214–241.

Smith, Edward E. and Kathryn T. Spoehr, The perception of printed English: A theoretical perspective, in B. H. Kantowitz (ed.), *Human Information Processing: Tutorials in Performance and Cognition* (Hillsdale, N.J.: Erlbaum, 1974).

Smith, Frank, The use of featural dependencies across letters in the visual identification of words, *Journal of Verbal Learning and Verbal Behavior*, 1969, 8, 215–218.

Smith, Frank, *Psycholinguistics and Reading* (New York: Holt, Rinehart and Winston, 1973).

Smith, Frank, *Comprehension and Learning* (New York: Holt, Rinehart and Winston, 1975a).

Smith, Frank, The role of prediction in reading, *Elementary English*, 1975(b), *52*, 3, 305–311.

Smith, Frank, Learning to read by reading: A brief case study, *Language Arts*, 1976, *53*, 3, 297–299.

Smith, Frank, Making sense of reading — and of reading instruction, *Harvard Educational Review*, 1977(a), *47*, 3, 386–395.

Smith, Frank, The uses of language, *Language Arts*, 1977(b), *54*, 6, 638–644.

Smith, Frank, Conflicting approaches to reading research and instruction, in Lauren Resnick and Phyllis Weaver (eds.), *Theory and Practice of Early Reading* (Hillsdale, N.J.: Erlbaum, in press).

Smith, Frank and Peter Carey, Temporal factors in visual information processing, *Canadian Journal of Psychology*, 1966, *20*, 3, 337–342.

Smith, Frank and Kenneth S. Goodman, On the psycholinguistic method of teaching reading, *Elementary School Journal*, 1971, 177–181.

Smith, Frank and Deborah Lott Holmes, The independence of letter, word and meaning identification in reading, *Reading Research Quarterly*, 1971, *6*, 3, 394–415.

Smith, Frank, Deborah Lott, and Bruce Cronnell, The effect of type size and case alternation on word identification, *American Journal of Psychology*, 1969, *82*, 2, 248–253.

Smith, Frank, and George A. Miller (eds.), *The Genesis of Language* (Cambridge, Mass.: M.I.T. Press, 1966).

Smith, Mary K., Measurement ot the size of general English vocabulary through the elementary grades and high school, *Genetic Psychology Monographs*, 1941, *24*, 311–345.

Sperling, George, The information available in brief visual presentations, *Psychological Monographs*, 1960, *74*, 11, Whole No. 498.

Spragins, Anne B., Lester A. Lefton, and Dennis F. Fisher, Eye movements while reading and searching spatially transformed text: A developmental examination, *Memory and Cognition*, 1976, *4*, 1, 36–42.

Swets, John A., The relative operating characteristic in psychology, *Science*, 1973, *182*, 990–1000.

Swets, John A., W. P. Tanner, Jr., and T. G. Birdsall, Decision processes in perception, *Psychological Review*, 1961, *68*, 301–320.

Taylor, Insup, *Introduction to Psycholinguistics* (New York: Holt, Rinehart and Winston, 1976).

Taylor, Stanford E., *The Dynamic Activity of Reading: A Model of the Process* (Huntington, N.Y.: Educational Developmental Laboratories, Inc., Bulletin No. 9, 1971).

Taylor, Stanford E., Helen Frackenpohl, and James L. Pettee, *Grade Level Norms for the Components of the Fundamental Reading Skill* (Huntington, N.Y.: Educational Developmental Laboratories, Inc., Bulletin No. 3, 1960).

Taylor, W. L., "Cloze" readability scores as indices of individual differences in comprehension and aptitude, *Journal of Applied Psychology*, 1957, *41*, 19–26.

Thorndike, E. L. and I. Lorge, *The Teacher's Word Book of 30,000 Words* (New York: Teachers College, 1944).

Tinker, Miles A., Fixation pause duration in reading, *Journal of Education Research*, 1951, *44*, 471–479.

Tinker, Miles A., Recent studies of eye movements in reading, *Psychological Bulletin*, 1958, *54*, 215–231.

Tinker, Miles A., *Bases for Effective Reading* (Minneapolis: University of Minnesota Press, 1965).

Tough, Joan, Children's use of language, *Educational Review* (Birmingham University) 1974, *26*, 3, 166–179.

Treisman, Anne M., Strategies and models of selective attention, *Psychological Review*, 1969, *76*, 3, 282–299.

Tulving, Endel and Wayne Donaldson (eds.), *Organization of Memory* (New York: Academic Press, 1972).

Tulving, Endel and Cecille Gold, Stimulus information and contextual information as determinants of tachistoscopic recognition of words, *Journal of Experimental Psychology*, 1963, *66*, 319–327.

Tulving, Endel and Donald M. Thomson, Encoding specificity and retrieval processes in episodic memory, *Psychological Review*, 1973, *80*, 5, 352–373.

Tulving, Endel and Michael J. Watkins, Structure of memory traces, *Psychological Review*, 1975, *82*, 4, 261–275.

Vachek, J., *Written Language* (The Hague: Mouton, 1973).

Venezky, Richard L., English orthography: Its graphical structure and its relation to sound, *Reading Research Quarterly,* 1967, *2,* 75–106.

Venezky, Richard L., *The Structure of English Orthography* (The Hague: Mouton, 1970).

Venezky, Richard L., *Theoretical and Experimental Base for Teaching Reading* (The Hague: Mouton, 1976).

Venezky, Richard L., Research on reading processes: A historical perspective, *American Psychologist,* 1977, *32,* 5, 339–345.

Wardhaugh, Ronald, *Reading: A Linguistic Perspective* (New York: Harcourt, 1969).

Watt, W. C., On two hypotheses concerning psycholinguistics, in John R. Hayes (ed.), *Cognition and the Development of Language* (New York: Wiley, 1970).

Weber, Rose-Marie, The study of oral reading errors: A survey of the literature, *Reading Research Quarterly,* 1968, *4,* 96–119.

Weber, Rose-Marie, First-graders' use of grammatical context in reading, in Harry Levin and Joanna P. Williams (eds.), *Basic Studies on Reading,* New York: Basic Books, 1970).

Weir, Ruth H., *Language in the Crib* (The Hague: Mouton, 1962).

Wheeler, D. D., Processes in word recognition, *Cognitive Psychology,* 1970, *1,* 59–85.

Wilkinson, Andrew M. (ed.), The context of language, *Educational Review,* 1971, *23,* 3.

Woodworth, Robert S., *Experimental Psychology* (New York: Holt, 1938).

Woodworth, Robert S. and H. Schlosberg, *Experimental Psychology* (New York: Holt, Rinehart and Winston, 1954).

Zipf, Paul, *Semantic Analysis* (Ithaca, N.Y.: Cornell University Press, 1960).

NAME INDEX

SUBJECT INDEX*